Children, Family and the State

Children, Family and the State

Decision-Making and Child Participation

Nigel Thomas
Lecturer in Applied Social Studies
University of Wales
Swansea

Consultant Editor: Jo Campling

First published in Great Britain 2000 by
MACMILLAN PRESS LTD
Houndmills, Basingstoke, Hampshire RG21 6XS and London
Companies and representatives throughout the world

A catalogue record for this book is available from the British Library.

ISBN 0–333–76037–9

First published in the United States of America 2000 by

ST. MARTIN'S PRESS, LLC,
Scholarly and Reference Division,
175 Fifth Avenue, New York, N.Y. 10010

ISBN 0–312–23626–3

Library of Congress Cataloging-in-Publication Data
Thomas, Nigel, 1950–
    Children, family, and the state : decision-making and child participation /
    Nigel Thomas ; consulting editor, Jo Campling.
      p. cm.
    Includes bibliographical references and index.
    ISBN 0–312–23626–3 (cloth)
     1. Child welfare—Great Britain. 2. Children—Government policy—Great
    Britain. 3. Decision making in children—Great Britain. I. Campling, Jo. II.
    Title.

    HV751.A6 T47 2000
    362.7'0941—dc21

                                                00–033351

This book is printed on paper suitable for recycling and made from fully managed and sustained
forest sources.

10 9 8 7 6 5 4 3 2 1
09 08 07 06 05 04 03 02 01 00

Printed and bound in Great Britain by
Antony Rowe Ltd, Chippenham, Wiltshire

To my family

Contents

List of Tables and Figures		ix
Foreword, by Malcolm Hill		xi
Acknowledgements		xiii
1	Introduction	1
2	Theories of Childhood	5
3	Psychology of Childhood	21
4	Rights of Childhood	36
5	Children, Parents and the State	50
6	Children Looked After by the State	70
7	Doing Research with Children	96
8	Patterns of Participation	115
9	Children's Views	132
10	Adults' Views	153
11	Making Sense of the Research	167
12	Children's Decisions and Children's Place	190
Notes		202
References		219
Index		238

List of Tables and Figures

List of Tables

8.1 Children invited to meetings at different ages 123
8.2 Children's invitation to meetings related to
   purpose of meeting 123
8.3 Children invited before and after use of
   Looking After Children forms 124
8.4 Children invited to meetings according to legal status 124
8.5 Children's attendance and relationship between
   family and agency 125
8.6 Children invited and relationship between
   family and agency 125
8.7 Children's attendance when invited and
   family–agency relationship 125
8.8 Influence of children's views and
   child's attendance at meeting 126
8.9 Child's influence related to difference of
   view with social worker 127
9.1 People who children mentioned most often 137

List of Figures

9.1 How children rated their review meetings
   ('pots and beans') 147
9.2 Children's ranking of factors in participation
   ('diamond ranking') 152
11.1 Matrix of attitudes to participation by
   children with disabilities 172
11.2 The 'climbing wall' of participation 176

Foreword

As the 1990s gave way to a new century and millennium, it has been possible to recognize many advances for children in the United Kingdom. The UN Convention on the Rights of the Child has now been ratified for over 10 years. While some of its provisions remain controversial or misunderstood, it is increasingly invoked as a touchstone for civilized approaches to children. The Children Act 1989, the Children (Scotland) Act 1995 and the Children (Northern Ireland) Order 1995 all placed the child's welfare at the heart of all decision-making and gave emphasis to children and young people's rights to participate and have their views taken seriously. Academic movements, especially within sociology and anthropology, have also given greater credence to children's competencies and perspectives than has often happened hitherto in studies of children or theories about them. The numbers of children looked after away from home has fallen significantly in most parts of the UK over the last 20 years. Legal duties towards children deemed to be in need have been strengthened and the responsibilities of local authorities towards vulnerable young adults have been extended.

Yet major problems undoubtedly remain. Child poverty grew substantially during the final part of the last century. Elaborate child protection systems may possibly be reducing the numbers of children at risk, but the 'secondary' suffering of children from protracted investigations and court cases can often more than outweigh the benefits of protection. Terrible accounts of extensive abuse of children in residential care during the recent past have prompted renewed vigilance, recruitment checks and training initiatives, so that hopefully such dreadful mistreatment will not occur again on the same scale, but we cannot afford to be complacent. As ever, the resources available for services are limited, so often legal aspirations are put into effect in a restricted, patchy fashion. A raft of new government initiatives focused on social inclusion or exclusion is likely to bring considerable benefits, but there are significant problems of coordination and geographical inequity.

This is a complex scene to portray in detail and I am pleased to introduce a text by Nigel Thomas which deals with the issues in a thorough and thoughtful, yet very readable manner. This volume embraces children in general, while having a particular focus on vulnerable children. It critiques common adult conceptions of childhood, at the same time as giving a central place to the viewpoint of children themselves. As well as reviewing state–family relationships in general, the book provides an interesting account of research carried out into the experiences of children looked after by local authorities. It reviews the plans and decisions made for and – sometimes – with them. Valuable insights are given into processeses and techniques for communicating with children, which will be of interest to practitioners as much as researchers. Specialist and general readers alike should find much to enjoy and learn from in the chapters ahead. This is a welcome addition to the small but growing body of publications that illuminate children's worlds, needs and rights from the inside as well as the outside.

Malcolm Hill
Centre for the Child & Society
University of Glasgow

Acknowledgements

I want to thank the many people who have helped with this book: Jo Campling for her advice and encouragement; my colleagues in the Centre for Applied Social Studies at Swansea, above all Sonia Jackson, for their advice and help and for allowing me the time to complete the work; Claire O'Kane who worked with such energy and creativity on the Nuffield research with me, and on whose work I have drawn in particular for Chapters 9 and 10; the advisory group for that research, especially our consultant Allison James who also read drafts of this book; the Nuffield Foundation itself, the local authorities who permitted the research, and the children, parents, carers and social workers who gave so generously of their time and ideas; all the other academic and professional colleagues with whom I have discussed the research or the ideas developed here; the children and families with whom I worked when I was 'in the field' in an earlier sense; and my own family for all that they have given me and all that they have tolerated from me. My gratitude for the help and support I have received does not qualify my responsibility for the ideas and the work presented here.

1
Introduction

This book began simply but became more complicated. It began with the idea of studying the operation of the new arrangements in the Children Act 1989 for planning and review of children 'looked after' by local authorities. When the Act was implemented in October 1991 it was clear to many of us then working in the care system that the expectations created would be challenging. Local authorities were to be obliged before making any decision in respect of a child to take account of 'the wishes and feelings of (a) the child; (b) his parents; (c) any person who is not a parent but who has parental responsibility for him; and (d) any other person whose wishes and feelings the authority consider to be relevant' and also to safeguard and promote the child's welfare (Children Act 1989, section 22). These obligations could produce tension between the wish to respect everyone's wishes and at the same time to come to the 'right' decision in the child's interests. I wanted to look at how that tension might work out and be managed in practice. In particular I wanted to see how much the child's wishes and feelings would really be heard and how much notice would really be taken of them, amidst all the competing voices and claims for attention from parents, relatives, professional colleagues and so on.

My first research was done in the local authority where I was working at the time, although later I ventured much farther afield. As I prepared for the early research I also read and thought about the theoretical issues involved, and as I did so the plan gradually changed. I became more interested in the idea of children's involvement in decisions about their welfare. In the year in which the Children Act was passed, the United Nations adopted the Convention on the Rights of the Child. This ascribed to 'the child who is capable of forming his or her own views the right to express those views freely in all matters affecting the child, the views of the child being given due weight in accordance with the age and maturity of the child' (United Nations 1989, Article 12). The Convention was ratified by the UK Government in November 1989, shortly after the Children Act came into law. So the inclusion of children in decisions was based at least in part on the idea that they had a right to be heard. I wanted to see where this idea came from and whether there were any problems with it. The inclusion of children also seemed to be based on the idea that it was in some way good for them, developmentally, to be involved, and I wanted to explore this too. Both the Children Act and the UN Convention implied that children's inclusion depended on their level of understanding, and that this varied with age; I needed to find out what was known about this variation. The last point connected with arguments about whether children were competent to make decisions or even to express their views, and arguments about whether children's dependence and (relative or apparent) incompetence were natural features of their age or whether they were sociological variables.

Thus the theme of the book had broadened to encompass questions about the phenomenon of 'childhood' and children's place in the world. The subject matter had spread from child welfare or social work to include elements of psychology and anthropology, sociology and history, law and philosophy. At the same time the experience of doing empirical research was leading me to look at how adults and children communicate with each other, and how conversations between them are read and interpreted. It was becoming increasingly apparent that the practical business of involving children in decisions about their care depended on communication, and so did the research in which I was engaged. In addition it seemed that some of the answers to basic questions about the place of children in the social world might be found in conversations between children and adults. The foundation who supported my research were fortunately happy for me to use it to explore these theoretical questions alongside the more practical ones.

This book has therefore been written from a number of different, if overlapping, perspectives. It is about what happens when children are looked after by the state and about what makes for good professional practice. It is also about some larger theoretical questions concerning the place of children in the world and their relationship to adults. Whether children belong in an adult or a child world, whether what they do is work or play, whether they are competent or incompetent – whether they belong to the individual or the social, to family or society, to the state or to their parents, to education or to welfare – whether they represent purity or danger, dependence or independence, power or weakness, ascendancy or subordination – all are moot points. But they are not only academic points; the relationship between adults and children, and the place of children in the world, are personal matters too. This book is written by someone who was 'a child' and is now 'an adult', without having undergone any obvious metamorphosis; who is now 'a parent'; and who lives in a world in which children are sometimes highly visible and sometimes oddly invisible. It is conceived and written out of my own experiences of childhood in a family, in school, with friends; and of parenting and looking after (or looking out for) children, as well as from academic study or professional experience.

Decisions about children who are 'looked after' by the state represent a site where the contested place of children can be examined. In some respects these children represent an extreme case; it might be asked how typical their situation is, or how representative they are of children in general. The problem with this question is that it assumes a concept of 'children in general' which is itself suspect, and so repeats the marginalisation of certain groups of children. Some of the issues and concerns presented by the children studied here are indeed particular to them as a group or as individuals, and much of what we learn from them is particular to their own situation. On the other hand, some issues seem to be common to many children, and what we can learn about these is highly general. It seems to me that these children's situation is worth studying both for the particular and for the general. In a world in which childhood has increasingly been constructed in 'welfare' terms, and in which 'welfare' decisions are increasingly individualised, a primary measure of society's valuation of children as subjects is the extent to which they are enabled to take a part in decisions about their own welfare, wherever they live. If they cannot be part of that process, how on earth can they be a part of the economy or of the polity? That is a question to which I will return in the concluding chapter.

Outline of the book

The first part of the book reviews the place of children in society from a series of different perspectives, with a focus that narrows gradually to the particular subject of decisions about children who are looked after by the state, and their involvement in those decisions. Chapter 2 looks at theories of childhood, the evidence that 'childhood' is different in different social contexts, and the significance of age. Chapter 3 reviews theories of child development and asks what can usefully be said from a psychological perspective about children's competence and their needs, especially in the middle years of childhood. Chapter 4 focuses on the rights of children and on the relationship between rights to welfare and protection, rights to participation, and age. Chapter 5 considers the relationship between children, parents and the state, the basis of adult authority, the relevance of the concept of the child's 'best interests' and the arguments for including children in decisions about their welfare. Chapter 6 reviews the development of state care for children in Britain in terms of its underlying assumptions and objectives for children, and examines the evidence about decision-making in care and the extent of children's inclusion in recent years.

The second part of the book looks at the process and outcome of research into children's participation in decisions. Chapter 7 discusses research methodology, especially in relation to qualitative research with children, and explains how the research presented here was planned and undertaken. Chapter 8 reports the findings of the quantitative part of the research, including a large survey of decision-making processes in 225 cases, and discusses what they can and cannot tell us about children's participation. The next two chapters are based on qualitative research, including a detailed study of 47 'looked after' children. Chapter 9 concentrates on what the children said about decision-making processes, and Chapter 10 on what adults – parents, social workers and carers – had to say. Chapter 11 analyses the findings of the research in a number of different ways, and includes an attempt to develop some typologies. The final chapter draws together some threads from both parts of the book, with further reflections on the place of children in society and in decision-making.

2
Theories of Childhood

Let us start with some fundamental questions. What is childhood? What sort of phenomenon is it? What are children like, and how are they different from adults? Is childhood something natural, or is it a social construct? This is not the first time these questions have been asked, and it will not be the last; the fact that they are regularly asked indicates that childhood is a contested phenomenon. There are many competing views of childhood that offer different answers to these questions; competing views held by historians, by sociologists and anthropologists, by psychologists and doctors, by lawyers and teachers, by politicians and economists (in so far as they think about childhood or children), by poets and novelists, or by ordinary people – parents, other adults, and children. Some of these views are implicit in theories about other aspects of life, or in the way we talk, what we do and how we live. Others are highly explicit and theorised, whether they are to be found in academic papers about the social construction of childhood or in everyday statements such as 'boys will be boys' or 'children should be seen and not heard'. In both cases they involve questions or assumptions about the nature of the difference between children and adults.

Discussions of the nature of childhood usually start with history, and in particular with Philippe Ariès's account of the transition from medieval to modern childhood. Ariès has been enormously influential in establishing the view that childhood should be analysed as a social construct; influential not just among historians, some of whom have in fact been very critical of him, but among sociologists and social anthropologists. Ariès's pronouncement that 'in medieval society the idea of childhood did not exist' (Ariès 1979, p. 125) has probably been quoted more than any other statement on the history of childhood.[1] Its only rival is Lloyd de Mause's 'the history of childhood is a nightmare from which we have only recently begun to awaken' (de Mause 1974, p. 1). Both are memorable statements, 'soundbites', and like many soundbites they are seriously misleading. However, they do each encapsulate a 'story' of childhood (Stainton Rogers 1993) that is commonly told: on the one hand that childhood is a modern invention, and on the other that only in modern times have children received tenderness and care. It is worth looking at each of these stories a little more closely.

Childhood as a modern invention

The passage from Ariès continues: 'this is not to suggest that children were neglected, forsaken or despised. The idea of childhood is not to be confused with affection for children: it corresponds to an awareness of the particular nature of childhood, that particular nature which distinguishes the child from the adult, even the young adult. In medieval society, this awareness was lacking' (Ariès 1979, p. 125). He does not seem to be arguing that childhood as a period was not distinguished from later stages of life, because elsewhere he says:

> The 'ages of life' occupy a considerable place in the pseudo-scientific treatises of the Middle Ages. Their authors use a terminology... childhood, puerility, adolescence, youth, senility, old age... so often repeated and so commonplace that they passed from the realm of science to that of everyday experience. It is hard for us today to appreciate the importance which the concept of the 'ages' had in ancient representations of the world.
>
> (pp. 16–17)

Rather Ariès is arguing that children, although distinguished from adults, were not seen as fundamentally different from them until the modern period. He bases this argument on several grounds: that there was no defined categorisation of childhood beyond infancy until the seventeenth or eighteenth century; that children were not shown realistically in paintings until the fifteenth century; that there was no special dress for children beyond infancy until the sixteenth or seventeenth century; that children played the same games as adults after infancy, probably until the seventeenth century; that children were routinely exposed to salaciousness until the sixteenth century; that the period of schooling was not clearly related to age until the seventeenth or eighteenth century; that the family is absent from the pictorial record until the fifteenth century, suggesting that the family was not of great importance to people; that as late as the fifteenth century children were still being sent away from home from the age of seven or nine.

Several of these arguments are questionable. Imprecision and inconsistency in the words used to refer to children are still with us. The argument from painting, although often repeated, has been dismantled by Fuller (1979) who has shown how children were shown realistically in many works of art, although not in all. In any case it is arguable that the subject matter of painting is as much a matter of artistic convention as of social reality.[2] Special dress for children appears to have been a fashion of the eighteenth and nineteenth centuries that is already disappearing; and in any case it is hard to see why a concept of childhood as distinct from adult should necessarily imply different styles of dress. The evidence on children's games is more mixed than Ariès suggests (see Thomas 1989). A more general difficulty with Ariès' statements about the medieval era is that his book is not really about that period at all. Historians like Shahar (1990) who have made a detailed study of medieval records have painted a very different picture of childhood, one which in general more closely resembles our own experience.[3]

In addition it is not always clear what Ariès himself means by childhood, partly because his pronouncements are contradictory and confusing, partly because the French 'enfance' is equivalent both to 'infancy' and 'childhood' in English. At times he seems to suggest that the period up to age seven has always been acknowledged to be distinctive, but that the period from seven to fourteen has moved from being part of an adult world to a childish one. Wilson (1980) has trenchantly criticised Ariès' scholarship: his argument is muddled, his use of evidence often erratic, and above all he is 'present-centred'; his text provides little sound evidence for the statement that childhood is a modern invention, and inadvertently provides evidence to the contrary. However, this has not prevented his work being widely quoted as establishing that childhood is a creation of modern times.[4]

Wilson suggests that Ariès's mistakes are characteristic of the initial stages of historiography, both in his use of evidence and in his 'present-mindedness'. However, Ariès's work set the context for research into the history of childhood, opening an important line of enquiry into changes in the conception of childhood held at different periods in history. For sociologists and psychologists it has given force to the argument that the 'natural state' of childhood is in fact a social construct. The irony that Ariès himself was susceptible to seeing all childhood through the lens of its modern construction does not detract from that argument at all.[5] The challenge remains to identify the precise ways in which conceptions of childhood have varied through history.

Childhood as a tale of woe

The other story told about the history of childhood is that children were brutally treated until some point in the recent past. De Mause (1974) represents perhaps the most dramatic example, with a reading of history based on successive stages each with its characteristic mode of parent– child relations. The explanation is 'psycho-historical': in the past parents projected their anxieties into their children and so treated them cruelly or rejectingly, and it is only gradually over successive generations that a more empathic and child-centred response has developed.[6] Others have seen a similar trend although they have explained it in more conventional historical terms. Stone (1979) traces successive developments in the style of family life in England, from 'distance, deference and patriarchy' to what he calls 'affective individualism' (p. 22). He believes that the earlier styles were associated with either neglect or brutality towards children: in the earlier period the high level of infant mortality militated against affection between parents and children, whilst in the seventeenth century the emphasis on patriarchal authority and moral discipline produced a high degree of severity.[7] Shorter (1977) also traces a progression from harshness and brutality to tenderness and care: 'Children were brutalized by the daily routines of life as much as by savage outbursts of parental rage' (pp. 171–2). This pattern did not give way to modern child care until the latter part of the nineteenth century. 'Good mothering,' according to Shorter, 'is an invention of modernisation' (p. 170).[8] Other authors who subscribe to the view that children were badly treated in the past include Sommerville (1982), Hunt (1972), Demos (1970) and to some extent Pinchbeck and Hewitt (1969, 1973), although the latter are mainly interested in the ways in which children are treated by the state. Most do not follow Shorter's crude account of modernisation as progress; for instance Stone suggests that 'the only steady linear change over the last four hundred years seems to have been a growing concern for children, although their actual treatment has oscillated cyclically between the permissive and the repressive' (1979, p. 425).

It is easy to be swept along by some of these accounts. The judgements are confident and the anecdotes vivid. Authors like Stone have amassed an impressive amount of evidence. More sober examination, however, reveals a highly selective use of that evidence, unwarranted or illogical interpretations and sweeping and often inconsistent pronouncements.[9]

Linda Pollock (1983) set out to test the accounts in a systematic way, examining a wide range of diary and autobiographical material from England and America from the fifteenth to early twentieth centuries, and cataloguing and analysing it meticulously. She concluded that there was no evidence to support the view that parents in the earlier period had less regard for their children, failed to recognise their particular needs, or treated them more severely. Peter Laslett's extensive study of English parish records established that for ordinary people household size had not fallen dramatically since the middle ages, and that there was nothing remarkably modern about the 'nuclear family'. In passing he notes that 'Ariès' insistence that there was an enormous change in the institution of childhood and in the attitudinal structure of the family, between medieval and modern Europe, is ... not verifiable from the evidence of English community listings ... nor indeed from any of our data' (Laslett 1971, p. 260).[10] Where Ariès confidently takes the absence of children from paintings as an indication that they were not considered, Laslett is more puzzled:

> The perpetual distraction of childish noise and talk must have affected everyone almost all the time, except of course the gentleman in his study or the lady in her boudoir; incessant interruptions to answer questions, quieten fears, rescue from danger or make peace between the quarrelling. These crowds and crowds of little children are strangely absent from the written record, even if they are conspicuous enough in the pictures painted at the time, particularly the outside scenes. There is something mysterious about the silence of all these multitudes of babes in arms, toddlers, and adolescents in the statements men made at the time about their own experience. Children appear, of course, but so seldom and in such an indefinite way that we know very little indeed about child nurture in pre-industrial times, and no confident promise can be made of knowledge yet to come.
>
> (Laslett 1971, pp. 109–10)[11]

It is hard to escape the thought that historians find in the history of childhood what they are looking for.[12] The discovery of callousness or neglect on the part of parents in the past can enable us to feel more comfortable about our own child-rearing. It is particularly easy to castigate poor parents in the past, who have no voice in the records, on the basis of extrapolation from the limited evidence of bourgeois parenting. The history of childhood sometimes seems to consist of men in book-lined studies writing about what other men in book-lined studies wrote about children in a previous era. Certainly it tends to be the story of adult conceptions of childhood and of parent–child relations. What hardly impinges at all is the voice of children themselves. Keith Thomas (1989), in a brilliant essay, suggests that the evidence is available to write a different story, if it is sought with care. In general, however, it is easier to find evidence of adults' perspectives rather than children's, and in most cases those adults are men rather than women, rich or prosperous rather than poor or averagely well-off, highly-educated rather than uneducated. Similarly the evidence is likely to concern boys rather than girls, and very often those who went on to achieve fame or fortune if they did not already possess it. The history that is written tends to reflect this bias in the available evidence.

Age and expectations

What then can we say with confidence about childhood in history? Few who have studied the evidence would now argue that the concept of childhood did not exist in the past. In many respects there seems to have been considerable continuity in how children were regarded, at least by their parents. Many parents valued their children, treated them with affection, worried about their future. Others behaved with cruelty or neglect, whether as a result of ignorance, pathology or conviction. To seize on examples of either as evidence of a general pattern may be as wrong in relation to the past, where the evidence is so patchy, as it is when similar generalisations are ventured in relation to the present. At the same time the physical and social world in which children lived was very different, and their lives must have been different too. It can be difficult to separate general changes that affected children along with adults from those that were specific to children. However, there are indications that the expectations which adults had of children, and the expectations which children had of and for themselves, were different in the past; not so much perhaps for children under seven, where physical dependency was of abiding and perhaps defining importance, but for older children and for adolescents (see Cunningham 1995). The most striking aspect of this change in expectations is perhaps in the economic contribution made by children. For most of history, it appears, children at least from the age of about seven have made a substantial contribution to the economic activity of the households in which they lived or the families to which they belonged, whether through work on family farms and smallholdings, in crafts and trades followed at home, or working outside the home as servants or apprentices. What seems to have changed in the modern period, beginning with Western Europe and North America and beginning with boys, is that increasing numbers of children have spent an increasing number of years in formal schooling rather than in direct economic activity.[13] Although the case that before this happened they were not regarded as 'children' has not been made, the meaning of childhood, both for children and adults, must have been very different.[14]

At the same time there is evidence that the years of childhood and youth were structured by age in the past in ways that resemble modern patterns, even though the content of each stage was different in different periods and for different social groups. In particular, key transitions often seem to take place around the age of seven and again at twelve to fourteen. In medieval Europe education for church service – 'reading school' or 'song school' – generally began at age seven and lasted until ten or twelve; grammar school would continue from this age until usually sixteen, although this was more variable than it is now (Shahar 1990; see also Ariès 1979).[15] Young noblemen would remain with their mothers until seven or nine and then go into service as a page, according to Shahar who adds: 'Serious military training commenced at the age of about twelve' (p. 210).[16] She suggests that in the Middle Ages the period from seven to fourteen in the case of boys, and from seven to twelve for girls, was regarded as a single stage, although there was a gradual change through those years in what was expected of a child.[17] As Wilson points out, Ariès also provides evidence suggesting that what happened in medieval Europe at age seven was a shift not to adulthood but to a different stage of childhood.

It seems that the period up to seven has always been regarded as a time of dependency when the mother, foster-mother or nurse is the most important person in a child's life. The next stage, from seven to twelve or fourteen, appears to be largely structured as a time of training and education, whether at home, in apprenticeship in another household, or in school. However, in Europe in the period between the fourteenth and nineteenth century this period also began to be construed as a time of dependence and irresponsibility, culminating in the late nineteenth century when most children in this group were removed from employment to full-time schooling. Cunningham (1995) warns against overrating the economic contribution of children in agriculture. He argues that in peasant economies their labour was probably not of *net* value below age fifteen, and that as important as children's present labour was their future contribution to the family economy. On the other hand, he adds that for children:

> For the great majority of them the major change in the first half of the twentieth century was that they lost any productive role within the economy, and increasingly gained a new role as consumers. This undoubtedly altered the way in which children were viewed by parents ... Children did not necessarily experience it as liberation. There is much evidence of children's self-esteem rising at the point where they began to contribute to the family economy.
>
> (p. 177)[18]

As Thane (1981, p. 18) puts it, 'the nineteenth century saw an increase in the spheres of life in which the child was assumed not to have equal civil rights with the adult.'[19] In the twentieth century the period of dependence, and expectation of formal training rather than employment, has extended into adolescence and youth.[20] Increasingly, young people up to the age of eighteen are being formally defined as 'children', suggesting a more definite opposition than hitherto between children and adults.[21] Sommerville (1982) suggests that before 1800 children may have seen themselves primarily in terms of their respective social class rather than as an age group. In the twentieth century, on the other hand, Oldman (1994) argues that children may usefully be seen as a social class in their own right, so marked is their opposition to the world of adults.

Childhood in different cultures

Another way in which to learn about how much of what we call childhood is biologically given, and how much of it is socially constructed, is to compare childhoods in different contemporary cultures. This work was pioneered by what became known as the 'culture and personality' school (see Benedict 1934; Mead 1963, 1943; Mead and Wolfenstein 1955). Taking a view of development that owed a great deal to Freudian psychology and which assumed that certain maturational processes were constant, Mead and Benedict attempted to show how different modes of child-rearing produced different personality types. Their work was in general done in 'primitive' societies; in Mead's perhaps naïve view this has two advantages: 'contrast with our own social environment which brings out different aspects of human nature and often demonstrates that behaviour which occurs almost universally within our own society is nevertheless due not to original nature but to social environment; and a homogeneous and simple social background, easily mastered, against which the development of the individual may be studied.' There may also be an idea that if there *are* universal human types then 'primitive' societies are likely to reveal them.[22] Mead appeared to find marked differences in personality types and traits between the different cultures she studied, which she related to patterns of child care and upbringing. The Samoans brought up their children without shame or guilt, in clearly marked age groups where children had definite responsibilities related to their age, and they grew into adults well-adjusted to their culture, contented and conforming. The Manus on the other hand gave their children little to do and little structure apart from elaborate taboos and a strong sense of shame, and this appeared to produce a personality type which was often selfish, demanding and aggressive.

Mead and Benedict's fieldwork has been criticised as superficial (see for instance Freeman 1983a).[23] More fundamentally, it has been argued that the frame of analysis employed by the culture and personality school fails to take account of a number of salient factors. As La Fontaine (1986) puts it, Mead's model 'is based on a far too simplistic set of connections between social behaviour, personality and childhood experience, and virtually ignores all social life outside the domestic sphere.' Whatever the inadequacies of the causal model, the point remains that Mead and her colleagues discovered wide variations in child-rearing practices and in the social organisation of childhood in the groups they studied, to the extent that it does not seem too fanciful to speak of children inhabiting different worlds. The same applies to later studies in the same tradition such as the 'Six Cultures' project (Whiting and Whiting 1975), Bronfenbrenner's (1971) comparative study of Russian and American child-rearing and Konner's (1977) account of the !Kung.

More recent cross-cultural work is characterised by a combination of anthropological and psychological approaches, attempts to introduce a greater precision, and a new emphasis on cognitive development. Leiderman, Tulkin and Rosenfeld (1977) argue that cross-cultural comparison can provide 'natural experiments' and enable us to tease out the features of child development that are culturally specific from those that are universal. Their collection of papers provides much evidence of common patterns, as well as of cultural difference. For instance Brazelton reports evidence that cultural variations in parental practice have little effect on the age of walking and talking. Kagan studied separation protest in Guatemala, Israel and the Kalahari, and found that in all cases protest began after 9 months, peaked between 12 and 15, and then declined. The same pattern appeared in children in the US, whether White or Chinese and regardless of whether they were in day care or 'home-reared'. Kagan relates this to the notion of 'object permanence' and argues that it is based on changes in memory function produced by maturational processes in the brain. More generally, Ainsworth suggests that there are 'genetic determinants of early social behaviour that for all societies place certain limits beyond which a society cannot push its efforts to mold the child to conform to social demands – at least not without visiting gross and maladaptive anomalies of development inimical to the survival of that society'. LeVine proposes that 'customs represent adaptations to environmental pressures experienced by earlier generations of parents seeking to realise the universal goals of parenthood'.[24]

Super and Harkness (1982) argue that 'there appear to be two major pathways of cultural divergence in the emotional training of infants and young children: (1) the direct expression of parental values and beliefs, and (2) the less intentional structuring of the child's developmental niche by the physical and social resources for caretaking' (p. 62). Comparing the development of emotional reactions in American and Kipsigis children, they conclude that 'the elements of expression are universally human, but they are organised, practiced [*sic*], and regulated by culture.' (p. 71) Some studies have sought to engage directly with parents' implicit theories of child development. Gergen, Gloger-Tippett and Berkowitz (1990) compared expectations of young children in a group of German women and a matched group of American women. Both groups showed consistency in expectations of the order and age at which children would exhibit certain characteristics, suggesting that they held a conception of development as an organic 'unfolding', rather than a mechanical process; and the differences between the two national groups did not decrease with experience of motherhood, suggesting that cultural expectations were more powerful than the actual experience of children's behaviour. Differences also appeared to be linked with other culturally distinctive beliefs.[25]

So we learn from cross-cultural research, as we did from the work of historians, that conceptions of childhood do not exist in isolation from other cultural patterns and concepts. Within the same 'culture', differences in social class and economic circumstances have an effect on patterns of child-care (Leiderman and Leiderman 1977; Moss and Jones 1977; Tulkin 1977). Studies in contemporary Britain have explored the different patterns of child-rearing and family life followed in different social groups, and how these are negotiated in encounters with the dominant culture (Rapoport, Fogarty and Rapoport 1982). Others have looked at how child care practices and outcomes differ for boys and girls and for children with different abilities (Stein 1984; Belotti 1975; Statham 1986).

There is clearly a wealth of variation in the shape of childhood in different cultures. The expectations adults hold of children at different ages, and presumably the expectations children have of themselves, in terms of skills, understanding, knowledge of proper behaviour, vary from one culture to another. The social worlds occupied by children vary, in the number of adults with whom they relate, in the extent to which they are segregated by age, in their relationships and their preoccupations. The levels of responsibility taken by boys and girls at different ages, and even by children and young people altogether, vary enormously. Societal beliefs about childhood, its purpose and its character also vary.

On the other hand certain features appear to be consistent. In every culture one can see a succession of changes in societal expectations of individuals which are to a greater or lesser extent age-based. The transition from one to another may be sharp or gradual. Usually they are irreversible although not universally, and they may or may not include an overriding dichotomy between 'childhood' and 'adulthood'. They are generally associated with an increase in power and influence; and they often seem to occur at the same age stages that we saw recurring in European history. Schildkrout (1978) tells us, for instance, that seven is the age by which Hausa children are expected to develop *hankali* (understanding or sense). Rogoff and colleagues (1976) surveyed a large number of ethnographic records for key changes in expectations of children and found for many of them a strong association around ages seven and twelve.

The sociology of childhood

Sociologists and social anthropologists have until recently shown relatively little interest in children or childhood, as La Fontaine (1986) has pointed out. Children tended to be seen as unfinished persons and not as full participants in social relationships. The dominant concept was *socialisation*, which contains the idea not only that children are shaped to the requirements of a particular culture or society, but that they are in effect *made social* in the process. The principal agent in this process was seen as being the family.[26] Tensions, however, begin to appear in the theory of socialisation when one attempts to take account of children's *agency*, as in the interactionist approach exemplified by Denzin (1975).[27] Speier (1976) comments that traditional interests in development and socialisation 'have neglected what we are calling the interactional foundation to human group life. The traditional perspectives have overemphasised the task of describing the child's developmental process of growing into an adult at the expense of a direct consideration of what the events of everyday life look like in childhood' (p. 170). Both the sociological and the psychological traditions are being asked to acknowledge that children's lack of active presence in society is mirrored by their lack of active presence in theory. In the words of Hardman, writing in a social anthropological framework in the early 1970s, children can be seen as a 'muted group' (1973, p. 85). Seeing children instead as social actors is a key element in the 'emergent paradigm' of the sociology of childhood identified by James and Prout (1990a), which has its theoretical roots both in sociology and in anthropology.

The other key element in that paradigm is that childhood is seen as a social construction. Whatever their defects, both Ariès and the 'culture and personality' school have shown that childhood is in some sense socially defined and created. Although the biological processes involved in maturation and ageing are real, the pattern and meaning of these changes is structured and mediated by society and culture. A seminal text in theories of social construction is that of Berger and Luckmann (1971), who analyse the way in which concepts produced in social interaction by social actors tend to become reified. 'Reification,' they write, is

> the apprehension of human phenomena as if they were things, that is, in non-human or possibly supra-human terms. Another way of saying this is that reification is the apprehension of the products of human activity *as if* they were something other than human products – such as facts of nature, results of cosmic laws, or manifestations of divine will.
>
> (p. 106)

Childhood is a clear example of a reified human phenomenon. As Denzin (1975, p. 2) puts it, 'Children must be viewed as historical, cultural, political, economic, and social productions. There is nothing intrinsic to the object called "child" that makes that object more or less "childlike".' Or as Jenks (1982) writes, 'The social propensity to routinize and naturalize childhood, both in commonsense and in theory, serves to conceal its import behind the cloak of the mundane; its significance and "strangeness" as an historical and social phenomenon become obscured...Childhood is not a natural phenomenon and cannot be understood as such.' The identification of certain age stages as 'childhood' and their occupants as 'children' in opposition to a taken-for-granted world of 'adults' is always in some sense arbitrary. Ariès, in his equation of a particular concept of childhood with childhood as such, was perhaps as bound by this as anyone. The concepts of childhood and adulthood of course depend on each other. Ariès might equally well have said 'in medieval society the idea of adulthood did not exist'.

Theories of social construction, and the practice of theoretical deconstruction, can sometimes appear to turn their back on any notion of reality or of real understanding. Contributions like those of Stainton-Rogers (1992) or Burman (1994), although illuminating, sometimes threaten to leave us with little but the knowingness of the author. The work which I want to look at in the new sociology of childhood attempts to avoid this pitfall in two ways: by not rejecting the insights produced by anthropologists and psychologists, while taking account of the particular frame of reference in which they were produced; and by grounding its own empirical study in the lived experience of children and of adults, but especially of children. Prout and James (1990) identify the key features of the new paradigm as follows:

1. Childhood is understood as a social construction. As such it provides an interpretative frame for contextualizing the early years of human life. Childhood, as distinct from biological immaturity, is neither a natural nor universal feature of human groups but appears as a specific structural and cultural component of many societies.
2. Childhood is a variable of social analysis. It can never be entirely divorced from other variables such as class, gender, or ethnicity. Comparative and cross-cultural analysis reveals a variety of childhoods rather than a single and universal phenomenon.
3. Children's social relationships and cultures are worthy of study in their own right, independent of the perspective and concerns of adults.
4. Children are and must be seen as active in the construction and determination of their own social lives, the lives of those around them and of the societies in which they live. Children are not just the passive subjects of social structures and processes.
5. Ethnography is a particularly useful methodology for the study of childhood. It allows children a more direct voice and participation in the production of sociological data than is usually possible through experimental or survey styles of research.

6. Childhood is a phenomenon in relation to which the double her-
meneutic of the social sciences is acutely present (see Giddens 1976).
That is to say, to proclaim a new paradigm of childhood sociology is
also to engage in and respond to the process of reconstructing childhood in society. (pp. 8–9)

Prout and James link their work, not only with the insights provided
by historians of childhood and with the work of anthropologists in the
'culture and personality tradition', but with new developments in the
psychological understanding of childhood represented for example by
Kessen (1979) and Richards and Light (1986).[28] Their perspective draws
attention to aspects of the structure of meaning associated with notions
of childhood that might otherwise be invisible. For instance James and
Prout (1990b), like Jenks (1982), have pointed to the ways in which
childhood is constructed in temporal terms: children are seen as preparing for the future or as representing the past, not as living in the present.
Hockey and James (1993) explore the ways in which dependency is
constructed and age groups marginalised at both ends of the life course.
Adulthood is identified with independence, and dependency is attributed to the essential nature of children – and of old people, who are
metaphorically associated with children. In reality, Hockey and James
suggest, dependency 'is primarily a social relationship based on the exercise of power'.

The new perspective has produced stimulating research, much of it in
Northern Europe and Scandinavia (which may in itself be an illustration
of cultural variation in the perception of childhood). Solberg (1990)
looked at the use of time and work in a group of Norwegian families
and found that variations between families in levels of responsibility,
in degrees of autonomy, and in the perceived 'bigness' of children were
to some extent negotiated between parents and children. A research
focus on children's own perspectives enabled her to counter the conventional problematising of 'latch-key children' with the perception
that, for the children she studied, time at home without adults constituted an opportunity. Qvortrup (1990, 1994) has taken a more macrosociological view of the way in which children's lives are rendered
invisible in social accounting, and what might be some techniques for
bringing them to light (see also Saporiti 1994). This echoes Laslett's
(1971) comment that children, like other relatively powerless social
actors, are 'subsumed' in adult-male-headed households in the historical
records. Ennew (1994) has examined the ways in which children's lives
are structured for them in terms of particular adult conceptions of time.

She also looks at how children's activity is trivialised in the concept of 'play', an argument put forward earlier by Denzin (1975). Morrow (1994) has studied children's work, both in paid employment and within the household, concluding that

> the social construction of childhood as a period marked by dependency and an absence of 'responsibility' prevents us from 'knowing' about those cases of children working and taking responsibility. An analysis of children's everyday lives outside school reveals that children have continued to work, but their labour has been made 'invisible' behind a conception of 'the child' as dependent, non-productive, and maintained within the family unit.
>
> (p. 142)

James (1993) has studied how young children use perceptions of bodily characteristics and differences in negotiating and understanding self and social relationships, and Alderson (1993) has shown how children with serious illnesses may have a mature and sophisticated understanding of medical intervention.

Implications for research

The new perspective presents a challenge to the dominant view of childhood in modern Western society. This is a view that equates 'the child' with 'the family' and regards children as anomalous if they are not contained either within a family or within a formal social structure established for that purpose, such as a school. It is a view that appears to have gone with a progressive raising of the *de iure* or *de facto* age at which children are able to be financially independent or geographically mobile (see Ward 1978, 1994). It is a view that continues to define children as incompetent adults, despite a growing body of psychological evidence that questions this (see next chapter). It is a view that trivialises attempts by children, individually or collectively, to assert some control over their situation as 'kiddies' lib' or as 'children divorcing their parents'. This chapter has concentrated on academic conceptions of the nature of childhood, not on everyday conceptions or those contained in the popular media, in political discourse, or in fiction. However, those other conceptions are ever present as a ground for more 'scientific' analysis; as Gergen et al. (1990) ask, 'if limits to the conception of the child are principally social in origin, then in what sense can science transcend culture?' Speier in his critique of socialisation theory argues that 'the intellectual and analytic position of sociologists is essentially ideological in the sense that they have used an adult notion of what children are and what they ought to be that is like that of the laymen in the culture' (1976, p. 170). The 'emergent paradigm' may not transcend completely the conceptions of childhood held in contemporary society. However, in so far as the contemporary world gives an unprecedented opportunity for contact with alternative conceptions from different historical periods and global cultures, and perhaps also from contending political perspectives, it may be that it is possible for the new paradigm to situate itself as 'on the side of' children, theoretically and practically, in a way that might not have been possible in the past.

The shift in focus from what adults do to children and how adults see children, to what children do and how they see themselves and their world, is a pattern which can repeat itself in history, sociology, anthropology and psychology, and also in education, law and social welfare. When we look directly at the part played by children in decisions about their own lives, it is important to do so on the basis of assumptions to which I hope this chapter has led: that children are not simply objects of other people's actions but subjects of their own; that what children are now is important, as well as what they will become in the future; that what childhood is like – and what children can do – is contingent on social structures, cultures and values, and therefore subject to variation; and that according to children and young people there is an inescapable link between their full value in social research and according them their full value in social life.

3
Psychology of Childhood

'Childhood' is a social construct, but this does not mean that all differences between those we call children and those we call adults are socially constructed. There is evidence that some are (or at least that they are effects produced in social interaction, which is slightly different). At the same time there is a biological base of maturational processes that cannot be ignored if we are to make sense of differences between childhood patterns. Taking this dual perspective as a framework, let us see what is known about children's psychological development, especially in the middle years of childhood, and consider its implications for children's participation in decisions about their welfare.

The concept of *development* underlies most psychological theories of childhood. Borrowed from biology, it implies that the characteristics of an organism change over time according to a pattern. The idea of succession often becomes an idea of stages, sometimes with the notion of an adult or 'fully-fledged' stage for which the preceding ones are merely preparatory.[1] In modern psychological theories development is *epigenetic*; that is, the stages of development are not completely fixed, but include the potential for adaptation. Development may be seen as the outcome of a process in which several factors are involved: genetic material, some of which is common to a species and some unique to an individual; the environment in which growth takes place, which is in itself complex and many-layered; and the individual's own adaptive capacity.

Whereas in the past discussion of development was dominated by the question of whether genetic or environmental factors are more important, researchers are now concerned to understand the interactions between these factors, and have also begun to pay attention to the individual's role in directing his or her own development.[2] At the same time advances in understanding the structure and chemistry of the brain have begun to comprehend the enormous complexity of its sysems and networks, and to indicate the many different pathways which development can take during the life course. It is clear that the physical organisation of the brain, which continues to develop throughout childhood and even into adult life, sets some parameters for the operation of both cognitive and emotional processes. However, what these parameters are, how variable they are, and how they operate, are questions which are far from resolution. In this chapter it will not be possible to make more than passing reference to these questions, but they are worth mentioning at this stage because they provide an important backdrop for the discussion.

In what follows I focus first on children's cognitive development, then on social development, and finally on emotional development. In each case I give a brief general overview before looking specifically at what can be expected for children in the middle years of childhood, and at any particular implications for children who are looked after away from home. Although it will be clear that emotional, social and cognitive development can only be understood in a connected way, it is necessary to treat them separately to some extent. I then look briefly at the concept of children's needs, at children's understanding of difficult decisions, and at the understanding of differences between children, before drawing together the implications of the discussion for the research described later in this book.

Cognitive development

Discussions of children's cognitive development generally start with Piaget, whose theories have held centre stage in psychology and educational theory for several decades. Piaget's theories and his methods, which were based on observation and close questioning of children, embody a respect for children's attempts to understand the world and an assumption that those attempts are necessarily incomplete and inferior to fully developed adult structures of thinking. The development of structures of thought is seen as progressing through a series of distinct stages which are *global*, in the sense that thinking in all areas is limited to one mode of thought until the child moves on to the next stage. Although representational or symbolic thought develops in early childhood, it is generally not until the age of seven that children are able to perform what Piaget called *operations*, or mental actions such as combination or manipulation which form part of an organised system of thought; and not until the age of eleven or twelve that these operations begin to be *formal* or logical rather than *concrete* (Piaget 1926, 1969, 1976).

It has been argued that Piaget underestimated children's abilities at several stages. Experiments with infants have indicated that awareness of other people and 'object permanence' is discernible far earlier than he thought. Some failures of operational thinking demonstrated by Piaget's subjects have been shown to be artefacts of his research methods. It has also been suggested that the formal operational thinking which he regarded as the summit of development is a culturally-specific mode of thought not used in other parts of the world, and not by all adults in modern Western society. Donaldson (1978), working in a Piagetian tradition, has argued that children's thinking is *embedded* in social contexts and that their ability to understand a concept can depend on whether the situation in which it is employed makes 'human sense' to them. This perspective has given rise to a number of complementary strands of research and thinking. One is to look for better ways of engaging with children's ideas and concepts so that they can be fully revealed, rather than obscured as they were by some of Piaget's research. For instance, Donaldson and Elliott (1990) have shown that children's explanations of causation in terms of *intention* are much more sophisticated than Piaget allowed when he concentrated on *temporal order*. A second strand has been to develop Vygotsky's insight that intellectual growth is a social process in which the contribution of a teacher is important. This has produced powerful concepts such as 'scaffolding' and 'contingency' in an attempt to understand what it is that happens when children learn from others to extend their thinking into new areas (Bruner 1983; Wood 1986; Vygotsky 1962, 1966, 1978; Van der Veer and Valsiner 1994). The third strand builds on another observation of Vygotsky, that what a child learns is not a set of universal abstract concepts but a culture. Light describes a child as 'apprentice to a culture', and has argued that concepts such as conservation only have meaning in the social contexts in which they are used (Light 1986; Light and Perret-Clermont 1989).[3]

More recently the idea of *global* stages has been called seriously into question by the development of theories of modularity and domain-specificity. There is evidence that competence in one area is not necessarily associated with competence in another.[4] In addition studies of the operation of memory, processing and attention have shown how these basic cognitive skills are enhanced by the effects of experience, which brings specific knowledge, practice and the opportunity to develop 'metacognitive' skills. It may be that this applies both in relation to particular domains – children who play chess have been shown to have a better memory for chess positions than adults who do not – and more generally. Experience is not simply a function of age but is often correlated with it.[5] Flavell (1985) suggests that it is theoretically possible to explain the entire difference in thinking ability between children and adults by the effects of experience, although he believes that there is some more fundamental difference. The evidence is now good that short-term and working memory capacity increases during early and middle childhood, and that this in itself can explain some advances in reasoning ability, although it is unclear whether this is a result of superior processing capacity or of more developed strategy (see for instance Oakhill 1984).[6] It is clear that physical changes in the structure and organisation of the brain, particularly of the cortex, continue until puberty and to some extent beyond. It is likely that such changes have an effect on mental function, and there is speculation for instance that changes around puberty mark the closure of a critical period for language acquisition (Rymer 1994). However, clarity in relation to the effects of brain maturation on changing cognitive processes is still lacking.[7]

Are there then any fundamental differences between children's thinking and adults' thinking, or any inherent limits on what children can understand at different ages? Flavell suggests that there must be, although he admits that the evidence is unclear. Meadows (1993), in a comprehensive review of the state of knowledge about cognition in middle childhood, resists drawing any general conclusion. Perhaps the best that can be said is that there may well be inherent limits on capacity related to maturational processes, but that it is not clear what they are, and that it would therefore be unwise to make too many assumptions of the 'children below the age of eleven cannot ... ' variety.

However, it would be equally unwise to expect children to display a full range of cognitive skills regardless of their age. Even if the generally superior performance of adolescents and adults can be fully explained by the effects of experience and practice, this does not mean that it is not significant. Although the failure of Piaget's younger subjects to produce judgements of conservation, to take another perspective, or to employ sophisticated causal explanations may be an artefact of his experimental procedures, the fact remains that older children succeeded in the same tasks. This suggests that one thing that happens with maturation is that our capacities to understand and explain become more stable and consistent in their application across a range of contexts. This process does not cease in adolescence or early adulthood, as has been shown by studies of the effects of expertise on adult scientific or logical judgements. However, in middle childhood it appears that some important conceptual frameworks may be especially precarious and need some shoring up from the context if they are to function effectively.[8] Lloyd (1990), looking at the ability of primary-school-age children to communicate complicated instructions, found that they tended to understand ambiguity but not to express it verbally, and that they needed support in dealing with unclarity or misunderstanding. Seven-year-olds were 'much less likely' than ten-year-olds 'to respond to an inadequate message with a request for further information (p. 64).

McLane puts the point neatly in her contribution to Garbarino et al.'s guide to eliciting information from children:

> Recent research indicates that Piaget probably exaggerated the differences in children's thinking at different stages of development. However, there is ample evidence to demonstrate that there are important differences in how children think, know, and understand and that children are not simply ignorant or inexperienced adults. Rather than describing them as stages, it may be more useful to think of developmental differences as reflecting gradual but perceptible shifts in ways of participating in and understanding experience. Thus, it is important for adults to try to understand that a child's interpretation and understanding of a situation may be quite different from their own.
>
> (Garbarino et al. 1992, p. 41)

Children in the 8–12 age group are likely to scan a situation rather than focus on one striking characteristic, to make inferences about reality rather than simply rely on perceived appearances, to attend to transformational processes rather than concentrate on fixed states, and to understand that operations are reversible. In these respects they have advanced beyond younger children who can do these things only with a great deal of help. Unlike younger children, they are believed to have a 'theory of mind': to be aware of their own thought processes, to understand that other people will have different thoughts, and to be able to make assumptions or predictions about what those thoughts may be (Frye and Moore 1991). On the other hand, their thinking may still be concrete and empirical rather than hypothetico-deductive, and focused on what *is* in reality rather than what might be possible. In many respects their understanding may develop markedly during the years from eight to twelve, for instance in their ability to conceptualise

processes taking place over time (Maurice-Naville and Montanegro 1992).
One should not assume that they are incapable of what Donaldson
would call more 'disembedded' thinking; but one should not rely on
their ability to utilise it. It is also possible that in situations that are stressful they will revert to more 'primitive' patterns of thinking. This is why
it is important not to consider cognitive development in isolation from
emotional experience and social understanding.

Social development

According to Isaacs (1930), Piaget saw the development of social awareness as the key to intellectual development. In his view the infant and
even the pre-school child had very limited awareness of other people as
separate and autonomous entities, and it was the coming of that
awareness at around age seven that stimulated the critical, questioning
approach that produced operational thinking. Nowadays Piaget is seen as
understating the social dimension of learning in childhood, in comparison say with Vygotsky, for whom learning and development were
nothing if not social.[9] Aside from the social aspects of intellectual
growth, however, the growth of social awareness is in itself worthy of
study. Mead (1934) and the social interactionist school showed how
social relationships are the key to the individual's developing sense of
identity. Burkitt (1991) has argued that most explanations of social
relationships are based on a dichotomy between 'the individual' and
'society' that is profoundly misleading. He draws not only on Mead and
Vygotsky but also on Marx, Foucault and Elias to argue for an analysis
which sees humanity as created in social practice, and 'individuality' as
nothing but an abstraction from this.

The implications of such a view for childhood are considerable. From
the illogicality of describing a baby's lack of awareness of a distinction
between self and outside world as 'egocentric', we move to a position
which recognises not only that the personality develops in social interaction but that the idea of personality is meaningless outside social
interaction; and to a more profound understanding of the social basis
of cognition (Light 1986). To see the dichotomy between individual and
society as ultimately meaningless, however, does not mean that it is easy
to talk about development without employing the distinction. We may
therefore have to think on more than one level (just as post-Einsteinian
physicists still employ Newtonian concepts such as gravity for certain
kinds of analysis). Conceptualisations based on the individual and
his/her environment can be most fruitful in explaining the processes of

development and its variations. Bronfenbrenner's (1979) typology of spheres of environmental influence is a good example of how such thinking can help us to conceptualise these processes.

At one level, the environment may be equated with those people with whom the child has direct contact. Studies of development have regularly focused on the infant's first relationships with parents and primary caregivers, especially mothers. Attachment theory sees these early relationships as the foundation of a healthy personality throughout life (Bowlby 1953, 1975). Although Bowlby's maternal deprivation hypothesis may not have survived in recognisable form, the conceptual framework of attachment theory has proved more robust (Rutter 1981). Bowlby's successors have concentrated on measures of the quality of attachment. Ainsworth identified three distinctive patterns of attachment from the behaviour of children when briefly separated from their mothers: *secure, anxious/avoidant* and *anxious/ambivalent*. Secure attachment is consistently most common, but the proportions displaying avoidant and ambivalent patterns appear to vary in different cultures (Ainsworth et al. 1978).[10] The patterns of attachment behaviour shown by children were associated with their mothers' behaviour when they were observed in daily interaction, and Ainsworth concluded that maternal 'sensitivity' to the child's responses was the key to developing secure attachment.[11] Murray and Stein (1991) show how the lack of response shown by depressed mothers produces insecure attachment, and that this is associated with difficulties later in infancy.

Further support has been given to this conceptual framework by research with older children and adults. Patterns of attachment laid down in infancy as a result of parental behaviour tend to persist, both because parental behaviour persists anyway and because children's behaviour tends to reinforce it for better or worse. It is suggested that gradually these patterns become internalised in the child's model of self, and govern the 'developmental pathways' along which the individual will travel. Holmes (1993) found that adults who were securely attached tend to be those who are able to give coherent narratives; and it is particularly relevant to my theme that Main found a very high correlation between the ability of ten- and eleven-year-olds to give coherent spoken autobiographies and measures of their security of attachment both as babies and currently (Main, Kaplan and Cassidy 1985, cited in Bowlby 1988; Main 1991).

Of course, the quality of attachment is not the only interesting thing about the relationship between child and parent-figure.[12] Baumrind's analysis of styles of parenting and their apparent effect on children's personalities is still influential, although its validity has been questioned (Baumrind 1973, cited in Maccoby 1980; for a summary of the criticisms see Das Gupta 1995). Bruner (1983) and Snow (1991) have argued that parental input is of critical importance in language development, although cross-cultural studies cast some doubt on this.[13] Detailed study of what happens in teaching and learning suggests that a child's relationship with a primary caregiver may be more important than schooling in developing skills and knowledge about the world (Wood 1986). Increasingly, however, researchers have become aware that relationships other than those with the primary caregiver can be important to the developing child. Other relatives and friends can be of considerable significance to children, sometimes more than adults realise. Brothers and sisters, for instance, have a lot to teach about social relationships. Dunn and her colleagues have shown how very young children may, if observed carefully in naturalistic settings, show surprisingly sophisticated understandings of motivation. They suggest that learning to comfort, to tease, to compete and to compare in day-to-day interactions with parents and siblings is an important way in which young children's understanding of social interaction and of moral principles is exercised and developed (Dunn and Kendrick 1982; Dunn 1988).

The evidence suggests that by the age of eight children may have a highly developed awareness of social interaction, with an ability to read others' motivation and an understanding of deception.[14] In most cases they will have a strong sense of who they are, which is beginning to be based on traits of character and later on interpersonal relationships, rather than simply on overt physical characteristics.[15] Relationships with their peers tend to be of increasing importance for children who are beginning to look out into the world rather than mainly to their family, both for recreation and for their values and opinions. School and schoolfriends assume greater importance, and by age ten or eleven children are beginning to have projects and plans which are not defined for them within their family setting.[16] These, however, are general patterns which may vary greatly for individual children, especially those with attachment difficulties.

Emotional development

Emotional development in childhood can be studied in terms of the range of emotions to which children have access, or in terms of their understanding of their own and other people's emotions. One influential account is based on psychoanalysis and describes childhood as a series of emotional events or dramas in which certain tasks must be accomplished in order for healthy development to progress, and in the course of which the personality is formed.[17] Freud described middle childhood as a period of 'latency' in which the powerful psychosexual dramas of early childhood were resolved or in abeyance and the struggles of puberty and adolescence were still to come. For Erikson (1950, 1968), this is the period of 'industry versus inferiority', a time for getting on with the business of making one's mark in the world and learning to use one's talents, rather than of struggles over trust, autonomy or identity; in short, it is a time for establishing competence. This is not to say that life may not at times be stormy for the nine-year-old or the eleven-year-old, or that uncertainties about attachment and independence may not persist. However, the picture we are given of the emotional life of middle childhood is one characterised by consolidation and steady development rather than full-blown dramas.[18]

There is some suggestion that the range and subtlety of emotions available to children of this age is rather greater than it was in earlier stages. This is not the same as children's understanding of their emotions. Harris (1989) has shown that children at an early age are capable of *expressing* two emotions at the same time, but that the *belief* that it is possible to have two emotions at the same time only develops much later. This is relevant to my research, since many of the situations and issues that arise for children being looked after away from home are likely to involve ambivalence. Harris's account would suggest that a child who has ambivalent feelings about a situation may verbally describe only one feeling but act out another, which observation in practice tends to confirm.

There is more than one link between cognition and emotion. Harris has studied the cognitive understanding of emotion; perhaps as important is the effect of emotion on cognitive development. Meadows suggests that this has been little acknowledged, although Merleau-Ponty (1964) discusses the story of a child whose development of grammar at a critical stage appeared to be influenced by the experience of acquiring a sibling. Dunn (1988) observed that young children's reasoning ability appeared to advance most in situations which had an emotional charge for them, for instance when they were angry. This contrasts with the obvious thought that emotional turmoil or stress can affect cognitive development adversely; for example, children who have had emotionally upsetting experiences such as separation from a parent appear to do less well at school. The difference may be between temporary agitation on a basis of stability, such as an everyday family argument, and the more unsettling effect of major changes that provoke anxiety or reduce confidence. Dunn's research was conducted in relatively stable, happy, prosperous families with warm and positive relationships between parents and children. The situation may be very different for children who are being looked after away from home. Some of them will have been abused or ill treated. They may have experienced a number of abrupt separations from parent figures for different reasons. The process of being received into care or accommodation may in itself have been difficult or upsetting. All these factors will be likely to have unpredictable effects on their emotional state and also on their cognitive abilities. Some children faced with these experiences become emotionally 'frozen', while others expend their energy in 'acting out'. Some may regress to earlier stages of development. One child may lose interest in school work and fail to progress, especially if his schooling also has been disrupted, while another may throw herself into her school work as a distraction from the pain which she would otherwise be feeling. Harris observed the latter strategy in children sent to boarding school.

Of course, it is not impossible that children who are in an unsettling situation or have had adverse experiences, and whose cognitive skills have developed more slowly as a result, may still be stimulated to new forms of thinking by certain stresses; however, this is speculation. How far children are damaged by adverse experiences, and how well they are able to recover lost ground, is a vexed question in psychology. The material collected by Clarke and Clarke (1976) suggests that children can recover from the most damaging experiences, but that their resilience may depend both on their previous experiences and on the care they are subsequently given, as well as on genetic or constitutional factors. In fact the care given to children who are looked after by the state is often less than optimal, as we shall see in a subsequent chapter. Nevertheless it seems from the foregoing that it would be wrong to assume that such children are disabled by their experiences from taking an active part in decisions about their future. On the contrary, it may be that their experiences of dealing with change, and in some cases of being compelled to take responsibility for aspects of their own care at an early age, make them in some ways better prepared than many other children to take part in decisions. It is also possible, if their self-confidence has been damaged by their experiences, that being able to take part in decisions about the future direction of their lives may represent the beginnings of recovery. Maccoby concluded from her review of the literature that 'participation in decision-making facilitates children's acquisition of social competencies' (1980, p. 386).

Children's needs

The concept of 'children's needs' is capable of misuse. Woodhead (1990) has shown how statements about needs contain an elision from 'is' to 'ought' and so make dissent difficult. Separating a statement into its components – a hypothesis about consequences and an assertion about their desirability – reveals how both are context-dependent and even a matter of choice. We have already seen how hypotheses about inputs and outputs in child-rearing may be true for one culture and not for another. If anything this is even more the case when we come to statements about what is desirable or what constitutes well-being. Clearly the question of what constitutes thriving for an organism cannot be entirely arbitrary, but there are many ways to achieve successful adaptation and the choice may depend partly on cultural context and partly on individual variation.[19]

Kellmer-Pringle (1974) characterised children's needs in terms of nurture and sustenance, a sense of identity, stimulation and opportunities to explore, chances to develop autonomy, and so on. Woodhead's analysis would suggest that many of these categories are specific to a particular culture or class, or to a professional or personal viewpoint. Nevertheless they are also categories with which many would agree. If the aim of development is to produce active and vocal members of society who can engage in dialogue and negotiation, then it is probably important to create opportunities to exercise choice and autonomy from an early age. It is arguable that such opportunities are also important in achieving mental health and a sense of well-being. There is evidence that babies as young as twelve months are less fearful of an upsetting stimulus if they are given a measure of control over it (Gunnar 1980). From the other end of the age range, having an internal rather than an external 'locus of control' seems to be associated with various measures of success and well-being, including mental health, among adolescents and young adults; and it seems likely that an internal locus of control is promoted in part by childhood experiences that give a sense of efficacy, although it may also be a matter of individual genetic variation.[20] We can probably say, then, that for certain outcomes in terms of success and well-being in later life, as well as for mental well-being at the time, participation in decisions as a child is likely to be of benefit.

As well as general statements about children's needs, statements are also made in social work discourse about the needs of individual children. One problem with such statements is that they may suggest that adults can *know* what a child's needs are and that children themselves are not capable of this knowledge. A study by Yamamoto et al. (1987), in which children and adults in different cultures were asked to rate the stressfulness of a number of life events for children, showed that children were more accurate and consistent in their ratings than adults. This raises the question whether children on occasion may be better judges than adults of what is in their interests.

Children's understanding of difficult issues

It may be argued that, even if children's maturity and understanding have been underestimated, some kinds of decision are too difficult for them to understand. The issues may be too complex cognitively or conceptually for them to grasp, or the emotional and social implications may be too entangled for children to be able to engage effectively with them, at least without distress. The question of distress and its place in the understanding of difficult transitions has already been mentioned. Here I want to focus on the question of children's ability to grasp difficult questions – questions that might be thought too 'adult' for them to deal with successfully. A number of authors have addressed this area; for instance Short (1991), Glachan and Ney (1992).[21] Stevens (1982) used small-group discussions and written questionnaires to find out how children at seven, nine and eleven years conceived of political processes, principles and institutions. Using a straightforward Piagetian framework to conceptualise their thinking at these ages, she found that it needed to be stretched to fit the evidence she gathered. Even the younger children seemed to have an ability to grasp political principles, almost 'an innate capacity for the grammar of politics' (p. 94). It appeared that a strong understanding of rules, law and government is actually learned from the experience of being in school and dealing with the power and authority of teachers – and from seeing the limits of that power and authority. It also appeared that children's understanding developed as a result of the discussions with the researcher.[22] Although some key concepts were surprisingly well understood by the seven-year-olds, the depth and complexity of understanding was much greater among the nine-year-olds, and by eleven the discussions which Stevens was able to have were really quite sophisticated. She relates this development in part to language skills.

As children acquire a political vocabulary political imagination develops, and with it the urge to find language for expressing ideas. By the age of nine, much of the political language of adult life has been acquired. By eleven, many children have as good a working vocabulary for politics as many adults could claim, and a framework of ideas which, even if developed no further, will enable them to grasp the facts of current affairs, understand something of relationships between principles and issues in politics, and make their choices at general elections.

(pp. 147–8)

There were striking differences in the kind of understanding, and also in the level of interest, revealed by boys and girls. Stevens' explanation of this echoes Gilligan's (1990) account of different developmental and moral perspectives. There also appeared to be significant differences in understanding and explanation between middle- and working-class children, which Stevens explains in terms of Bernstein's (1972) concepts of 'restricted' and 'elaborated' codes. However, both sexes and classes by the age of nine were demanding respect for their ideas and showing respect for those of others.

Differences between children

The question of differences between children based on sex and gender, class, ethnic background and ability is one which cuts across an account based on age in complex ways. Statistical differences between boys and girls, for instance in linguistic or mathematical ability at different ages, may be read erroneously as if they apply to individual children; on the other hand the difference in perspective or 'voice' which Gilligan (1982) found does appear to have some general applicability. Class and ethnic differences are especially contentious. Bernstein's argument about linguistic codes has been criticised, for instance by Labov (1972) whose analysis of the speech patterns of urban black youngsters suggested that the 'elaboration' may be there if one looks for it.[23] However, it is clear that in institutional environments such as schools that are dominated by a particular way of speaking, children who speak in a different way risk being perceived as less competent than they are, and that this applies whether the difference is one of language, dialect or 'code'. In a way this underlines the importance of a 'child-centred' approach, which starts by trying to understand a particular child's perspective and assumptions and builds on that to something of more general application.[24] This is particularly so when we consider children with 'learning disabilities' or 'special needs', where all the difficult questions about cognitive capacity and level of understanding, of what can be achieved with support and what without, and of what counts as support and what as substitution, are repeated with a new level of uncertainty.

The children in the care system with whom this book is principally concerned include children from all these different groups. They certainly include boys and girls from poor families with little formal education, and children who have had difficulty in school or even been excluded from school. They may include children from different ethnic, cultural or linguistic backgrounds, and children who have been identified as having a learning disability. They are often children who have experienced failures of attachment, poor early care, lack of affection, of consistent discipline or of a clear moral framework. On the other hand they are children who have had a variety of different experiences of life, more or less well known to those caring for them, which they have tried to understand in their own terms, and whose effect on their cognitive skills, emotional well-being or social competence is not easily predictable.[25] In these circumstances it may be as well not to make too many assumptions about what children can and cannot understand or 'cope with', but rather to let children as far as possible be our guide to what is suitable for them.

Implications for research

This review of children's psychological development has a number of implications for children's participation in decisions when they are looked after away from home, and for research into that participation. First, we should not underestimate children's capacities: their ability to reason and conceptualise; their understanding of causes and consequences; their grasp of social relationships, motivation and morality. Although children's capabilities are limited to some extent by immaturity, it is not entirely clear where those limits lie and not entirely predictable how they will operate for a particular child. There should therefore be a *presumption of competence*.[26] Second, children's understanding is likely to vary with their experience, and we should pay attention to the experiences and the understanding of particular individual children in considering how best to involve them in planning their lives. Third, children's ability to engage with issues and contribute to discussion may depend crucially on how the issues are explained to them, the context in which this takes place, and the meaning which this has for them. Fourth, it is likely that children's ability to take an effective part in decision-making will improve with practice; and fifth, that taking part in an effective way, and thereby exercising some degree of control over what happens to them, will in itself be of psychological benefit. All these conclusions are especially important for those working with children to engage them in planning for their future when they are not living with their families. They are also important for those who attempt to engage with children for the purposes of research into those processes.

Finally, we should not underestimate the effects of worry and bewilderment on children's ability to take part in discussion. While writing this chapter I was in my local town when I met a friend of my younger son, a boy of eight years, fairly competent if a little shy. I passed him twice in a few minutes before realising that he seemed troubled. It turned out that he had lost his mother and was quite upset; but he had not been able to tell me, whom he knew fairly well, or speak to the staff in the shop he had been in with his mother, although it turned out that they were very kind and also knew him. When I established that he was lost and tried to help him, he was very compliant and did exactly as I suggested; but he did not think to tell me that his mother had been taking him to the dentist. Fortunately the shop staff knew this and we found his mother at the dentist's looking for him. What struck me about the incident, occurring as it did when I was concerned with these questions, was how difficult it was for a child who wanted help and was keen to cooperate, either to tell someone what he was worried about or to provide information relevant to finding a solution to his problem. It seemed that these difficulties were at least in part a result of the very stress and worry that made it so important for him to communicate. When we turn to look, in the following chapter, at children's rights to take part in decisions about their lives, it will be as well to remember just how hard it can be sometimes for them to exercise autonomy in a world which is controlled and defined for them by adults.

4
Rights of Childhood

Do children have a right to participate in decisions about their lives? Does it even make sense to talk of children having rights, and if so what rights? In this chapter I look at the philosophical basis for theories of children's rights and at some arguments about the potential for conflict between different kinds of rights. I argue that it does make sense to talk of children having rights; that these can include rights to welfare and protection as well as rights to freedom and participation; that conflict between the two kinds of rights is a practical matter rather than one of fundamental principle; and that the exercise of rights is distinct from their possession and varies with circumstances, in which age is one – but not the only – factor.

The concept of children's rights

Since Rodham (1973) described children's rights as 'a slogan in search of definition', definitions have appeared at an alarming rate without resolving some fundamental disagreements about the meaning and value of the concept.[1] Veerman (1992) reprints 42 separate declarations or charters of children's rights made in recent years by official or semi-official organisations. Earlier statements, like the United Nations Declaration of the Rights of the Child adopted in 1959, often emphasise rights of children to certain basic standards of welfare or protection, while more recent statements often stress rights to self-determination and autonomy.[2] Some, notably the United Nations Convention on the Rights of the Child (United Nations 1989), include both. Some argue for optimal, rather than basic, standards of care or protection as of right. At the same time practical measures to promote children's rights have gathered pace, despite setbacks. The United Nations Convention has been ratified by most of the world's governments and has achieved wider support and greater prominence than almost any similar United Nations initiative. It has begun to be used in many countries, including Britain, as a basis for challenging the ways in which children are treated and attempting to secure improvements (see for instance Lansdown and Newell 1994).

At the same time the philosophical and the legal basis for statements about children's rights have continued to be questioned. Stier (1978) argued that 'the quality of the optimal relationship between the state and its child citizens in terms of meeting children's needs is more appropriately captured by Hart's notion of *duty*' (p. 57). O'Neill (1992) suggests that 'obligations' make a better basis than rights for the relationship between children and those responsible for their welfare. It is, she claims, 'hard for rights-based approaches to take full account of ways in which children's lives are particularly vulnerable to unkindness, to lack of involvement, cheerfulness or good feeling' (p. 28). One might counter that it does not invalidate a rights-based approach to show that it does not accommodate everything one might want to say about relationships between adults and children.

Freeman (1983b) argues in favour of children's rights to self-determination, but is sceptical about whether the fulfilment of basic human needs counts as a right when it does not constitute a valid claim against a particular individual. He quotes the UN Declaration of the Rights of the Child (wrongly cited as the Declaration of Human Rights): 'the child shall have the right to adequate nutrition, housing, recreation and medical services'. 'No one,' says Freeman, 'would gainsay this. But who is to bear the responsibility of meeting these needs in environments where resources are insufficient, as they are in much of what now tends to be called the "South"?' (p. 25). This seems unnecessarily restrictive of the concept of rights. Given that Freeman is talking about moral rather than legal rights, it is surely possible to say that a right may constitute a claim on anyone in a position to meet it; which could be a parent, or someone holding power in the society where the child lives, or in relation to that society. Common speech can imply that children in the poor world have a right to sustenance which people or governments in the rich world have a corresponding duty to meet. Is this statement meaningless, or based on a misuse of the concept of rights? It is not immediately evident that this must be so. Even if one argues that a moral right does not make sense unless it is capable of translation into a legal one, one can see ways in which such welfare rights might be expressed in national and international law.[3]

The argument is not really about whether children *ought* to have adequate nutrition, housing, health care, education and so on, which few would dispute. Nor is it about whether there is an obligation on adults, whether parents or the state, to ensure that these needs are met. Again, few would deny this, although there may be disagreement about the precise nature of such obligations. Rather is the argument about whether such needs and obligations should be framed as moral or legal rights. In relation to the other kind of rights to which children are said to be entitled, namely rights of self-determination, the issue is rather different, as we shall see.

Rights of self-determination

Powerful statements of children's rights to determine their lives have been made by Farson (1974) who argues that 'The acceptance of the child's right to self-determination is fundamental to all the rights to which children are entitled' (p. 27), and Holt (1975) who proposes 'that the rights, privileges, duties, responsibilities of adult citizens be made *available* to any young person, of whatever age, who wants to make use of them'. This includes the right to vote, to be legally responsible for one's life and acts, to work for money, to direct and manage one's own education, to travel, to live away from home, and 'the right to seek and choose guardians other than one's own parents' (pp. 15–16). Holt's proposed rights, applied to children regardless of age or maturity, have been regarded by some as an abusers' and exploiters' charter. As Wald (1979) points out, however, even if one rejects the package as a whole, Holt's and Farson's claims can be 'a challenge to prove the basis for existing restrictions and to abandon those that do not withstand scrutiny.'

Purdy (1992, 1994a) has taken up this challenge. She takes issue with the argument that children ought to have equal rights of self-determination with adults, on the basis that it hinges on a view of morality which attaches undue importance to individual rights, freedom and justice and ignores the connectedness of human needs, and that it understates the limits on children's understanding and wisdom. The core of her argument is that children need protection while they learn to exercise sound judgement and acquire the knowledge they need to manage well in the world, and that adults are responsible for providing education, care and protection until young people are ready to look after themselves without undue risk of avoidable harm. This is a position from which many people would not dissent. The argument that rights are not everything and that we also have a duty to care for each other is important and has a sound basis in feminist ethical philosophy.[4] However, there are difficulties, which Purdy inadvertently exposes. In philosophical terms she rejects 'the capacity to plan for goals' as a test of rationality sufficient to justify holding equal rights; the test she attributes to 'liberationists'. She proposes instead 'the capacity for planning systematic life-enhancing projects or having a rational life plan' which would 'exclude from equal rights young children and quite possibly most older children as well' (Purdy 1992, p. 27). The concept of a 'rational life plan' as a criterion is one she borrows from Palmeri (1980), although she uses it to argue rather differently.[5] This capacity, claims Purdy, depends on 'the cognitive capacity to judge what is in one's own interest and the character traits necessary to act on it.' But if the basis of adult rights is the capacity to develop a rational life-plan, what does this imply about adults who lack this capacity, either because of limited intellectual ability or simply very poor judgement? Are they to have adult rights, or not? What is the difference between such adults and children? The argument could be – although Purdy does not put it explicitly – that unlike children such adults have achieved full rationality for themselves as individuals, and the duty to protect them from their mistakes therefore ceases to apply. However, this depends on an assumption that arrival at adulthood marks the termination of development, which is not an easy position to sustain. As we have seen, it is hard to identify a clear qualitative difference between adults and children.[6]

In some ways Purdy overstates her case, and she has been sharply criticised by philosophers for flaws in her reasoning (McGillivray 1994; Campbell 1994; for a response see Purdy 1994b). She rejects Rawls' contract theory and proposes a modified utilitarianism without taking real account of Rawls' criticisms of this approach (Rawls 1972; see also Rawls 1962, 1967; Wolff 1968). Nor does she notice that a similar modification of utilitarianism has been used by Cohen (1980) as the basis of a strong defence of granting adult rights to children, despite the fact that Cohen at times appears to be her chief target.[7] In addition Purdy's view of childhood is extremely culture-bound. In arguing that the proper maturation of teenagers is dependent on protecting them from ill-advised decisions about where to live, whether to go to school, whether to have sex, she ignores the fact that millions of the world's teenagers do take those decisions for themselves. Just as the liberal philosophers she criticises seem to see the world from the point of view of a gentleman in his club, she appears to see it from the point of view of an affluent, educated North American mother. Above all, she fails to distinguish sufficiently clearly between younger children and adolescents, although at points she appears to concede that adolescents should have a range of civil rights at least similar to those held by adults. Others such as Freeman (1983c) have argued forcefully for children and young people's rights to a degree of autonomy without going so far as Holt and Farson. (In fact Freeman's substantive position has a good deal in common with Purdy's, but is proposed as a defence of children's rights rather than an attack on them.)

The basis for having rights

The debate about children's self-determination rights is not so much about whether the concept of *rights* is applicable to the sort of claims under discussion; clearly it is. The arguments here are different ones: first, about whether children are capable of bearing rights at all; second, about how far such rights, if granted, should extend. The possession of rights can be held to depend either on the exercise of *will*, or on the fact of having an *interest*. Theories of rights based on will, or power, can be traced back to Kant (see Paton 1948). Campbell (1992) argues that such theories, in their stress on self-sufficiency and autonomy as the basis for participation in the rational community, are 'inadequate as an expression of the moral significance of persons, particularly children.' He puts forward instead an *interest* theory of rights, according to which 'children have rights if their interests are the basis for having rules which require others to behave in certain ways with respect to these interests.' This provides Campbell with the basis for a powerful argument for basing adult obligations to children on children's rights, which include the right to choose.

Worsfold (1974) considers a number of different ways of founding a theory of children's rights. He argues that entitlement to rights 'cannot be resolved without reference to some broader framework, a comprehensive theory of justice, to which all parties can agree,' and that statements of rights should meet the test set by Cranston (1967) of being practicable, universal in application, and of paramount importance. According to Worsfold 'practicable' implies that rights 'must cohere and be theoretically consistent within the society's conception of justice', not that they have to be 'popular or practical to implement'; and 'universal' does not preclude rights which have different implications for different members of society, but has to do with the capacity for rights more than with their exercise (Worsfold 1974, p. 149). The final criterion (paramount importance) echoes Dworkin's notion of rights as factors which 'trump' other considerations (Dworkin 1978, cited in Worsfold 1974).

Worsfold argues that the modified social contract theory proposed by Rawls (1972) provides the necessary foundation and satisfies Cranston's test. Rawls uses a hypothesis of impartiality – the 'original position' – whereby members of society choose rules of justice and fairness without knowing their own eventual position in society, to derive two fundamental principles: 'that each person should have a personal liberty compatible with a like liberty for all others' and 'that societal inequalities are to be arranged such that all individuals must share whatever advantages and disadvantages the inequalities bring (Worsfold 1974, pp. 151–2). Children are included in these arrangements to the extent that they are *capable*, that is rational and capable of accepting the principle of fairness. Worsfold argues that this provides a justification for children's participation in decisions. It also provides a basis for some form of paternalism, but one which protects against abuses of authority and which provides that children must have the opportunity to participate in a decision-making process even when paternalism is operating.[8] He concludes that Rawls's procedural conception of justice 'provides a framework within which the granting of children's rights is practicable'; that 'the notion of impartiality ensures that all shall be considered equally in the division of societal advantages and disadvantages'; and that 'the primacy of personal rights...is a central tenet of the theory' and extends to children 'as well as other members of society' (Worsfold 1974, pp. 156–7).

Rawls' argument includes rationality as a requirement for participation in the social contract, or at least of the capacity for rationality. There is a tradition going back to Locke of allowing rights to all in principle, but accepting that the ability to *exercise* them is limited by capacity, particularly in the case of children but also in the case of some adults.[9] This is an important and useful conceptual distinction, as we see later.

Archard's argument for 'rational autonomy'[10]

Archard (1993) suggests that what I have called 'welfare rights' are appropriately based on interests, while rights to self-determination must be based on the capability of making and exercising choices.[11] He further argues 'that all children have interests and thus merit rights to their own welfare', which may be exercised by them directly or on their behalf by adults. Rights of self-determination, however, 'can only be exercised by those thought capable of doing so...The argument over whether children should have *and* exercise these rights turns on whether children are thought capable of exercising them' (Archard 1993, p. 65).

Archard distinguishes between two general approaches to this question, which he calls the 'liberationist' and 'caretaker' theses. The liberationists, exemplified by Holt and Farson, appear to regard children's incompetence as an ideological construct. Sometimes (especially in discussing older children) they argue that it is not based in fact. On other occasions, according to Archard, they simply dismiss it as irrelevant. The 'caretaker' thesis on the other hand places great emphasis on children's incompetence as a basis for paternalism. Archard sees this assumption as having dominated discussions of the relationship between children and adults, ever since Locke rejected Hobbes' notion of children as the property of their parents in favour of a concept of responsibility as the basis of parental rights. Other philosophical exponents of the position are Mill (1910) and more recently Feinberg (1980). In essence it is a viewpoint which places great emphasis on self-determination not as a simple right but as the goal of human development. The attainment of self-determination requires that an individual's freedom be curtailed until he or she becomes capable of exercising it fully. Feinberg characterises this as the child's 'right to an open future.' Similarly Freeman (1983c), seeking a path between 'liberationist' and 'caretaker' positions, argues for compulsory education on the grounds that to allow a child to choose not to be educated would in effect deprive her or him of future choices. In a later article he suggests that

> the question we should ask ourselves is: what sort of action or conduct would we wish, as children, to be shielded against on the assumption that we would want to mature to a rationally autonomous adulthood and be capable of deciding on our own system of ends as free and rational beings?

> (Freeman 1987, p. 310)

Archard argues that the capacity for choice is based on *rational autonomy*, defined as composed of rationality, maturity and independence. *Rationality* he equates with cognitive competence. Adherents of the 'caretaker thesis' often accept Piaget's account of the development of cognitive competence, but Archard argues that this is flawed because Piaget's ideal of adult cognitive competence is a Western one and not universally applicable, because even in the West not all adults always achieve this level of rationality, and because children demonstrate important competencies earlier than Piaget allows: 'It is all too easy to cast children as cognitively incompetent when the standard of competence by which they are measured is both culturally specific and unrealised by many adults, but, even so, children may be cognitively more competent than we assume' (Archard 1993, p. 66). Particularly in relation to older children, Archard argues that it is 'not fair' to presume that they are 'obviously incompetent' compared with adults.

Maturity is identified by Archard with emotional stability. Again he concedes the argument up to a point – 'there are reasons to think young children more likely than adults to make decisions while in the grip of strong emotions which can change from one moment to the next' – but concludes that it is easy to overstate the differences between adults and children, especially older children. *Independence* is related to Kant's concept of 'the capability of self-maintenance' (Kant 1887, cited in Archard 1993). In the strongest sense this means self-sufficiency, but the extent to which adults can be regarded as self-sufficient must be limited by the complexity and interdependence characteristic of modern societies, as well as by personal factors such as unemployment or disability; whereas in pre-industrial and even early industrial societies children may make a significant contribution to the household income.[12] A broader interpretation of 'self-maintenance' is the ability to act out one's choices, which may be impeded by physical or mental immaturity. As Archard points out, these limitations do not apply to all children, and they do apply to some adults. Finally, independence may be defined as having a mind of one's own: 'Independent people in this respect have a clear idea of what they think and want. When they make choices these are their own and do not simply follow the example of others. There is no doubt that children can be independent in this sense.' Although Archard does not make the argument, it is perhaps an even more telling objection to the use of independence as a criterion for rights that it could oblige us to exclude adults who are dependent, such as those with severe multiple disabilities, from normal civil rights.

All in all Archard appears to conclude that the concept of rational autonomy provides a basis for rights of self-determination which apply to children as well as adults; that it justifies denying rights of self-determination to some children all of the time, and to some children some of the time; but that it does not justify the restrictions on the liberty of children, particularly of older children, which currently exist.

The right to vote and the right to have sex

Political and sexual rights are useful test cases for many arguments about what rights children should have and at what age. The right to vote is an index of participation in the wider community, with the implication that one's choices will have effects for other people. The right to take part in sexual activity and to make sexual relationships is an index of how far one is trusted to take charge of one's own body and well-being, and of one's moral life. Franklin (1986a) supports Holt in arguing for the right of children to take part in the political process by voting whenever they decide they are ready to exercise that right. He counters the objection that it is ridiculous to extend the vote to two-year-olds, by suggesting that they are unlikely to have any interest in voting. Arguments about the lack of knowledge or experience of children, or the risk that they will choose on the basis of irrelevant considerations, are countered by drawing attention to the reality of adult political wisdom and voting decisions.

Hughes (1989) is critical of Franklin's arguments. She contends that 'from one point of view, the demand for the enfranchisement of children demands too much. It does not allow for learning who we are in the political community before taking the full responsibility which is involved in acting with full political authority.' On the other hand, she suggests, it 'requires too little' in that full democratic participation must include standing for office as well as voting. 'It is oddly paternalistic,' writes Hughes, 'to think that children should make do with anything less.' Her conclusion is that to take both the democratic process and children's rights seriously requires that 'political maturity, responsibility, and commitment ... must be learnt in other contexts before they can be expressed in a performative act' (Hughes 1989, pp. 49–50). It could be objected, of course, that adults are not required to learn any of these things before voting. Archard suggests that being subject to the laws, in the sense of being legally accountable for one's conduct, can entitle one to a say in their formulation.[13] This would imply that the age of voting should coincide with the age of criminal responsibility. Archard also refers to Stevens' evidence that many children of eleven have an adequate understanding of politics, comparable with that of many adults (see Chapter 3 above).

With sexuality the issues are different, and perhaps more complex. Holt does not appear to regard the question as difficult; were he writing twenty years later, with the greater awareness of child sexual abuse that we have now, it is possible that he would have approached the issue differently. For Holt it is a simple question of young people's right to do what they want with each other, and parents' lack of right to impose their own values. His arguments have some force, but he ignores the question of what constitutes valid consent where there is a marked imbalance of power. Ives (1986) attempts a more sophisticated analysis, suggesting that children possess 'at least three sexual rights: the right to freedom from sexual exploitation, the right to express their sexuality, and the right to sex education'. He dismisses Finkelhor's statement that children 'can never consent', but is not able completely to resolve the question of when a child can and cannot consent. He refers to a proposal that the age of consent be replaced by a general test of capability of 'real consent', but without enthusiasm (p. 143).[14]

Archard (1993) discusses the question of consent in a way that begins to do justice to its complexity. He suggests that the key to protecting children from exploitation is to empower them to say no, but acknowledges that this may imply a corresponding right to say yes.[15] Further, it represents a major challenge to conventional relationships between adults and children. 'It is a tragic irony,' says Archard,

> that the very habits of obedience to elders which support parental instructions to avoid strangers make it easier for adults to exploit children sexually. Victims of sexual abuse often testify to the fact that they submitted to the assaults because they had been taught to respect and defer to adults. If children are to learn to say 'no' to adults it cannot just be a localised and parentally-approved negative that is encouraged.
>
> (1993, p. 78)

He also suggests that some relationships might be defined, as apparently they are in some European countries, as special ones in which the power imbalance is such that a valid consent cannot be given, or in which some additional evidence of positive consent is necessary: for instance relationships between doctor and patient, teacher and pupil, or parent and child.

In both cases – that of political participation and that of sexual consent – Archard proposes a reduction in age thresholds to include teenagers. In the case of sexual consent he specifically recommends fourteen as the threshold for both homosexual and heterosexual sex. In the case of voting he does not specify a precise age; I assume that by 'teenager' he means someone aged thirteen or over. Lindley (1989) also makes a case for treating teenagers differently, and suggests that they are oppressed by those who insist on treating all children as though their principal need was for protection. He makes a cogent case for extending to teenagers a range of adult rights roughly equivalent to those proposed by Holt for all children.

Conflicts between different kinds of rights

Both protectionists and liberationists sometimes write as though there were no difference between a one year old and a sixteen year old, or at least no difference as important as that between both of them and an adult; and those writers on children's rights who discriminate between children at different ages tend to focus on the two ends of the continuum. It is not hard to see the needs of young children, say up to seven, as chiefly to do with care, protection and nurture, while talk about rights of self-determination may be of limited or theoretical relevance to them. Equally there is persuasive force in the suggestion that many adult rights should be allowed to adolescents, or at least that the onus is on those who would wish to deny such rights to make their case. Where it may be most difficult to achieve agreement, and where many writers avoid treading, is in the area of rights and needs of children in the middle years of childhood, those between these two extremes. This may be where the conflict between different kinds of rights becomes especially significant, and we see later that this can be a real difficulty in practice.

Farson (1974) draws a distinction between those interested in protecting children and those interested in protecting their rights, and suggests that one may be incompatible with the other. Rogers and Wrightsman (1978) distinguish between a *nurturance* orientation, which 'stresses the provision by society of supposedly beneficial objects, environments, services, experiences, etc. for the child...what is good or desirable is determined for the child by society or by some subset of society, not by the child'; and a *self-determination* orientation, which 'stresses those potential rights which would allow children to exercise control over their environments, to make decisions about what they want, to have autonomous control over various facets of their lives.' Rogers and Wrightsman tested the validity of the distinction by administering a 'children's rights attitude scale' to four groups consisting of high-school students, education undergraduates, other undergraduates, and adults. The questionnaire elicited support for statements reflecting each orientation in the areas of health, education/information, economics, safety/care, and law/justice/politics. They discovered that there were significant differences between the groups, although in all groups there was general support for both kinds of rights, and especially for nurturance rights. The group consisting of high-school students was simultaneously the least enthusiastic about nurturance rights and the most enthusiastic about self-determination rights.

Rogers and Wrightsman have been criticised by Franklin (1986b) and Archard (1993) for creating a 'dichotomy' between two kinds of rights, with the 'clear implication...that children are either regarded as independent, active and strong persons equal in all significant respects to adults, or treated as dependent, passive, vulnerable individuals who do not merit the same moral status as their older and superior caretakers' (Archard 1993, p. 87). It may well be that such a dichotomy does exist in the minds of many. All that Rogers and Wrightsman claim, however, is that their research shows that the distinction is a valid one, but that the two categories are not mutually exclusive. It seems a useful distinction, and as Franklin points out it is logically prior to the more elaborate classifications of rights employed by Wald (1979) and Freeman (1983c).

Is there a dichotomy, or is the opposition, as Franklin suggests, 'more apparent than real'? There is a question about whether both kinds of rights can be constituted in similar ways and held by the same people, or whether perhaps there is a progression for groups of people from one kind of right to the other. Archard argues that those who lack rights of self-determination can still have their wishes considered, but he does not consider whether those who do have rights of self-determination may still also have welfare rights. Franklin points out that adults are also subject to protections, which may sometimes be experienced as infringements of their autonomy but usually are not.[16] Houlgate (1980) appears to argue that if children are granted adult rights then consideration of their welfare cannot outweigh those rights. On the other hand he also concedes, in criticising Rawls' justification of paternalism in terms of children's irrationality, that adults are not always able to judge their own interests or make sensible decisions.

Perhaps we should accept that rights do not have to be absolute, and that Dworkin's 'trumps' analogy may sometimes be misleading. If we allow that every person has full human rights but that the *exercise* of those rights varies with circumstances, we may find a way to encompass some of the contradictions involved in children having rights both to protection and to self-determination. At the same time we may leave space for the mutual obligation to care which some have argued is antithetical to 'rights talk', but which can perhaps be persuaded to lie alongside it. It may be argued that this dilutes the concept of 'rights' to the point where it becomes meaningless; but it is not clear that an all-or-nothing version of rights is the only one that makes sense or is even very helpful in organising real social groups. Wringe (1980) makes a similar argument in relation to rights in school:

If rights may be overruled it may be felt that little is gained by showing that pupils, or indeed anyone else, have them. This would be mistaken. Firstly, if rights are admitted, educational or other advantages must be weighed not only against each other but also against the undesirability of overruling individual rights. If this is done, it follows that the latter consideration may sometimes prevail. Secondly, if a right is not invalidated by being overruled, it continues to stand as a pressing argument for working towards a solution where it can be implemented. Thirdly, quite apart from action that follows from the particular rights of pupils, the recognition that in general they have rights establishes unequivocally that they are to be seen in a certain way and that account must be taken both of their interests as seen by adults and of their own purposes and point of view.

(p. 286)

Having rights in practice

To some extent the exercise of rights can be dependent on the ability and need for them. Rights to self-determination can be framed in such a way that they apply to those who are able to exercise them, while welfare rights may apply to anyone who is vulnerable for whatever reason. For instance, an adult would normally have the right to provide himself or herself with the means to existence; but an adult who was severely disabled, or temporarily incapacitated by illness, or imprisoned, might have a legitimate claim on others in a position to provide those means. It would be nonsense to say that someone in a coma had the right to earn a living, or the right to vote; but that does not mean that such a person has relinquished all rights, and it may be that by their situation they have acquired rights to care and protection which they did not previously need. In this way it could be possible for each person to hold a combination of rights to welfare and to self-determination appropriate to them and their circumstances.[17] There is, however, also a specific question in particular cases, where a person may have a welfare right which imposes responsibility on another person, and the exercise of this responsibility conflicts with the first person's exercise of some right of self-determination. An adult example could be that of a severely disabled, physically dependent person who wished to commit suicide. An example from childhood might be that of a ten-year-old who wished to refuse dental treatment. It is in relation to children in the middle years that these conflicts arise most frequently and are often most difficult to resolve. As McGillivray puts it,

> Autonomy is always relative; what is meant by autonomy for children is the measured right to self-determination, the increasing

freedom to make one's own mistakes. The central issue in the rights debate is to what extent we leave children of what age to experience the unadulterated social consequences of those mistakes.

(1992, pp. 220–1)

If one accepts that adolescents ought to have substantial rights to determine their own lives, then perhaps their rights to welfare begin to be secondary to their self-determination rights and are to be claimed by them for themselves. On the other hand if one concedes that babies and infants are often not the best judges of their own interests, then their rights to welfare are primary and have to be claimed for them by responsible adults. In the middle years of childhood, however, the competing demands of self-determination and 'best interests' can often be very evenly matched. If we accept that children have rights to both, then to give due weight to both can be a considerable challenge. It is a challenge that the Convention on the Rights of the Child (United Nations 1989) lays down when it asserts the right of every child to protection from abuse and neglect, to an adequate standard of living and to education, and at the same time the right to freedom of association, thought and expression and to have his or her views considered.[18]

Clearly these statements have a rhetorical force, and this is an important part of their purpose. However, they also have a force and a meaning in rational moral and political discourse, and in law. If these rights that children have confer obligations on those who are in a position to meet or deny them, then children's rights may make demands on a wide variety of social actors. In a democratic society this can include any citizen. It certainly includes those who have charge of children, particularly those who have charge of children under some basis of compulsion. It is no accident that much that has been written and done in the promotion of children's rights is about the school setting, since that is where many children and young people are compelled to spend much of their time (see for instance Adams et al. 1971). Above all, perhaps, these obligations fall on parents, and on the agencies of the state. The relationships between children, their parents and the state constitute a complex web of mutual demands, obligations and expectations; and this is especially true when there is a question of the state intervening in, or taking over, the parent's responsibility for the care of a child.

5

Children, Parents and the State

My intention in this chapter is to explore some assumptions about relationships between children, parents and the state that underlie law and social policy, and to examine their implications for children's involvement in decisions. This means looking at the nature of parental rights and responsibilities, the obligations of the state to provide services to children and families, the rules governing state intervention in family life, and the ways in which disputes about children are adjudicated. I also consider the impact of Children Act 1989 and of recent court judgements in England and Wales, and review some problems with the concept of 'the child's best interest'. Finally I suggest some principles for including children in decisions when both their families and the state are involved, against which actual practice in decision-making may be tested.

All the negative or limiting assumptions about children and childhood found in some of the accounts reviewed in earlier chapters – whether those accounts are sociological, psychological, historical, philosophical or lay – recur in the fields of family law and social policy. Children are silent or muted. They are seen as incompetent, as unable to judge what is best for them. Their interests are identified with those of their parents, or are seen in terms of a future and not a present orientation. Finally, they are identified as a separate kind of being from adults, with their own distinct, and disabling, status.

The nature of parental authority

Most legal and philosophical accounts of parental rights accept that the position of parents is a social construction. The view that parental authority is a natural right is no longer tenable; if nothing else, the evidence of cultural variation has seen to that. There is less agreement about what kind of social construction it is. One view is that children are the *property* of their parents. Barton and Douglas (1995) suggest that this is not as untenable as some philosophers have argued, although they do object that it 'feels uncomfortable' (p. 22).[1] This is weak; a more substantial objection is that it is clearly not the case in most contemporary societies that parents can dispose of their children as they see fit. In general we are free to do whatever we want with our property, including giving it away, selling it, or destroying it, so long as we do not contravene another law or rule. Even a domestic pet we can sell or give away as we please, although we may be prevented from treating it cruelly. Our children, however, are not ours to dispose of, and there are many limitations on how we may behave as parents. It was not always so; and perhaps the view of children as property has more relevance to ancient or medieval societies than it does now.

Another view is that children are in *trust*. According to Barton and Douglas this implies that parents hold rights on the presumption that they are best placed to bring up their children, and only to enable them to carry out their responsibilities. They suggest that this view of parenthood 'may be incoherent' because the situation does not readily fit the legal forms required and because many parents continue to exercise their role despite evidence that others might do it better (Barton and Douglas 1995, p. 25).[2] Barton and Douglas imply that the position of parents may best be characterised as a combination of ownership and trusteeship, holding together the view that having children is a private undertaking and parents have the right to bring up their children in the way that seems fit to them, and the view that we all have a collective interest in the upbringing of future citizens and in ensuring that children are treated decently.

However, it is arguable that trust is becoming more valid than property as an account of the rights of parents. Children were more like parental property in the past than they are now – the objections made in the late nineteenth century to the first legal intervention to prevent parental ill-treatment of children illustrate this. The shift from one view to another is still continuing, although unevenly. In the USA Ruddick observes that 'the language of the law still reflects the older view of children as their parents' chattels' (1979, p. 127). Ruddick suggests that the 'trust' analogy does work; from contract theory he derives the idea that parents make an implicit commitment to care for a child in ways that ensure its future, and not to do it harm; this is a commitment *to the child* rather than to the state, on the model of a two-party trust. He argues that this allows for parental latitude in decision-making, which serves children's interest in having parents who are committed to the task. 'Parents free from intervention take more pride in, and hence more responsibility for, their children and treat them more consistently' (Ruddick 1979, pp. 127–8).

Blustein (1979) focuses on parental duties rather than rights, but many of his arguments are similar. Procreation cannot provide sufficient basis for parental duties, and ultimately the source of child-rearing duties can only lie in social practices, which vary quite widely. In ancient Sparta and in Nazi Germany natural parents often had a very limited or non-existent role in the upbringing of children – the extreme case of 'children of the state'. Blustein suggests that every social practice is an attempt to accommodate the interests of children, parents and society as a whole, and that those interests are interdependent: 'mutual adjustment of interests, not their ranking or aggregation, is required' (p. 120). Dingwall and Eekelaar (1984) argue that parents are 'agents' or 'trustees' who exercise their parental rights on an implied licence from the community.[3] This makes them entitled to help and support as well as to regulatory control. However, they also suggest that 'all children have an equal *prima facie* claim against the present adult world, for optimal conditions of upbringing compatible with society's fundamental economic and ideological structure' (p. 25).

 ## The state's interest in children's welfare

Providing such conditions may be one of the objects of 'family policy', but states differ in the extent to which they openly adopt such policy. Kamerman and Kahn (1978) distinguish between *explicit* and *implicit* family policy, between purposes which may be 'manifest' or 'latent', and between consequences which may be 'intended or unintended, direct or indirect, mutually consistent or inconsistent'. They suggest that some countries have family policies that are explicit and comprehensive, in that there are relatively clear over-arching goals which those policies are designed to achieve. Other states accept the existence of family policy as a field and therefore evaluate policies to some extent in terms of their impact on families. A third group only have 'implicit and reluctant' family policies; these include the United Kingdom and the United States.[4]

Land and Parker (1978) agree that the United Kingdom has resisted an explicit family policy. However, within a range of policies there are assumptions about how families should operate which may amount to a 'hidden agenda' of policy-making. They suggest that

> what is being protected are particular patterns of responsibilities and dependencies within the family and a long-established division of labour between the sexes and between generations. By presenting these as 'natural' or 'normal' the state can support and sustain them without appearing intrusive, thus preserving the illusion that the family is a private domain. At the same time, such strategies deny that there is an ideological dimension either to family life or to the policies themselves. Great care is taken in the delivery of services and benefits to the family not to upset the pattern of power and dependency within it.
>
> (p. 332)[5]

This has a particular relevance for this book, in that one problem with promoting children's involvement in decisions when they are in state care may be that it represents a challenge to conventional power relationships in families; and this is something the state is generally reluctant to do.

Fox Harding (1996) also suggests that 'Britain is ... very far from a *laissez-faire* model which does not attempt to mould family life at all' (p. 186). She argues that the British approach includes both *laissez-faire* and authoritarian elements. Of course the last century has seen a much greater level of intervention by the state in children's lives: in protecting them from abuse and neglect; in providing basic health care and education; and also in making and enforcing rules about what they can and cannot do.

Donzelot (1980) has claimed that in fact the primary purpose of intervention is to control, not just the children and families who are directly subject to intervention, but all members of working-class families. He argues that there was a fundamental change in the relationship between the state and the family between the society of the *ancien regime* characterised by a patriarchal alliance between the state and the head of the family, and the modern apparatus where the state is represented by 'experts' who make alliance with the mother through which the family is brought under surveillance – the *tutelary complex*. This development, he argues, was the state's response to the challenge of controlling the working-class family and dealing with poverty without encouraging destitution or fomenting rebellion; or, implicitly, by redistributing power and wealth. Assistance to families is linked inextricably with surveillance, so that a family's own need is used to bind them into the power system.

Donzelot has been criticised for supporting patriarchy (Barrett and McIntosh 1982), and there are problems with his analysis. He does not explain why, if the purpose of the tutelary complex is to control working class families, the penetration of parental advice seems much greater among the educated middle class; and his focus is entirely on relationships between adults. As in much writing on family policy, children only appear as problems for adults to deal with, never as subjects in themselves.[6] Parton (1991) puts the question differently: 'how can the state establish the rights of individual children while promoting the family as the natural sphere for raising children and hence not intervening in all families and thus reducing its autonomy?'

There is an assumption that the state has a legitimate interest in the welfare of all children; that they do not simply belong to their parents. In Tudor England, as Pinchbeck and Hewitt (1969) show, destitute children were sometimes regarded as 'children of the state' and a potential asset, but there seems to have been a clear difference between them and children maintained by their families. The modern concern with the welfare of all children, rather than simply the destitute, may be linked to the twin developments of political democracy and mass armies at the end of the nineteenth and beginning of the twentieth century. Political democracy produced concern with the development of children's minds; the demands of warfare with their bodies. As a result it became important for the state to concern itself with what went into both: with education on the one hand, and health and nutrition on the other. It could be argued that the State's concern with the welfare of children is at bottom no more than a concern with maintaining order; but this would be to discount the much more varied motivation of the philanthropists, trade unionists, doctors, teachers and social workers who struggled to improve child welfare services. A culmination of this concern with the welfare of all 'the nation's children' was probably the period immediately after the Second World War, when optimism about democracy and solidaristic social organisation were at their highest. Steedman (1986) has written movingly of how state welfare provision in the 1950s was able to give a sense of being valued and having 'a right to exist' to a child whose own family failed to give her that message: 'I think I would be a very different person now if orange juice and milk and dinners at school hadn't told me, in a covert way, that I had a right to exist, was worth something' (p. 122).[7]

The state's intervention in parental conduct

If one of the central questions of family policy is about what services are provided to support families, the other is about when the state should intervene to regulate the conduct of parents. In modern societies the autonomy of all parents is significantly reduced by compulsory education and universal health surveillance. However, there are circumstances in which it is seen as legitimate for the state to intrude further into individual families and regulate, modify or even replace their parenting. What is the ideological justification for this? Dingwall (1994) argues that

> The family is a site where the moral conditions for liberalism are reproduced. If its internal regime is unjust, then not only are the freedoms of some members diminished, but public life is also threatened because of the impairment of members' capacities to participate in the institutions of liberal democracy. It is here that the argument for intervention rests, that no group can be permitted to disable those under its control for participation in civic life.
>
> (p. 64)

Of course the extent of state intrusion into parental autonomy is not the same for all social groups. Others besides Donzelot and Parton have argued that surveillance and intervention fall more extensively and heavily on the working class or the poor (Jenkins 1975; Holman 1988; Frost and Stein 1989; Jordan 1990; see also Stedman Jones 1971). This is partly because some reasons for intervention are more likely to apply to families with fewer resources or more sources of stress, and also because the network of surveillance is often combined with the provision of services used by these groups. The state of course is not the same as society, and the wider family and community have an interest in the quality of care given to children (community sanctions may have been more important in the past when the state's role was less). However, to the extent that outside intervention in how families care for children is undertaken by agencies of the local or national state, it is likely to be experienced as 'other' by most social groups, but especially by those who are more excluded, marginalised or distanced from the prevailing culture: for instance the long-term unemployed, ethnic minorities, homosexuals, or people with disabilities.[8]

There is disagreement both in academic writing and in real life about the proper boundary between the authority of parents and the power of the state to intervene. There is disagreement about when the state may intervene – whenever a child's best interests are not being promoted; or when certain specified minimum standards are not met; or only when children are being flagrantly ill-treated; or only when normal care arrangements have broken down. There is disagreement about whether the state's primary duty is to children, and to some conception of their best interests aside from their families, or whether it is first to families as social units that include children. Some years ago Fox (1982) established that these different perspectives, which she characterised as 'kinship defender' and 'society-as-parent protagonist', were actually held by different professionals and academics specialising in child welfare. She later developed her analysis to incorporate four distinct value positions: *laissez-faire*, state paternalism, parents' rights and children's rights (Fox Harding 1991).

Fox Harding characterises the *laissez-faire* position in terms of 'a belief in the benefits for society of a minimum state' and 'a complementary belief in the value to all, including children, of undisturbed family life'. This tends to support existing power relationships within families between men and women and between parents and children: 'Parents' and children's interests are, largely, identified, and by implication the interests of the two separate parents are also identified; the family as a whole has a life as a unit whose boundaries the rest of the community should respect' (pp. 15–16). *State paternalism*, on the other hand, is distinguished by 'a strong sense of identification with the suffering child ... the child is seen as essentially dependent, vulnerable, and with needs which are different from those of the adult.' Parents' duties rather than rights are emphasised, and

> much greater faith is placed in the value of beneficent state action to protect children's welfare. The state not only has the *duty* to intervene where there is inadequate care or suspicion of it, but also the *capacity* to provide something better for the child. The state decision-makers – courts and social workers – are seen as able to make sound and valid assessments of what would be best for the child.
>
> (pp. 60–1)

The *parents' rights* perspective

> favours extensive state intervention but not of the coercive kind. Birth families should be supported in their caring role; children should not enter substitute care except as a last resort or on a 'shared

care' basis; having entered care, most of them should be kept in touch with their original family and should wherever possible return to it.

(p. 107)

As with the first perspective, this approach tends to emphasise the identity of interests between parents and children, rather than the difference. In the *children's rights* perspective, in contrast,

> the emphasis is on the *child's* own viewpoint, feelings, wishes, definitions, freedoms and choices, rather than the attribution by adults of what is best for the child – and therefore, it might be inferred, the very existence of a child care 'system', with the function of making *decisions about* children, is called into question.

(p. 155)

Fox Harding argues that this perspective is fundamentally different from the other three, but in some ways more marginal to child care policy and practice, at least at present.

This typology is helpful as a framework for interpreting the relationship between children, parents and the state. Fox Harding suggests that all four strands were significant in British policy-making in the 1980s, with the result an 'uneasy synthesis' in which the dominant elements were parental rights and state paternalism.

The state's support of parental authority

A challenging version of the *laissez-faire* position is that taken by Goldstein, Freud and Solnit (1973). They argue forcefully that parental autonomy is actually in children's interests; to focus on their 'best interests' is to encourage over-interference, and in reality it is not possible to do the job of parenting well without having nearly total authority.[9] (They even propose that courts should not make orders governing contact between a child and a separated parent, on the grounds that the custodial parent must have complete discretion as to whether or not to allow such contact.) Fundamental to their argument is the concept of the 'psychological parent' of which a child can only have one, or one set. Without much evidence beyond their combined wisdom, and in fact against much psychological evidence, they assert that a child is incapable of forming attachments to more than one set of parent figures. The work of the 'psychological parent' is essential to the child's healthy development, and should not be impeded except in cases of gross failure.

Richards (1986) has dismantled Goldstein et al.'s argument: psychological evidence shows that children *can* relate to separate adults; the courts do have a role in setting expectations of appropriate conduct; and the argument is based on an idealised fantasy of a particular type of family.

Goldstein et al.'s conclusion is that parents' authority should not be intruded upon except in narrowly defined situations where there is a major and demonstrable threat to the child's well-being. In such cases, parental responsibility should normally be taken from the offending parent and transferred to another. Their definition of situations in which parental freedom may be intruded upon is not in fact very different from that contained in much contemporary legislation, for instance the Children Act 1989 in England and Wales. However, their account of the forms that intrusion may take is rather different. Not for them the notion of 'partnership' or 'shared care'; for Goldstein et al. parenting is all or nothing. Rather than parenthood as ownership, this is parenthood as sovereignty. As Owen (1992) puts it, 'the sovereignty argument allows the family to be treated as a benevolent dictatorship, which can be justifiably swept away and replaced by another dictatorship if it becomes corrupt' (p. 128).[10]

In all these discussions children tend to be regarded as objects – of parental duty, of state intervention – and not as subjects. What seems often to be taken for granted is that children will do as they are told by whichever adult is assumed to have authority over them. An exception is Blustein (1979), who devotes some attention to considering whether children owe duties to their parents. He concludes that they have a responsibility to facilitate their parents' exercise of their functions when they are young, and that they have obligations to their parents when they are grown up.[11] Seymour (1992) explores children's and parents' rights with the example of a 15-year-old who decides to leave home. He asks not only whether she has the right to leave home, but whether her parents have the right to stop her. They certainly do not have the right to do so by direct action, he suggests. They can invoke the law, but a law designed 'to provide procedures for children thought to be at risk because of their unruly behaviour' and 'to establish mechanisms by which the state can control troublesome juveniles and so protect itself from the threat which they pose. Thus the fact that Mary's parents may request the police or welfare authorities to invoke these laws does not mean that they have personal rights which the law will enforce' (p. 103). Seymour is writing against a background of Australian law, and his comments would also apply in the British context. In the USA, on the other hand, parents do have some power to call on the state to enforce their parental authority, although the end result of such action is again likely to be separation. There appears to be no equivalent in the modern world for the *lettres de cachet* for which Donzelot (1980) appears nostalgic.[12]

Ultimately the justification for expecting children to obey authority seems to depend on one of two assumptions. One is that children are developmentally immature and need to be dependent and have their lives directed until they are ready to take charge. The other is that children are a potential source of disorder, a threat to social stability or established interests.[13] Hendrick (1994) has suggested that throughout the development of modern welfare services children have been viewed simultaneously as threats as well as victims: 'children who were victims posed a variety of *threats* to public health, social stability, family cohesion, and educational progress' (p. 13). But ordinary children may also be seen as representing a threat, because of their unfamiliarity with or disregard of conventional rules of social interaction, because of their spontaneity which produces embarrassment and their vulnerability which produces danger, or simply because they are seen as holding the future both for their parents and for society as a whole.

The Children Act 1989 and the position of children

The web of powers and responsibilities that extends between children, their parents and the state is complex, ambiguous and contested. There is no dominant view of the relationship that is officially prescribed or generally supported, and there are contradictions in most of the positions taken. The central tensions come from the state's wish to support families without undermining their 'independence', and the desire to ensure that children are brought up 'properly' without interfering officiously in family life or parental autonomy; delegating responsibility to welfare professionals is one way to distance the state from head-on collision with families. To the extent that children's rights to participation and autonomy have become part of official policy, the same ambiguities apply. If it is difficult for the state to overcome its reluctance to intrude in order to protect children from physical or sexual abuse, it is even harder to do so in order to defend a child's right to an opinion. Article 12 of the United Nations Convention does not apply to decision-making within families, and few countries have begun to establish rights for children to be consulted in such decisions. Where possible, for instance in decisions about education, the assumption that parents represent their children's wishes and interests continues to be made.

All these ambiguities are contained within the Children Act 1989; its brilliance as a piece of legislation lies in its ability to contain such contradictions whilst appearing to be based on clear and strong principles. The Act takes a position on all the questions considered in this chapter. It locates parental rights within 'parental responsibility', which parents do not relinquish although others may from time to time acquire it. It provides that other family members, and children themselves, may intervene in matters of children's upbringing. It defines the duty of local authorities to provide services in terms of children's need to achieve a reasonable level of health and development. It sets a criterion for compulsory intervention based on significant harm to the child caused by inadequate parental care. It provides that the law should intervene in private disputes only if it is in the child's interest to do so, and on the presumption that it will normally be in the child's interests to remain in contact with parents and other significant figures. Finally it provides for children to be consulted and to have a voice in decisions about their lives, taking account of their age and understanding.

The Act has reframed legal interventions into children's lives in order to reflect these principles. Custody and access orders, with their emphasis on parents' rights and powers, are replaced by residence and contact orders made only if the child's interests demand it, with shared parental responsibility and a presumption of reasonable contact. Local authority accommodation of children is redefined as one of a range of services to be provided to children in need, rather than a last resort in cases of failure. Compulsory intervention is based on grounds of harm or likely harm to the child rather than on a range of parental inadequacies. Throughout the Act there is an emphasis on working with the grain of children's family networks and on planning in consultation with people of significance to the child. Stress is laid on establishing and taking into account the wishes and feelings of the child, parents and other family members or people whose views are likely to be of importance. Courts are expressly directed to discover and take account of these views, as are social work agencies. Guardians *ad litem* now have to be appointed in virtually all public law cases, with a duty to advise the court as to the child's best interests and to ensure that the welfare principles are adhered to. Above all the Act provides a framework in which competing accounts of children's welfare, parents' rights and the state's obligations can be contested.

'Gillick principles'

Another major change in the legal position of children has come from the decision of the House of Lords in *Gillick* v. *West Norfolk and Wisbech Area Health Authority*, usually referred to as 'the Gillick judgment'. This had an impact on children's rights within families, in that it appeared to establish an increasing right of children to determine their lives provided that they understand the implications of their decisions. Scarman's judgment held that 'the parental right to determine whether or not their minor child below the age of 16 will have medical treatment terminates if and when the child achieves a sufficient understanding and intelligence to enable him or her to understand fully what is proposed' (1986 1 Family Law Report 224).

It became clear in subsequent cases that the implications of the judgment were not as far-reaching as had originally been thought, at least when interpreted by judges (see Freeman 1987, Lyon and Parton 1995, Roche 1996). For instance, Donaldson ruled in 1991 that parents could still consent to treatment on behalf of a 'Gillick-competent' child who was refusing it, and that the court had even wider powers to override the wishes of the child. This was confirmed by subsequent judgments of Donaldson and of Sir Stephen Brown, President of the Family Division. It has been argued that the original judgment represented merely a transfer of authority from one group of adults to another – parents to doctors. On the other hand Coleman (1993) suggests that

> For at least two reasons... the Gillick case has made the position of the under 16s worse rather than better. First, the complexity of the case, and the legal wrangles surrounding it, have left teenagers confused and uncertain where they stand. Second, the publicity accorded to Mrs Gillick, as well as the tightening up of definitions, has left doctors with less room to manoeuvre and has caused almost all medical practitioners to exercise greater caution than before.

Nevertheless Scarman's original statement has commanded wide assent among those dealing with children in the courts; particularly when echoed by the principle in the Children Act 1989 that a child's wishes should be given due consideration having regard to his or her 'age and understanding'. The Children's Legal Centre (1988), considering investigations of abuse, proposes a right of all children to be consulted and, if of sufficient understanding, to decide what should happen. They quote the Official Solicitor's evidence to the Cleveland inquiry: 'children should be regarded as having increasing rights to consultation and control which should be accorded due respect even before they have reached an understanding and intelligence which is judged to entitle them to make a decision'.

The question arises of how a child's level of understanding is to be established. Seymour (1992) wonders if the Gillick judgment

> has opened the way for case-by-case decisions in a range of situations whenever children are old enough to argue that they have the capacity to make informed assessments. If this view is accepted, it might be seen as establishing a new right for older children, one which could be defined as: *an entitlement, in all disputes, to have their actual capacities determined, rather than being subject to presumptions based on their ages.*
>
> (pp. 100–1)

He argues that if accepted this presents a challenge to our concept of childhood, but suggests that in practice the effect is likely to be minimal because the decision as to whether a child has the requisite capacity will depend on whether her proposed course of action is seen as being in her best interests; in other words 'the suggested right will be read down and will not mean what it says' (p. 101). These are issues to which I will return later.

The best interests of the child

There is an underlying assumption that, when the state becomes involved in making decisions about individual children, those decisions will be based on consideration of the child's welfare. In the past the criteria might have been to do with social order, moral propriety or the inheritance of property. Since 1948, however, the law in England and Wales has held that decisions by agencies providing care must be based on the child's welfare except where the safety of others takes priority. The Children Act 1989 made the child's welfare the *paramount* consideration in all court proceedings about the care or upbringing of children, and reaffirmed the duty of an agency providing care or accommodation to promote the welfare of the child and to consider the child's interests when making decisions. At the centre of our child welfare law, then, is a concept of the best interests of the child as something that can be determined objectively.[14]

The notion of 'best interests' has inherent problems, which may be described as the *problem of indeterminacy* and the *problem of culture*. The problem of indeterminacy is that we cannot know incontrovertibly what is in a child's best interests, nor always agree on what values are important. Mnookin (1983) argues that 'what is best for any child or even children in general is often indeterminate and speculative, and requires a highly individualised choice between alternatives' (p. 8). He points to the uncertainty of predictions about children's development. A longitudinal study at Berkeley, California (MacFarlane 1964) 'attempted to relate personality development to specific variables and to show that these variables have the same effects on different children. In this respect it was unsuccessful. Many instances of what looked like severe pathology to the researchers were put to constructive use by the subjects' (Mnookin 1983, p. 10). Mnookin quotes Skolnick (1973): 'the researchers experienced shock after shock [as] it turned out that the predictions they had made about subjects were wrong in about two-thirds of the cases.'[15] Mnookin also refers to research by Phillips et al. (1971) who discovered that professionals of similar background and experience, studying files, frequently made different decisions as to which children should be removed from home and which should be supported at home. In the 50 per cent of cases in which they agreed, their reasons for their decisions were usually different.

Elsewhere Mnookin (1976) has argued that we can be more sure in some situations than others, and that we need legal and administrative standards which limit interventions to those situations where we have a reasonable level of certainty that we can at least choose the 'least detrimental alternative'.[16] He proposes that difficult and complex decisions about state intervention in family life should be governed by 'determinate rules' rather than 'indeterminate standards'. The rules are to be based on three principles: a high value accorded to family autonomy; an assumption that continuity and stability in relationships are important, especially for younger children; and a principle that 'legal rules ... should not contradict deeply held and widely shared social values' (p. 265). He does not favour giving children a determinative role but suggests that as children grow older more weight should be given to their views, and that for adolescents this weight might be predominant. This solution to the problem of indeterminacy has elements in common with that proposed by Eekelaar, which is considered in more detail below.

The problem of culture is first that standards of best interests only exist in a cultural framework, and one culture's version may simply not be accepted by another; second, that children have an interest in being an accepted part of their inherited culture which may have to be balanced against their other interests.[17] Both problems in practice involve questions of social and political values. In arguing for modesty in asserting children's best interests Mnookin, like Goldstein et al., is also arguing for families to be protected against too much state intervention; it could be argued that this represents a demand for respect for cultural difference no less than defences of corporal punishment or clitoridectomy. The often-quoted letter from Susannah Wesley to her son is an illustration of how a sincere regard for what are believed to be a child's best interests can lead to treatment which would be seen by others as highly abusive.[18]

However, my main concern is less with these inherent problems and more with what happens at the point where the best interests principle meets the principle of considering the child's wishes and feelings. The conflict is not simply one between children's rights and adult duties. If we take as a starting point the accounts of children's rights and adult duties contained in the UN Convention and in the Children Act 1989, we can distinguish:

1. a child's right to participation
2. a child's right to protection
3. an adult duty to promote the child's best interests
4. an adult duty to listen and consider the child's wishes and feelings.

It is apparent that there is potential for conflict within children's rights and within adults' duties, as well as between the two. It is this conflict that Eekelaar (1994) explicitly addresses in developing the concept of 'dynamic self-determinism'.

'Dynamic self-determinism'

Eekelaar argues that there is a need to reconcile the 'best interests principle' with children's rights, not simply because the implementation of the United Nations Convention demands it, but because the best interests principle is suspect without a framework of children's rights.[19] He argues that 'an acceptable conception of the status of minority in modern conditions can only be achieved through a reconciliation between the "principle" and children's rights' (pp. 44–5).[20] His solution is to reconstruct the principle in terms of (a) 'objectivization' and (b) 'dynamic self-determinism'. 'Objectivization' echoes Goldstein et al. and Mnookin, in replacing discretion where possible with general rules of disposal.²¹ Dynamic self-determinism provides the flexibility which would be missing from a totally 'objectivized' determination. The aim is to place the child

> in an environment which is reasonably secure, but which exposes it to a wide range of influences. As the child develops, it is encouraged to draw on these influences in such a way that the child itself contributes to the outcome. The very fact that the outcome has been, at least partly, determined by the child is taken to demonstrate that the outcome is in the child's best interests. The process is dynamic because it appreciates that the optimal course for a child cannot always be mapped out at the time of decision, and may need to be revised as the child grows up. It involves self-determinism because the child itself is given scope to influence the outcomes.
>
> (Eekelaar 1994, pp. 47–8)

Although Eekelaar's principle is developed with custody determinations in mind, it is consistent with arguments for 'open' adoption or for shared care with contact, as he partly acknowledges. Although Eekelaar does not mention it, the idea has a lot in common with Feinberg's (1980) 'right to an open future'. He does link it with the ideas of 'self-realization' in humanistic psychology and with forms of political liberalism – particularly the ideas of Raz (1986) about the value of autonomy and the ability to choose one's life-goals.

Eekelaar explains that 'dynamic self-determinism' does not mean giving way to licence, impulsiveness or self-destruction. Nor does it mean delegating decision-making to children, for two reasons. First, 'the method does not primarily seek to elicit *decisions* from children. Nor does it primarily seek the child's *views*, in so far as this implies a balanced evaluation of the whole situation, though if the child wishes to offer such an opinion, it should surely be listened to'. He allows that 'the child's wishes, if articulated, are likely to be a significant factor in the adults' decision,' but only when elicited in 'an environment in which the child's competence and personality can be assessed' – and this is a professional task: 'Applying dynamic self-determinism, this assessment should include [the professional's] interpretation of the child's expressed wishes (if any), their stability and their consistency with the process of self-realisation occurring within the child' (Eekelaar 1994, p. 54).

Second, he asserts that 'unless the child is competent...there can be no question of the child's opinion being determinative.' *Competence* he bases on Scarman's 'sufficient understanding and intelligence to enable [the child] to understand fully what is proposed' and further on Raz's notion of an autonomous decision as 'one wherein the desires chosen to be followed are consistent with (and intentionally so, not by accident) the individual's ultimate goals...[and] achievable within attainable social forms' (Eekelaar 1994, p. 55). The first part of this notion has something in common with Palmeri's (1980) concept of a *rational life plan*, which she uses to argue that children should have much greater autonomy and rights of participation in decisions. The final qualification, on the other hand, Eekelaar sees as 'helpful in constructing a concept of legal competence for children', because children do not always have the cognitive ability to predict the behaviour of others and so assess whether their goals are realistic. He adds the qualification that even a competent child may be prevented from taking a decision which is contrary to his or her most basic self-interest 'narrowly defined...in terms of physical or mental well-being or integrity' (Eekelaar 1994, p. 57).

In principle 'dynamic self-determinism' seems to provide a basis for reconciling children's rights with the 'best interests' principle. However, as outlined by Eekelaar it takes us less far than at first it promises. As Cohen (1980) put it, 'a child's ignorance of his or her own self-interest does not improve the adult's knowledge of that child's best interest' (p. 11). In fact there is some evidence that children may be better and more consistent judges of what is important in their lives than are adults (Yamamoto et al. 1987). For these reasons a version of 'dynamic self-determinism' that gives substantial weight to the part to be played by children of any age in dialogue about their interests is likely to be a better solution to the problem of indeterminacy, and to the problem of culture, than the non-interventionism advanced by Mnookin and by Goldstein et al. – which in effect usually leaves decisions with existing carers, for good or ill. It is surprising that Eekelaar does not place more emphasis on the child's right to participate in the decision by actually expressing a view and having that view heard. He also has little to say about the process of dialogue between children and adults over the child's situation and options for the future. These are issues which I discuss further when I come to review the findings of my own research.

Principles for including children in decisions

The idea that children's participation in decisions ought to increase with age, understanding and competence is a common one, as we have seen. Perhaps in 'democratic' families this is what happens: that all children are listened to attentively, but that as they get older one moves from an assumption that parents will listen and decide, to an assumption that the young person's wishes will have force unless this will result in harm. It is arguable that the task of professionals in planning and decision-making is to support this process in the families where it happens naturally, and to model it where it does not.

Eekelaar and Dingwall (1990) take the view that this is not enough, and that legislation should specify precisely when a child's wishes should determine the outcome. They suggest that the Children Act 'virtually ignores' questions of children's degree of autonomy: 'it does specify that, in certain contexts, courts or welfare authorities must give particular attention to the wishes and feelings of the children with whom they are dealing and special provisions have been enacted permitting children in some circumstances to refuse to undergo medical examination. But, apart from that, it seems that the decision-maker's views will normally take priority over those of the child if there is a disagreement. The Act has nothing to say about what happens when an ordinary person with parental responsibility has a difference of opinion with a child over how that responsibility ought to be exercised' (pp. 23–4). Lyon and Parton (1995) concede that the Act does extend children's rights of autonomy but suggest that this, 'rather than constituting children and young persons as subjects, has provided a new set of strategies and mechanisms for using the voices of children as elements in the newly constituted government of families' (p. 53).

The 1989 Act is certainly far from being a comprehensive charter of children's rights, and it is true that it says nothing directly about decision-making within families. It does, however, open to children the possibility of legal challenge to the arrangements made by their parents for their care, a fact which has caused some consternation both among the public and among professionals.[22] It is equally true that the obligation on courts and welfare authorities to consider the voice of the child does not make clear how the child's wishes and feelings are to be balanced against the views of parents and others when they differ. The magazine *Childright* (1990) has even suggested that the Act has weakened the rights of children in care or accommodation, taking a 'backward step' in adding to the duty to consider the wishes and feelings of the child, which had been in Section 18 of the Child Care Act 1980 and before that the Children Act 1975, a duty to consider the wishes and feelings of a parent or person with parental responsibility and of anyone else whose views the local authority consider relevant.

No primacy is given to the child's wishes, even a child who is old enough to understand the implications of the decision ... For the last 15 years Section 18's provisions about the wishes and feelings has [*sic*] on numberless occasions prevented social workers from infringing the rights of children in care. Let us hope that the much diluted duty does not enable social workers in future to tell the child: 'Well you think this, but others whose views are legally just as important think otherwise'.

The law does not, then, offer a path through these dilemmas about whose views should prevail. It may be, however, that it at least points the direction in which the path should go. The repeated emphasis on first ascertaining the wishes and feelings of the child, and then on giving them due consideration having regard to the child's age and understanding, clearly opens the way for principles to begin to be established that will give children an *increasing* influence on the outcome of decision-making. If we go back to the principles arrived at in the previous chapter, we see that our presumptions may be different in relation to different groups of children. In the case of young children, up to say seven years, it seems clear that most important decisions will need to be made by adults, whether parents or professionals, but that children should be given the opportunity to reflect on what is proposed and express their wishes and feelings in whatever way is most suitable for them. In the case of adolescents, from about age thirteen, many would agree that the 'default' position should be the opposite: that unless there are strong reasons to impose an adult view of what is in a young person's interests, his or her own wishes and feelings should prevail.

In the case of children of middle years the balance is more even. For the purpose of this research it seems useful to set out in advance certain principles regarding what might constitute effective and appropriate participation by children of this age in important decisions about their lives. The principles which I offer are:

1. That the child should have an acknowledged right to take a full part in the discussion which leads up to the decision (without being obliged to do so if they do not wish);
2. That the choices to be made and their implications should be clearly explained to the child;

3. That the child's views should be carefully attended to by all those responsible for making the decision;
4. That the decision should then be made by the responsible adults on the basis of what is considered to be in the balance of the child's interests (including the child's interest in having her or his views taken into account);
5. That the plan should be explained and recorded with explicit reference to the part which the child's views played in determining it; and
6. That if the child's wishes are not to be acceded to, the reasons for this should be explained to the child and to anyone else who has a legitimate interest.

6
Children Looked After by the State

If the relationship between children, parents and the state is a triangle, its shape is different when children are in the care of the state. The state's direct influence on children's lives is much greater, and the part played by parents much less. Since these are the children with whom this book is mainly concerned, it is time to look at the 'care system' and how it defines and addresses the needs of children. This chapter will follow a number of themes through the history of state care: the purposes of care, the kinds of children admitted, the aims of the system for children, the types of placement used, the standards of care applied, the monitoring of services and outcomes, and the process of decision-making. Following this it will look more directly at research into decision-making when children are looked after by local authorities, at children's own involvement in those decisions, and at some of the practice issues around communicating with children.

The history of state care in England and Wales is usually recounted from the seventeenth century onwards (Heywood 1965; Pinchbeck and Hewitt 1969, 1973). Less is known about what was done with neglected or destitute children in the middle ages, although it seems likely that any response was a community one rather than a state one. In any case the legal framework for relief of destitution set down early in the seventeenth century survived, with some amendment, until the second world war. Although the legal framework remained the same, the way it was used changed, and the period invites an historical overview. Heywood paints a picture of steady progress and increasing enlightenment, culminating in the triumph of the 1948 Children Act; hers is a 'Whig history'. It is possible to see a gradual progression, with more children brought within the system's purview, new needs met, greater attention given to the welfare and happiness of children, and increasing care taken in selecting and supervising placements. There was indeed a gradual extension of the system in terms of the needs it aimed to meet and the children it embraced.

At the same time it would be a mistake to see the story as simply one of steady progress and increasing enlightenment. Hendrick (1994) suggests that the purposes of providing care for poor children were more mixed than the story of philanthropy would suggest. He argues that the shape of services is crucially formed by the demand to restrict spending on the working class, on the one hand, and the need to neutralise the threat posed by delinquent or abused children, on the other.

The purposes of state care

The purposes of the state in providing care for children have indeed been varied. Apart from the obvious motives of relieving suffering and preventing crime, which tend to be emphasised in straightforward histories such as Heywood's, other purposes need to be taken into account if we are to understand what happens. Purposes may be environmental or aesthetic (to improve the appearance of the streets), political (to neutralise protest), economic (to turn dependence into economic usefulness), military (to provide soldiers and sailors), moral (to prevent depravity, or to assuage guilt) or social (to provide a service to parents). In the seventeenth and eighteenth centuries the object was principally to relieve destitution and the more obvious poverty, to maintain social order, and to ensure that those who could made an economic contribution, and that those who could not were as little of a drain on the public purse as could be managed. If possible this was to be done by turning economically dependent children into self-sufficient children. This meant that there was an emphasis on training, either through schools provided specially for pauper children (some of which were so good that they were colonized by the better-off) or through apprenticeship.

It was during the nineteenth century, however, that concern with the *moral* development of poor children began to predominate in the care arrangements devised for them. Heywood (1965, p. 46) quotes Mary Carpenter:

> The child ... must be placed ... where he will be gradually restored to the true position of childhood. He must be brought to a sense of dependence by re-awakening in him desires which he cannot by himself gratify, and by finding that there is a power greater than his

own to which he is indebted for the gratification of these desires. He must perceive by manifestations that he cannot mistake, that this power, whilst controlling him is guided by wisdom and love; he must have his affections called forth by the obvious personal interest felt in his own individual well-being by those around him; he must, in short, be placed in a *family*. Faith in those around him being once thoroughly established, he will soon yield his own will in ready submission to those who are working for his good...

In the twentieth century the purpose became ostensibly more and more concerned with the welfare and 'best interests' of the child. However, other concerns did not just disappear, and it is important to be alert to their presence behind the rhetoric about what is best for children. Hendrick argues that the child as victim and the child as threat are difficult if not impossible to separate, and that fear of what children may do to adult interests or to the established order is never far from the motives of the establishment in providing child care services. It may also be argued that pedagogy has always been about making children into what adults want them to be; about classifying and describing them. Even when the emphasis has been on children's individual needs and identities, it is possible that this is in part a cloak, deliberate or not, for moulding children too.[1] Alice Miller puts it strongly:

> I am convinced of the harmful effects of training for the following reason: all advice that pertains to raising children betrays more or less clearly the numerous, variously clothed needs of the *adult*. Fulfilment of these needs not only discourages the child's development but actually prevents it. This also holds true when the adult is honestly convinced of acting in the child's best interests.
>
> (Miller 1987b, p. 97)

The kinds of children admitted to care

During most of the period of the Poor Law the emphasis was on relief of destitution. For children this meant those whose parents were destitute, those who were abandoned, and orphans. Heywood suggests that the medieval system *absorbed* the destitute, making any more planned or organised response unnecessary, but that the economic dislocation of the Tudor revolution and the new ascendancy of family over community demanded the Poor Law. The service provided was for those who were destitute either because of circumstance or personal incapacity. Packman's categories of 'victims, villains and volunteered' (Packman, Randall and Jacques 1986) do not really feature until the last hundred years. Child criminals were dealt with for the most part through the penal system; intervention to prevent abuse and neglect was extremely rare; and there appears to have been no legally sanctioned way in which parents could *ask* for their children to be cared for by the state. Nevertheless it is possible that some of the same children found themselves dependent on the state, even if they had to be abandoned first.[2]

In the last hundred years, however, three new groups of children, or at least three new definitions of need, corresponding roughly to Packman's categories, have been brought within the system of state care.[3] Towards the end of the nineteenth century serious attention began to be paid to the question of abuse of children within their families, and the Act of 1889 gave the courts power to take a child away from a parent convicted of neglect or ill-treatment and commit him or her to a 'fit person'. This power was further consolidated and clarified in 1908 and 1933. Next, the latter Acts also established juvenile courts and a separate system of detention for young offenders, and made it possible for the local state in the form of education authorities to bring before the courts children who were in need of care and protection because their parents were failing to 'exercise proper care and guardianship' (Children and Young Persons Act 1933, section 61). Finally, in 1948 local authorities were given the duty to receive into care any child whose parents were unable to provide care for any reason. The importance of this change should not be overlooked, since it was intended to represent a profound shift in the relationship between the state and the parents of children in the care of the state.

What sorts of children are looked after away from home? Where do they come from and what are their needs? First, they originate overwhelmingly from certain social groups: poor working-class families in inadequate housing, often with disrupted parenting and disproportionately of mixed ethnic origin. Jenkins (1975) showed long ago that in the USA child welfare services are overwhelmingly directed at poor black and working-class families. Bebbington and Miles (1991) calculated that in the UK a child of mixed ethnic origin, living with three or more other children and a single adult in privately-rented accommodation with more than one person to a room and dependent on supplementary benefit, stood a one-in-ten chance of being received into care, whilst a white child in a smaller two-parent family in an owner-occupied home with more rooms than people stood a chance of one in seven thousand.

Most children are looked after for quite brief periods, although a count of the number in the system at any one time would suggest that the majority are long stayers. Lengths of stay and reasons for admission vary with age and gender, with small children of either sex often being admitted as a result of physical abuse or neglect and remaining away from home often for long periods, while adolescents are often admitted as a result of breakdown in family relationships, sometimes connected with offending behaviour (mainly in the case of boys) or sexual abuse (mostly girls), and again often remain away from home for some time. Children in the middle years are less likely to be admitted, and if they are it is very often for a short period to relieve a parent in difficult circumstances. However, there are a considerable number of children in this age group who were admitted when younger and have remained in care or accommodation.

Parker (1987) refers to 'the danger of generalising about children in care' (p. 2) and argues against the tendency to concentrate on what separated children have in common; as if delinquency and deprivation, for instance, are two sides of the same coin. 'It is of the utmost importance,' he writes, 'to recognise the significance of the sub-categories *within* the "in care" population: sub-categories which are based upon children's characteristics; their backgrounds; their problems and what happens to them' (pp. 3–4). Nevertheless the different groups do have much in common. Children who come to be looked after by public agencies have almost without exception suffered forms of deprivation or disturbance before their admission. Apart from poverty and poor housing, they are likely to have suffered from one or more of the following: the illness or incapacity of a parent; parental conflict, perhaps including extreme violence; parental departure, which may have been sudden or repeated; abuse or neglect; lack of warmth or consistency in care; lack of stimulation or support for learning, for instance in language; disrupted schooling; poor health; stigma and prejudice. All these factors are likely to have an effect on a child's response to care and to impinge on his or her ability to take part in discussion and planning about what should happen to them, as suggested in Chapter 3.

On the other hand some children who come into care or accommodation may have had experiences which have increased their confidence or self-reliance. They may have had to fend for themselves, to care for younger siblings or even to look after an ill or disabled parent.

Children of alcoholic or drug-dependent parents may have had to get their own food, to get themselves ready for school, to deal with visitors or fend off inquisitive neighbours or officials.

For all children the process by which they came to be in care or accommodation is likely to have been confusing, frightening or worrying. Whatever expectations they bring to this new situation from their previous lives – expectations of being treated well or badly, of being nurtured or deprived, of being listened to or ignored – begin to be confirmed, modified or re-interpreted in the light of their experiences of admission and their subsequent care. Is what is happening explained to them in ways that they are able to understand? Do they know why they are moving, where to and for how long? Are their surroundings familiar, or strange? Is there food that they like, or are used to? Do they have any choice over where they go, when they go, what they take with them?

The aims of the care system for children

Heywood (1965) argues that there was a decline in the importance of the family, and in the economic value of large families, following industrialisation and the restriction of child labour: 'Children, once a financial asset, now became, during their long dependency, a liability' (p. 133). If she is right, we should expect this to have an impact on the sense of purpose behind the state care of destitute, deprived or 'delinquent' children. We might expect the emphasis to move from maximising the usefulness of children to minimising their cost and nuisance, at least until some new, more intrinsic value was ascribed to them. This appears to be what happened. Although the work provided for children in workhouses and reformatories during the nineteenth century may have been gruelling, it does not seem to have been particularly productive.[4] The aims of the system were on the one hand to limit the numbers of children who came into care unnecessarily whilst at the same time tidying them up from places where they might have been a nuisance, and on the other to prevent them becoming a further nuisance through the demands they made on the system. Although the ostensible aims of the reformatories and industrial schools were to produce useful citizens, little real investment was directed to this purpose.

This began to change with the child protection legislation of the late nineteenth and early twentieth centuries. With children increasingly seen as victims who were not to blame for their plight, it became more desirable to provide good and even tender care for them. Around the time of the Poor Law Review of 1911 there was a renewed emphasis on boarding out which may be understood in these terms. At the same time the belief continued that the most useful thing that could be done for many children was to separate them completely from their families; for some this meant removal to the colonies. Heywood suggests that the understanding of children's emotional needs developed in advance of the social conditions which would have made it possible to put that understanding into effect. However, she detects at the turn of the century 'an effort, based on the experiments of the voluntary societies, to give the child more individual care and some sense of belonging to a community' (1965, p. 91).

The demand to consider the child's best interests was embodied in legislation from 1933, but this still meant for the most part finding a 'fit person' to replace unfit parents. The most profound change came with the 1948 Act. Just as the Act introduced the idea that children could be received into care as a *service* to their families, so the aim of care was now to give them a *family life* as close as possible to what they would have had at home had circumstances not been adverse, and wherever possible to aim for their return to their own family. In addition there was an explicit duty on local authorities providing care to make use of services provided for children living with their own families; the clear differentiation of 'Poor Law children' was to be a thing of the past.[5]

However much the Children Act 1989 was heralded as a new departure, the provision for local authority services in Part Three of that Act can be seen as a further step in the direction established in 1948. This is not to say that the 1989 Act did not make important changes; the redefining of 'need' in terms of the child's opportunity to attain a normal development, rather than in the narrower terms (of preventing reception into care) used in the 1963 Children and Young Persons Act, made it possible to reframe 'accommodation' as one of a range of positive services to assist families instead of a negative outcome to be avoided. However, the explicit aims of the system for children have not changed fundamentally since 1948.[6]

Types of placement

It would be a mistake to see the history of state care as a steady progression from institutional to family placement. 'Boarding out' goes back to the use of apprenticeship under the Tudors and before that to all the arrangements whereby children were sent to live and work in other households.[7] Throughout the Poor Law period both institutional care and boarding out were used at different times and in different ways in order to provide for children: from the apprenticeship of older children to the fostering of babies; from workhouses to 'cottage homes' to training schools of various kinds. The system came under increasing strain during the social upheaval of the seventeenth century, prompting the development not only of workhouses but also of foundling hospitals to accommodate increasing numbers of unwanted babies. When the numbers of destitute children created problems the response was large institutions, often mixing children with adults including criminals and mentally ill people.

However, there were successive attempts to provide something more suited to the needs of children, whether it was the orphan homes for children of respectable families, the ragged schools and other reforming attempts modelled on experiments in France and Germany, or the development by Poor Law administrators of cottage homes (with 'family groups' of up to thirty children and their 'mothers'), scattered homes and a revival of boarding out especially in the 1880s. Some of these developments were made possible by the 1870 Education Act, which meant that there were now local schools which children in these placements could attend. Foster parents tended to be poor themselves, and were supervised by committees of voluntary visitors.

Ambivalence about residential or institutional care was a feature of the later Poor Law years and grew after 1948. Packman shows how the emphasis on foster care in the new Act was belied by the opening of new residential institutions, in response to pressure on care services, just as the old ones were being closed. A similar ambivalence is detectable in relation to foster care. Although the 1948 Act espoused foster care wholeheartedly as the placement of choice, it was impossible to forget that the Act had its origins in a death of a child in foster care, and one of its chief purposes was to ensure that placements were effectively supervised. Suspicion of the motives of foster carers, and a feeling that there is a conflict between pecuniary rewards and family life, have bedevilled the issue of foster care allowances – and still do so.

Standards of care

The reformed Poor Law doctrine of 'less eligibility' was always problematic where children are concerned. On the one hand they do not normally have a choice about whether to be claimants, so that the issue of deterrence is less obvious than it might be with adults; and if the state wants them to be successful and productive citizens, this argues for providing a relatively high standard of care. On the other hand the state did not want to encourage people to abandon children in order to give them a better future. The difficulty was acknowledged by Florence Davenport-Hill (1889): 'the most one could do was to try to ensure that the boarded-out child should be brought up as well as, and no better then, the most respectable poor in the locality in which he was placed' (quoted in Heywood 1965, p. 87).[8] With the abolition of the Poor Law, however, the idea was that children deserved better.

The importance of the 1948 settlement was that it was part – even if added as an afterthought – of what was seen as a comprehensive settlement of the problems of social policy on a *democratic* basis. The social legislation of the 1940s represented a decision to build on the shared endeavour of the war years to avoid a return to the division of the 1920s and 1930s. Together with the provision of basic education and health services to everyone without charge, a comprehensive system of income maintenance, and a serious public housing programme, the Children Act drew on a determination that everyone should share in the fruits of victory and the good things to come, and a desire to reduce, if not actually eliminate, unjustifiable social distinctions. Where the Poor Law had always striven to define a sharp difference between the dependent and the independent, the legislation of the post-war settlement went some way towards recognising our mutual dependence.

This can be seen in the 1948 Act in the provision for substitute care. Local authorities had a duty to *receive into care* any child whose parents were unable to provide care themselves, and to work for the child's return to their own family so long as this was in the child's interests. For the first time there was provision for the state to care for a child *by agreement* with the family. Once the local authority had received a child into care it had a positive duty 'to exercise [its] powers with respect to him so as to further his best interests, and to afford him opportunity for the proper development of his character and abilities'; and 'to make use of facilities and services available to children in the care of their parents' (Children Act 1948, section 12). It was expected that children would be placed with foster parents unless it was against their interests to do so. The accent was therefore, as it had never been before, on *normalising* the lives of children who needed to be cared for by the state. The experience of wartime evacuation, when more than a million children in Britain were sent to live with other families, had perhaps contributed to a feeling that there was nothing extraordinary about children going to live with strangers and that one should try to make it as ordinary as possible for the children. Foster parents were to care for a child 'as if s/he were our own', in the words of the undertaking which they signed at the start of a placement.

The aim of the Curtis Committee had been to make care *personal*, in contrast to what they had seen in some establishments:

> The child in these Homes was not recognised as an individual with his own rights and possessions, his own life to live and his own contribution to offer. He was merely one of a large crowd, eating, playing and sleeping with the rest, without any space or possession of his own or any quiet room to which he could retreat. Still more important, he was without the feeling that there was anyone to whom he could turn who was vitally interested in his welfare or who cared for him as a person.
>
> (Curtis 1946, p. 134)

If the 1948 Act was revolutionary in anything, it was in the endeavour to provide care which gave children a sense of individual worth.

Monitoring services and outcomes

The inspection of care services and the maintenance of expected standards was always a fairly hit-and-miss business, despite the tireless efforts of some administrators to ensure that it was done. Boarding out in particular was subject to very loose forms of inspection, perhaps reflecting an ideology of family privacy. Even when structures for visiting were set up following the 1911 review, with voluntary committees established for the explicit purpose of monitoring foster placements, it was left very much to the volunteers themselves to establish both what they were looking for and how they looked. There was great reluctance to intervene more than strictly necessary or for a visitor to become a court of appeal for a child from the foster parent. In the inspection of foster homes in the past, especially before 1948, children's bodies were regarded as more informative than their words.

Enacted following the death of a child at the hands of a brutal foster father, the 1948 Act went to some trouble to establish requirements for regular visiting and review. The first child care officers were called 'boarding out visitors'. The Act was followed in 1955 by regulations that specified the selection process for foster homes and arrangements for visiting and review. The expectation was that a home would be visited by the officer responsible for a child in order to establish that it was a suitable placement. Placements were to be visited at specific intervals and a written report made on each occasion. Reviews likewise were to be undertaken at regular intervals which should never be more than six months. The years since the war saw successive refinements to this system, but even the 1988 Boarding Out Regulations did not fundamentally change its nature. The requirement was to review the child's 'health, conduct, progress and welfare' and the principal mechanism was that of seeing the child regularly in the foster home and reporting on those visits to a responsible person. There was now some requirement to establish the views of the people involved, including the child; but the focus was still on process rather than on outcome.

It was only with the Department of Health's *Looking After Children* project in the present decade that the results of the care provided to children, not only at the end of the process but from day to day and year to year, began to be an object of formal attention (Parker et al. 1991; Ward 1995). The new approach to monitoring was research-based. It sought to identify objectively the key components of good parenting and to provide practical tools – the 'assessment and action records' – for ensuring that those components were present in individual cases and as a source of aggregated data for use in management and research. Interestingly, the early versions of the records were addressed to adults, but in the version finally implemented by the Department of Health the forms for children aged over nine were addressed directly to the child. It is arguable that this represents an important shift in official policy towards involving children during the early 1990s.

The process of decision-making

Except for those decisions which had to be taken by a court, the process of deciding what happened to individual children in public care was until recently left to the officials charged with that responsibility.[9] It was not until 1975 that there really began to be any overall direction of decision-making processes. When such direction was introduced, it was a response to perceived defects of the system as it had been operating. The 1975 Children Act was intended to respond to the Houghton recommendations on adoption and custody, to concern about cases where children appeared to have been removed from caring foster homes to unsatisfactory birth families, and to the developing theme of children's need for 'permanence' which was emphasised by Rowe and Lambert's (1973) study of 'children who wait' for a permanent placement without in many cases any purposeful action being taken to achieve such an outcome.[10] The Act attempted to change the balance between the various interests represented in decisions about the future of children in public care, giving power to local authorities to step in where parents were not taking responsibility, and giving some independent power to long term foster parents to intervene on their own account. At the same time local authorities in making decisions about care were to have regard to the need to promote the welfare of a child 'throughout his childhood'. Furthermore and in a radical new departure, they were required to ascertain and take account of the child's wishes and feelings.[11]

A further step towards the formalising of decisions about children in care came in 1983 with the Code of Practice on Access to Children in Care and associated amendments to the 1980 Child Care Act (Health and Social Services and Social Security Adjudications Act 1983, s. 6 and Schedule 1). Prompted by research which showed how children in care often lost their links with their families unnecessarily, the new provisions allowed remedies for parents and family members who were unhappy with the local authority's refusal of access (see Millham et al. 1986). In part the Code represented a reaction to some of the perceived excesses of the 'permanency' movement; what is significant here is that it represents a further attempt to specify what sort of decisions agencies should take about children in their care, and how they should take them. A number of research studies in the 1980s had pointed to the unsatisfactory nature of much local authority decision-making for children in care or in need of assistance (Fisher et al. 1986; Packman, Randall and Jacques 1986; Vernon and Fruin 1986). Summarised by the Department of Health and widely disseminated among local authority staff and members, these studies had a pronounced effect on practice in the final years of that decade as well as contributing substantially to the framing of the new law (Department of Health and Social Security 1985; see also Department of Health 1989a).

In relation to decision-making about children in public care, the 1989 Children Act represents as radical a departure from the previous approach as did its 1948 predecessor in relation to the actual provision of care. For the first time agencies caring for children away from their families must have an explicit plan which identifies the child's needs and makes clear how they are to be addressed. Guidance and regulations specify how these plans are to be drawn up; a process which involves the participation of the child and family and consultation with other agencies. Similar provisions apply to reviews, whose object now is not only to monitor the child's previous progress but to plan for the future. Participants in plans and reviews are entitled to a record of the decisions taken.

The expectation is that important decisions concerning the child's care will be taken at formal planning and review meetings. This includes decisions as to where the child should live, arrangements for contact, health and education, leisure facilities and anything else necessary to ensure the child's well-being. Once in substitute care, children who are expected to stay for more than a few days are likely to have a range of needs to be addressed. In addition to their basic needs for nurture, sustenance, relationship and opportunities to learn, they may have needs for psychological help, for remedial health care, for special educational input, for the learning of new skills and behaviours or for the opportunity to make new attachments. In addition they will have needs arising from their situation, for the maintenance of links and continuities with their lives at home. These needs must be identified and formal decisions taken about how to meet them. This is in sharp contrast to what happens for most children living in their own families. First, these questions are less likely to be at issue for most children. Second, if they are, they are likely to be decided in a much more informal way. Third, there are no legal requirements governing the process by which such decisions are taken in families, although the outcome may be constrained in certain ways by the law.

Children who are looked after by the state are therefore in a unique position in that important decisions about their day-to-day lives have to be taken according to processes that are specified by law. This includes the requirement that children's own views be ascertained and taken into account along with the views of their parents and others. Decisions have to be recorded and the record made available to those taking part. On the one hand, this means that children who are looked after have rights and protections unavailable to their peers – perhaps reflecting their perceived vulnerability. On the other hand, their lives are unusually open to the public gaze. Meetings at which their personal affairs are discussed may be attended by a number of people not personally well known to them, who are there by virtue of their official position in the public organisations responsible for the children's well-being. This contrasts with the privacy and seclusion that characterise most children's lives in families, where their affairs may be very open to their parents' gaze but almost entirely shielded from anyone else's, except when they are at school or seriously ill.

Decisions in child care before 1989

One of the major roots of the Children Act 1989 lay in research conducted during the early 1980s into what happened when children came into the care of local authorities, and in particular into the processes by which decisions were made about where and how they should be cared for. The conclusions of those studies were highly consistent: decisions were often made by default, so that outcomes for children were very different from what anyone ostensibly wished or intended; children were often refused admission to care when their families asked for it, but removed in response to a crisis (Fisher et al. 1986; Packman, Randall and Jacques 1986); after admission there was often little communication with families and few attempts to promote contact with their children (Millham et al. 1986; Vernon and Fruin 1986). The result was that children who might have originally only been expected to be in care for a short period actually remained in the system for years, and children who originally had strong links with family and neighbourhood drifted into a situation where they were without roots or a sense of belonging.

Vernon and Fruin (1986) give a vivid account of what can only be described as a process of *non-planning*. They discovered that the key figure in most decisions to admit was the social worker, who clearly had considerable discretion in this respect. At the same time 'there was little evidence to suggest that social workers purposefully worked towards children's exit from the care system' (p. 69). Social workers' understanding of planning was not characterised by purposeful action towards clear objectives but by conforming their behaviour to what they expected would happen anyway, or by postponing choices until the situation became clearer. There was little organisational support for the planning process either formally or informally; managers were mainly concerned with crises and by default left any strategic planning of casework to their staff.[12]

It seemed clear that the 1975 Children Act had not solved the problems of a lack of purposeful planning identified by Rowe and Lambert (1973), and that by reducing the power of families it may even have exacerbated tendencies to make decisions without reference to them. Packman et al. (1986) found that families were far more likely to be involved in decisions when admission was 'voluntary', and that contact was also more likely to be maintained in these cases. However, cases involving compulsion are often those where children have been abused or involved in criminal activity, and it may be, as Owen (1992) argues, that reasons not directly connected with the child's legal status contributed to the difference in process in these cases. Vernon and Fruin found that in most cases the social workers did not take a separate decision about the most appropriate legal route into care for a child, but the legal route simply reflected the circumstances in which the child was admitted.[13] Fisher et al. found families often bemused and angered by the decision-making process, uncertain of their rights but aware of being manipulated. Packman et al. concluded that 'gate-keeping' practice was dominated by a 'rule of pessimism' about the care system and frequent determination to keep children out unless there was absolutely no alternative. The reverse of this coin was the unplanned, disorganised emergency admission, often to an inappropriate placement.[14] Parents were unclear on their rights and sometimes surprised to discover the powers of social workers and how they intended to use them.

Vernon and Fruin found social workers to be preoccupied with the past and present and often giving little thought to the future. They suggest that 'the risks of planning' – that something would go wrong or that one would appear with hindsight to have made a bad decision – deterred them from committing to a strategy for the future. In fact, they suggest, reviews often played a crucial part in a process whereby what we may call 'non-decisions' are taken and upheld[15]:

> it is apparent that reviews are not perceived as taking decisions and do not function in an explicitly decision-making manner. Their overall effect, then, in terms of outcome is to endorse what is currently happening on a case. In this sense this means that they reinforce the plan or approach already being followed
>
> (Vernon and Fruin 1986, p. 111)

Vernon and Fruin conclude that many children remain in care for long periods not because 'this has been a planned outcome on which firm decisions have been reached ... it is clear that such a decision is rarely taken or formally agreed,' but 'because over time and for a variety of reasons, it becomes accepted that they will not be returning home'. They found that the alternative of adoption was seldom considered even when the child's foster parents might wish to pursue it, so that 'children may thus remain in the care system by default' (p. 143). It is precisely this situation that the 1975 Act had been intended to address, but the diagnosis at that time was that too much parental power was the chief problem. In contrast, Fisher et al.'s picture of work with families following that Act is of a process fraught with misunderstanding and miscommunication, whereby parents were disillusioned, children felt powerless, and social workers were driven by their situation into responses that often seemed 'inflexible and monolithic' (1986, p. 53). Fisher et al. argued instead for 'shared parenting' and for systems and practices that supported families and reduced the abruptness of transitions between different levels of intervention.

In the light of this research the framers of the 1989 Children Act sought to ensure both that purposeful planning took place based on a consideration of what was best for children in the long term, and that family members were enabled to take an effective part in the decision-making process. These objectives may of course be perfectly compatible, if what is in a child's best interests is something which can be objectively ascertained and on which people can agree. Both assumptions may be justified at some times, but at others there may be deep-rooted disagreement about the child's interests, so that a duty to promote the child's welfare may be at odds with a requirement to work in partnership. Since the disagreement may even be three-way – parent, child and social worker having a different view of what is best – it is clear that having regard to everyone's wishes *and* doing what is in the child's interests can be a tall order.

Children's involvement in decisions in care

The rest of this chapter will concentrate on the question of how children are involved in decisions about their lives in the care system. It will look at earlier research into the views of children and young people and at more recent studies of decision-making processes since the Children Act 1989. It will also consider some of the work that has been done on methods of including children and young people in these processes.

What then has been the extent of children's involvement in decision-making about placement in recent years? The evidence is limited. The studies of decision-making drawn together by the Department of Health and Social Security in the mid-1980s looked closely at the processes of social workers' judgements and at agency policies (Department of Health and Social Security 1985; Fisher et al. 1986; Millham et al. 1986; Packman, Randall and Jacques 1986; Vernon and Fruin 1986). They also considered the extent to which parents and relatives influenced decisions, but they did not look separately at the part played by children. The exception is one telling comment by Packman et al.:

> Finally the children in question – the ultimate consumers of the service on offer – were the group least likely to be consulted, and there was discussion with less than one in ten before adults' minds were made up. In this regard, practice apparently did little to counteract the legal anomaly whereby the duty to ascertain the child's wishes and feelings in decisions which affect him or her applies once the child is in care but not beforehand.
>
> (1986, p. 79)

Perhaps because of the statutory duty to consider children's wishes and feelings, there has been slightly more research into their participation in decisions *after* reception into care. Studies of statutory reviews have focused on children's participation to a limited extent. McDonnell and Aldgate (1984) reviewed the literature available in the early 1980s and found 'little substantial evidence that reviews have enabled greater participation by children and their families in the making of decisions which affect their lives; indeed the evidence would suggest that reviews are still likely to be a fairly private event, between the social worker and his [*sic*] senior, although there are some small signs that this is changing.' They quote young people who contributed to some of the studies: 'I feel that the whole review system for me is a total façade. Although the decisions taken at reviews are carried out these decisions occur through the wishes of the adults involved whereas I am merely a bystander' (from Stein and Ellis 1983). On occasions when children were included in meetings the experience could be just as alienating: 'I think that bringing kids into that room where they don't know half the people and are scared stiff is one of the most painful experiences I have ever had'; 'I think you should be at least introduced to everyone when you go in' (from Page and Clarke 1977).

Although McDonnell and Aldgate's own survey of local authorities found that 97 per cent claimed to include children 'frequently' or 'occasionally', they do not give separate figures for the two responses, and this figure needs to be treated with extreme caution. Kendrick and Mapstone's (1991) review of research from the 1980s found levels of participation as low as 6 per cent (Rowe, Cain, Hundleby and Keane 1984), 5 per cent (Vernon and Fruin 1986), or even 2 per cent (Sinclair 1984). Gardner (1989) suggested that children were still not generally being included in reviews. Kendrick and Mapstone did find studies in Scotland in the 1980s where there was more evidence of young people being regularly included, but these generally related to older teenagers.

The Children's Legal Centre (1984) surveyed 63 local authorities and discovered that only 15 were in the practice of inviting children in their care to review meetings.[16]

Gardner (1985) found that the children she interviewed who attended reviews were generally positive about the experience. They were able to say what they wanted; there were not people present who they would have preferred not to be there; and although there were people not present who they would have liked to include, Gardner thought this was generally because they liked them and wanted them to see how they were doing. Nevertheless it seems possible from some responses that children might also have been hoping for advocacy: '...my solicitor, because I like her and it's all about my care order' ('Debby' in Gardner 1985, p. 16). In a subsequent study Gardner (1987) studied 'choice and control in care' more widely, rather than concentrating solely on the review process. She interviewed 50 children and 50 carers in 10 agencies. The children were all aged over twelve, and the majority over sixteen. Twenty-eight were in residential care, and the remainder in foster care.[17] The study looked at choice in relation to food, clothes and hours; smoking and medical examinations; friends, contact with relatives, and where to live. Seventeen of the children in residential care, and 6 of those in foster care, said that they had at no point been given any choice about their placement. Moreover 'one or two said they had been given no opportunity to express their wishes.' Of those who had been given some choice, the majority considered that social workers or social services took the ultimate decision. Ten thought that foster parents had some part in the decision, and 4 mentioned their own families.

There is some evidence that the involvement of children has improved since attention was drawn to the issue in the mid-1980s. Research in the early 1990s suggested that attendance at meetings was becoming the norm from the mid-teen years onwards (Dolphin Project 1993; Fletcher 1993; Lifechance Project 1994). Fletcher (1993) sought the views of children and young people with a carefully-designed questionnaire inserted into *Who Cares?* magazine. Over 600 young people in care responded and, although they cannot constitute a representative sample, what they had to say is interesting. Fletcher reports that 61 per cent felt that people listened to them at reviews and conferences, and that 84 per cent were asked before plans were made to move them. There was a difference in the level of negative response to both questions between residential care (17 per cent and 18 per cent) and foster care (12 per cent and 13 per cent), which may be of greater significance given that the children in residential care tended to be older

(92 per cent over thirteen years compared with 85 per cent in foster care), and might therefore be expected to be given more say rather than less. One in four respondents answered 'don't know' to the first question. Some of the comments made by those who felt left out of decision-making are poignant:

> 'I believe they like to think you are helping with decision-making but if you don't agree they will go against you.' (Seventeen-year-old)
>
> 'I never really say anything because I am worried about saying the wrong thing.' (Fifteen-year-old)
>
> 'They talk about you as if you are not there, so you just shut up – and listen without saying a word.' (Fourteen-year-old)
>
> 'I never go to meetings. My Mum tells me what happens at the meetings.' (Eleven-year-old)
>
> (Fletcher 1993, pp. 52–3)

A number of important points can be drawn from the research reviewed here. (1) Children and young people very often feel excluded from decision-making processes: because they are not allowed to take part; because they have insufficient confidence to take part; because they do not feel that anyone really listens to them; or because they think people disregard what they say. (2) Some children feel that they are really included, listened to and given an effective voice; and there is some indication that the number of such children is increasing. (3) There are fears that giving more say to parents and other interested parties may reduce children's influence on the outcome of discussions. (4) Most of the research evidence relates to teenagers, and there is really very little about the experiences of younger children.

Developments since 1989

All the studies referred to took place before the Children Act 1989. There was some expectation that the Act would make a major difference to children's participation. Hodgson (1990) wrote at the time: 'The Children Act 1989 ... sets out a philosophy of empowerment for children.' He emphasised the duty to consider the child's wishes and feelings and the consequent obligation to provide adequate information, and he drew attention to the new duty in section 20(6) to consult children *before* providing accommodation. Others have been less sanguine about this aspect of the Act. Fox Harding (1991) acknowledges that many provisions of the Act reflected, at least in part, a children's rights perspective. However, she also identifies elements of *laissez-faire*, paternalism and parents' rights in the Act, and argues that these are at least as important as the children's rights strand and partly undermine it.

It is only recently that research has begun to appear which examines practice in decision-making for children who have been looked after since the implementation of the 1989 Children Act. Grimshaw and Sinclair's (1997) major study of reviews and planning meetings used a combination of case record analysis, review observations, individual and group interviews with children, interviews with parents and interviews with social workers and review chairs. They found that 55 per cent of children and young people attended their reviews and planning meetings, but that attendance varied considerably with age ($p < 0.01$). They also found that the longer children had been looked after, the greater the frequency of their attendance ($p < 0.01$), and that attendance was higher for children in section 20 accommodation than among those in care ($p < 0.05$).

Grimshaw and Sinclair found little evidence of independent supporters for children at the meetings they observed. In observing meetings they used the modified ladder of participation from Thoburn et al., the ten 'rungs' of which are: controls; helps design service; partner; participant; involved; consulted; informed; placated; manipulated; powerless.[18] The rating was of 'the highest level of participation achieved by an individual concerning at least one significant issue in the meeting' (Grimshaw and Sinclair 1997, p. 150).[19] Using this method they found a spread of ratings but with more children in the 'consulted' or 'involved' cells rather than the 'participant' or 'partner' cells. Levels of participation and partnership appear to rise with age.

Grimshaw and Sinclair conducted twelve interviews and two focus group discussions with children and young people aged eleven and over who had experience of review meetings. From these interviews and discussions they learned that some young people were overawed and nervous at a gathering of adults, but that 'young people who felt they knew what would be discussed approached the meeting with greater calmness.' Young people rarely met the chair beforehand, and 'even after attending the meeting, some still did not know the chair's name.' They talked of 'the sense of being put under the spotlight, especially when faced with intrusive questions from adults who appeared as strangers to the young people'. Some complained of people 'butting in'. On the one hand, 'lack of preparatory work before a review meant that young people felt pressurised to agree. A brief introduction to the agenda was not sufficient to allow space for reflection.' On the other, 'young people disliked ritualistic questions...the feeling of being caught up in a mechanical ritual...seen as a way of filling in time'. Most young people 'clearly felt that they had been consulted about the decisions and had been given a choice,' but 'few said they had been informed at the meeting about any rights of redress if they disagreed with the plan...the main impression is that those young people who spoke of genuine consultation had benefited informally rather than by using any formal rights' (Grimshaw and Sinclair 1997, pp. 153–7). 'Young people were also unhappy about large meetings.... There were few individuals offering young people support.... Young people typically felt self-conscious about their meetings yet the meetings themselves were often not organised in ways that made them feel comfortable' (Grimshaw and Sinclair 1997, p. 165). These findings are very similar to those which I report later in this book.

Aldgate, Bradley and Hawley (1997) looked at the use of relief care for non-disabled children. The overall aim of the study was to examine the effectiveness of relief care provision under the Children Act 1989, and in particular how well it was meeting the needs of children and families. As part of their research the team interviewed children from age five upwards using a variety of methods. They discovered that 'the majority of older children (38 of 41) recalled being informed by someone about what was happening'. However, 'when it came to having the opportunity to talk about how they felt and have an input into the decision-making, just over half the children (22) thought that this had happened, 8 said it definitely had never happened while the remaining 11 were uncertain' (p. 176). The authors comment:

> There was a distinct feeling from children's comments that there had been little opportunity to protest or to change plans. Consultation was very much on the side of information-giving. By contrast, when children's views were compared with those of parents and social workers, it was clear that the adults thought children had been given the opportunity to air their views in rather more cases. Though differences between the views of the children and the adults were not statistically significant, it seemed likely from children's comments that they had felt more intimidated and coerced by any consultation than adults realised.
>
> (p. 177)

The study found that 13 of the 41 children had attended planning meetings, although 'in children's minds, a meeting was only registered as such when it took place outside the home. But in the nine cases where this did occur, both children and parents believed the meeting allowed the children to influence the shape of arrangements' (p. 177). The authors suggest that the separate components of consultation, which they identify as 'information giving, talking over anxieties and giving children the opportunity to influence plans', may need to be done separately. They also suggest that

> account needs to be taken of the natural power parents may wield over their children in any circumstances to get them to conform to the parents' agenda. Independent sessions with children either with social workers or, in some cases, if they are known, carers may be more objective.... Although no child in this study complained about the abuse of power by adults, it is all too easy to see how consultation could degenerate into tokenism. If short term accommodation is targeted at parents in the interests of preventing family breakdown, this needs to be made explicit to the children. Choice of being accommodated may not be an option. It is as much an abuse of power to set children up to make spurious choices as it is not to ask them for their views.
>
> (p. 178)

An important piece of action research which has been proceeding for several years now is the Children's Planning Initiative being conducted by the Children's Society in North-West England (Welsby 1996a). The project seeks to develop a new approach to decision-making for young people who are looked after, based on principles of justice. Rather than fit each young person into a pre-existing system, it aims to create a unique planning framework centred on the individual young person and their wishes and needs. A research component is built into the project, but its purpose is to assess the strengths and weakness of the new approach rather than evaluating existing services. I refer to this work again later.

All the indications are that changes in the process of planning for children are continuing to unfold. In addition to the variety of attempts by agencies and practitioners to put into practice the emphasis on partnership in the Children Act 1989, there is the impact of recent changes in law and practice in New Zealand. The 'family group conference' approach is based on giving the family network the primary responsibility for making plans within a statutory framework (Wilcox and colleagues 1991). These developments are gradually becoming better known in this country and a number of agencies are seeking to emulate them (see Marsh and Allen 1993; Marsh and Crow 1997; also Thomas, forthcoming). It remains to be seen to what extent the family group conference enables effective participation by children in decisions.

One area of practice where participation by parents, let alone by children, might have been expected to be slow to gain ground is the field of child protection. In fact by the late 1980s there were a number of moves to involve families more fully and openly in child protection decisions, which were significantly boosted by the enquiry into investigations of sexual abuse in Cleveland (Butler-Sloss 1988). The Department of Health guidance to child protection agencies, revised to take account of the Children Act, for the first time encouraged children's participation in case conferences (Department of Health 1991b). A number of agencies have followed this lead with enthusiasm (see Thoburn 1992). Shemmings (1996) studied children's participation in child protection conferences in two local authorities. Thirty four children were interviewed following their conferences, and the adults involved were asked to complete questionnaires. The answers reflect a range of experiences, many of which were positive. With only a few exceptions the children were glad they went to the conference. Some felt adequately prepared for the meeting and supported when they were there; others did not, and found the occasion very difficult as a result. Several children would have liked more opportunity to talk about their own concerns, and some who were made to leave for part of the meeting objected to this. Some had a discussion with someone after the meeting to go over what had been decided; others did not.

Communication with children

Social workers and their managers, foster carers and other adults faced with the task of helping children to be involved in decision-making processes may have to think carefully about the task and their reasons for undertaking it, as well as considering what kinds of skills and techniques may be helpful. Hoggan (1991) sounds a cautionary note. In using techniques to communicate with children, she suggests, 'we need to ensure that our motive is to open up real dialogue between adults and children, rather than to persuade children to accept our adult decisions.' She analyses the experience in Scotland of permanency planning for children aged between five and twelve, in terms of three stances on children's rights: protectionist, parentalist and libertarian.

Broadly favouring a 'protectionist' approach, she argues that the children generally experienced a more parentalist approach, and suggests the following reasons: a tendency to rationalisation and pragmatism; a tendency to avoid the pain of facing children's real feelings; a high level of adult power in situations involving care; negative assumptions about children's level of understanding; and the assumption that adults know best. She concludes:

> Children in long-term care can be placed in a 'no-win' situation by care workers. Because they have suffered loss, neglect or abuse they often have developmental delays or display difficult behaviour. We sometimes assume that these labels equate with a child being unable to express or hold any valid view.
>
> (Hoggan 1991, pp. 31–4)

A number of authors have written about how social workers and carers can communicate and work with children who are worried, distressed or 'damaged' by their experiences. A tradition going back to Clare Winnicott and Selma Fraiberg, and more recently including Fahlberg (1994) and Jewett (1984), uses insights from object relations and attachment theories to explore the meaning of change for children and of their relationship with the caseworker. McFadden (1991) looks explicitly for ways of understanding the complexity of the inner life of the child. Another tradition is less psychoanalytic, more practical and concerned with understanding the child's point of view and enabling him/ her to voice it. Crompton (1980) writes from experience of social work with children and emphasises the need for children to know the truth about their lives and to be supported in giving their own views. She emphasises the importance of play as a means of communicating, and of trust. She quotes Rich (1968) to the effect that 'the responsibility...for understanding what the child means...is the interviewer's' (Crompton 1980, p. 96). Above all she emphasises that the object of communication is at least as much for the child to learn what s/he needs to know as for the adult to find things out, illustrating the point with a story from Gripe's *Hugo and Josephine* of a child's first meeting with a schoolteacher:

> She realizes that Hugo doesn't understand, she says, but in school children have to sit still and be quiet. The teacher does the talking, and the children just answer when the teacher asks them a question. Hugo listens attentively to this, but looks frankly astonished.

'Now that's odd,' he says.

'What's so odd about it?' the teacher asks.

'There's no sense in our answering, when we don't know anything. We're the ones who ought to ask the questions.'

(Gripe 1962, quoted in Crompton 1980)[20]

Crompton also makes the point that children's talk needs a relaxed setting; the adult setting must adapt to the child, not the other way around.

Kroll (1995) points out how any work with children in care must start by acknowledging the power imbalance between adults and children and also the difficulty of working directly with a child without alienating the parents. She suggests that the key issues in this area of work are: how do we talk to younger people? how do we clear our minds sufficiently to pay proper attention to the child? how do we make real contact with a child, create a safe place and establish a good enough relationship? what can be achieved in the few sessions that are often all we get? how can a focus be maintained while at the same time leaving room for the child's own contribution? how can 'leading the witness' be avoided? how can the way the child makes the worker feel be used to assist the work? She argues that workers' needs include a child-centred philosophy, a range of helpful theories and useful techniques in addition to training, supervision and support. The philosophy must accord value to the child's point of view as an individual, not just as a member of a family (but parallel or interpretative work with parents is often extremely important). Theories need to encompass cognitive development and emotional processes including attachment and mourning. Techniques include play, drawing and other creative activities, but perhaps most important is what Kroll calls 'the art of "being" rather than "doing",' of simply spending time with a child and being receptive to what s/he may want to communicate (Kroll 1995, p. 98).

Thurgood (1990), in a review of the contribution social workers can make to listening to children who have been abused, argues for the importance of consistent relationships and of acknowledging children's individuality. She goes on to explore a number of ways in which workers can facilitate communication with children. Play can be used as a medium of communication as well as in therapeutic intervention: 'In play, children will open up areas of feeling they may not be able to put into words or would deny in conversation.' Painting and drawing 'may be an easier way of communicating than talking', as may writing for some children. Activity-based work 'offers a way for workers to build relationships with children and young people who would have no interest in a talking relationship.' Provision of primary care can be a sound basis for communication. Life story work can provide 'a focus for the child to achieve an understanding of their past and to work through feelings about it.' Group work can make it easier for some children to communicate more freely than in an individual setting (a similar point is made by McFadden). Finally, Thurgood emphasises both styles of talking to children and the importance of looking for non-verbal communication (all quotes from Thurgood 1990, pp. 59–64).

Some difficulties in putting these approaches into practice have been identified by Kroll and others. One relates to skill and confidence; practitioners may feel that direct work with children is a highly skilled area of work that they do not have the talent or the training to undertake. Another is that sensitive work with children takes time and other resources, and may conflict with other agency priorities. Finally, it is possible that working directly with children to help them articulate their views will lead to conflict with other interests such as those of parents, carers, social workers or agency managers. It will be interesting to see how significant these difficulties are when we come to look at what happens in practice.

7

Doing Research with Children

The rest of this book is based on empirical research into children's involvement in decisions. The research was intended to find out how far children are being involved in decisions since the implementation of the Children Act 1989 and to learn something about what factors enhance or impede their involvement. The first piece of research was carried out in a local authority where I was employed, and consisted of a small number of interviews with children together with a brief quantitative analysis of participation in decision-making meetings. This was followed by a study in seven local authorities which combined a much fuller quantitative survey of children's involvement in decision-making meetings with a larger series of open-ended interviews with children, social workers, carers and parents. Before looking at the research more closely, we need to locate it in relation to social research methods in general, and to some issues that are specific to research involving children.

Approaches to social research

The research belongs in general to the theory-building rather than the theory-testing category. It studies an aspect of social activity which has not been extensively studied previously, and about which there is not a body of theory or a set of hypotheses waiting to be tested. In looking at younger children's participation in decisions that affect their lives when they are looked after by the state, I am concerned principally to *find out what is going on*: to discover how and how far children take part in decision-making processes, what factors influence, enhance or impede their participation and what are the expectations of those involved, especially the children directly affected. More fundamentally,

I am seeking to understand better two theoretical questions: what counts as effective participation in these sort of circumstances, and how people may try to resolve conflicts between principles of participation and principles of adult and professional responsibility for children's welfare. The research is therefore exploratory in nature, and to the extent that it is successful the outcome is likely to be a better set of questions rather than a series of answers.

This does not mean that I embarked on the research without any hypotheses. There were working hypotheses, outlined in the funding proposal, which helped to generate some of the specific research questions.[1] There are also a number of underlying assumptions which I brought to the work, which have emerged or which I have tried to clarify throughout this book. Glaser and Strauss (1967) imply that the best theory is that which emerges from empirical data in the entwined processes of collection and analysis. There is a grain of truth in this, and I have tried to maximise the opportunities for it to happen in the course of this research. But theory also emerges through reading, and through the kind of practical experience which was the long forerunner to this work; and it would be perverse either to deprive oneself of what may be a valuable source of understanding or to pretend that it is possible to approach the material as some kind of theoretical innocent. This is especially so with this research, which relates to an area of activity with which I have had considerable involvement as a practitioner, a manager and a teacher. It can be a struggle to use the insights gained from this experience without falling into the trap of preconception; and it was certainly an advantage during the later research to work with a colleague who had less experience of the particular area of activity we were studying and who was perhaps able to ask some questions which I would have missed.

In disciplinary terms, the research is situated within a sociological frame rather than, say, a psychological one. It draws on traditions of sociological and anthropological research which are broadly concerned with social interaction and with meaning. At the same time it also has a foot planted firmly in a tradition of applied social research which is concerned to evaluate policy and practice. It may be thought that there is a contradiction between evaluating the technical effectiveness of social welfare practice in its own terms and a more critical perspective which questions the meaning of that practice. I prefer to regard it as a constructive tension rather than as a fundamental contradiction. My research is based on the assumption that applied research, both at the level of policy and at that of practice, is enriched by the insights of sociological method. Purely technical evaluation of practice that never questions ideology seems to me as arid and obtuse as pure 'deconstruction' with no commitment.

Two other divisions that are commonly drawn in social research are those between microsociological and macrosociological approaches and between qualitative and quantitative analysis. These differences also have the potential to be unnecessarily limiting on the scope of our thinking. At an early stage I was fortunate to discover Layder's (1993) 'multistrategy approach', which offers two conceptual frameworks that have been very helpful in thinking about this research. The first is a resource map for field research which encompasses 'macro' and 'micro' perspectives and avoids accepting a dichotomy between them. Layder suggests conceptualising the research project in terms of four primary levels of interest: the *self*, where the focus is the individual's self-identity, social experience and life-career; *situated activity*, where the focus is on the meanings and definitions that emerge in social interaction; the *setting*, where the focus is on intermediate social organisations (for instance social work agencies); and the *context*, where the focus is on 'macro' social organisations such as state and legal structures. Layder suggests that a particular piece of research is likely to have a selective focus on one or two areas while the others remain in the background, but that the framework provides a useful starting point for thinking about a research strategy and in some cases will be 'more directly involved with emergent theory' (p. 73). Some attention to each level will usually be needed to ensure that the analysis is thorough and relevant and that all useful data are included. Over-arching all of these levels is the historical perspective which Layder suggests should always be present to a greater or lesser extent.

The other framework which Layder provides is incorporated in a series of statements about methodology, drawing heavily on Glaser and Strauss but allowing more space than they do for a range of methods including quantitative as well as qualitative approaches. The statements are: that 'the use of qualitative analysis and data is a central requirement of field research which endeavours to give an account of the social activities taking place in some bounded social world'; that 'a multistrategy approach actively encourages the use of quantitative data and forms of measurement in order to complement the central core of qualitative analysis'; that 'quantitative data and analysis should also play a part in generating grounded theory. In particular quantitative data on macro processes can be linked with qualitative data on situated activities in order to generate substantive theory'; that the researcher should 'make as many methodological and analytic "cuts" into the data as possible', not only in order to provide a validity check ('triangulation') but to 'increase the possibility of producing grounded theory which is dense and robust'; and that where possible the multiple cuts should include all the layers of the research map outlined above, and where selective focusing is necessary this should not totally exclude either a macro or a micro perspective (Layder 1993, pp. 127–8). Layder's approach was extremely helpful in supporting my original inclination not to be bound by rigid categories of types of research, but to look at whatever sources of data and methods of analysis seemed likely to be helpful in elucidating the questions which concerned me. At the same time it provided help in thinking about diverse sources of information and levels of analysis without becoming confused or overwhelmed.

A few other writers on methods have been helpful. Glaser and Strauss (1967) argue that theories which emerge from the data have better 'fit', and that concentrating on verification impedes the generation of theory. They describe how hypotheses are developed in the process of data collection through *theoretical sampling* and *constant comparative analysis*, alternately maximising and minimising the differences between cases in order to develop the categories of analysis. They argue for the greater resilience of theory based on diverse data, for the use of conflicting data to enrich theory rather than excluding it because it tends to disprove a theory, and for collecting data until a category is *saturated* rather than according to a preconceived plan which specifies how many cases need to be sampled. I have not followed this approach consistently in the research which follows, mainly for practical reasons; but it has been useful both as an ideal type of one kind of social research and as a support for persisting in what I might otherwise have felt were rather messy ways of proceeding at times. Hammersley and Atkinson (1995) give a sound and thorough introduction to some of the things that are meant by 'ethnography'. Lofland and Lofland (1995), although I discovered their book rather late in my research, offer so much wise advice that speaks directly to the researcher about getting access, working in a setting, collecting data, analysing and writing about it, that it is now hard to remember how I thought about the work before I read them.

The research strategy

Returning to Layder, it may be helpful to indicate where my research concerns are located on his research map. The *context* in this case includes much of the material I have looked at in the preceding chapters: the conceptions of childhood, child development and children's rights that are influential in the culture generally and in academic or professional circles; ideologies of family responsibilities and relationships; the legal and policy framework for state intervention in children's lives. The *settings* are the social work agencies in which the research was done, and within those the sub-settings of specific social work teams, children's homes and foster homes; their styles, cultures, preoccupations, their rules whether written or unwritten. The *situated activity* which in many ways is the principal focus of this research consists of all the decision-making processes which take place around children: the reviews and planning meetings in which they take part; the discussions between social workers, managers, carers and family members to which they are not privy; and the day-to-day negotiations of family or institutional life. The *selves* with which we are mainly concerned are those of the children supposedly at the centre of these activities, settings and contexts: their sense of who they are, whether their needs are being met and how much control they have over their lives. Behind it all lie the history of childhood and of thinking about childhood, the history of state policies towards children, the histories of the agencies and institutions carrying out those policies, and the individual histories of the children and adults who are the subjects of the research.

In formulating a strategy to investigate the question 'what is happening about involving children in decisions about their care?' I tried to take account of all these dimensions. In terms of *context* it might be important to pay attention to the social characteristics of the areas and communities where the studies took place, since one possible hypothesis was that the social background of children makes a difference to their experience of participation. As for *setting*, I needed to consider to some extent the structures and policies of the agencies where the research was conducted, since these might well have an effect on the nature of children's participation. In fact these levels of interest were of less importance than initially expected; a decision was taken early on to focus closely on the *situated activity* of the decision-making processes, since so little seemed to be known about how this was being conducted either currently or in respect of the younger age-group. Secondly, I decided to make it a priority of the research to study the individual perspectives of the different participants in these processes, especially the children themselves. *Self* and situated activity, then, is the selective focus of the research. The practical strategy would be to talk to children and to the other participants in decision-making processes and also to observe those processes, while at the same time collecting information about the overall context of policy and practice and how this was interpreted in the specific agencies where the research was done.

I also wanted the strategy to incorporate the distinctive strengths of both qualitative and quantitative approaches. The most effective way to do this seemed to be to seek rich overlapping data on a small number of cases, while at the same time collecting information on a much wider population which could be analysed numerically. This survey could serve the dual purposes of checking on the representativeness of the smaller sample and of helping to generate questions which could be explored further in the qualitative research. In return I hoped that the qualitative analysis might help to explain some of the patterns which might emerge from the larger survey. The above elements of the strategy were established early in the research – or at least in the second study – and remained fairly constant. Other aspects developed in the course of doing the research; sometimes you don't quite know what you're going to do until you've done it. As we see in the following chapters, this applies particularly to the processes of interviewing and of learning about children's perspectives.

Research with children

The theoretical starting point of this research is that children's participation in decisions about their lives is both important and problematical. Important, because children have a right to be heard in decisions, because their sense of autonomy is an important part of their well-being, and because the law now requires that their wishes and feelings be taken into account. Problematical, because their rights may clash with adults' responsibilities, because their well-being may depend on their safety and security, and because the law sometimes requires that adults do what they think is best for children. Nevertheless the research has been rooted in a commitment to maximise the opportunities for children to express their views and engage in discussions about their care; to this extent it is not impartial. This commitment carried implications for the conduct of the research. First, it meant that from the start I wanted a major focus of the research to be on finding out what children themselves thought about these issues. A substantial part of the field-work activity has consisted of talking to children, and a good deal of thought needed to go into choosing the most effective way to do this. Second, it meant that I wanted to give children a real choice about whether they participated in the research.

In Chapter 2 I suggested that the 'emergent paradigm' defined by Prout and James (1990) was the most promising frame for research into childhood. I pointed to the work in psychology, in sociology and in social anthropology which attempted to respond to children as social actors, to recognise their subjectivity and to avoid preconceptions about their (in)competence. I also suggested that adopting this approach also demanded that children be given a voice in the conduct of the research. In summary what Prout and James say is: that childhood is best understood as a social construction; that it is not universal but varies with class, gender, ethnicity and other social variables; that children's social relationships are worthy of study in their own right; that children must be seen as active in the determination of their own lives and the lives of those around them; that ethnography is a particularly useful methodology because it allows children a more direct voice than is usually possible through other styles of research; and that to engage with a new paradigm of childhood sociology 'is also to engage in and respond to the process of reconstructing childhood in society' (p. 9).

Within the new paradigm, even those who take a macrosociological view seem to suggest that the future lies largely in 'ethnographic' work (see Alanen 1995). This offers a way of doing exploratory research without too many preconceptions about the answers, or indeed the questions. James (1993) suggests, following Geertz (1975), that this must be a reflexive ethnography, which takes note of the biography of the ethnographer and her or his relationship with the subjects. She also argues, again drawing on Geertz, that it should be an ethnography which gives voice to the subjects' own constructions of their situation alongside the researcher's. Where the subjects are children and therefore not often regarded as fully autonomous, as well as having a very different experience of life from an adult researcher, this may make particular demands on the research process. Because children are seen as vulnerable and certainly are relatively powerless, it is easy to take advantage of them in doing research – to rely on adults for consent, to fail to explain the purpose or rules of research adequately, or simply to use their time in ways that are not in their interests or of their choosing. It may be necessary to make space in research for children's own ideas of what is relevant, interesting or important. Both Waksler (1991) and Yamamoto (1993) have revealed how children often have their own distinctive view of these issues which may be very different from what adults assume to be the case. It may also be necessary for researchers to shed some of their adult defences in order to get closer to the world as children experience it; see Mandell (1991), Opie (1993) and discussion below.

What is striking and attractive about much of the new writing on the methodology of research with children is its *engagement*. Researchers see their work as the extension of a commitment not just to opening up childhood to scrutiny but to opening up the social world, including research, to children; not only making children more visible as members of society but making society more accessible to children. Mayall (1995) argues passionately that childhood research should be committed to challenging the oppression of children. Oakley (1994) develops Hardman's (1973) view that children are a 'muted group' and compares the attempt to bring them into research as subjects with previous efforts to do the same with women. A key difference of course is that most of the researchers who achieved this have themselves been women, whereas few if any social researchers are themselves children. Alderson (1994) argues fundamentally for greater respect for children in the design and execution of social research, as in many other areas of social life. In her own research she is at pains to demonstrate the ability of quite young children to understand issues that are both complex and painful and to produce 'mature' judgements on those issues (Alderson 1993).[2]

The view of childhood one holds is fundamental, and this may be explicit or implicit. James (1995, 1998) has suggested that 'envisioned in the different research strategies used by social scientists to study children are at least four ways of "seeing" children', which she identifies as 'the developing child', 'the tribal child', 'the adult child' and 'the social child'.[3] The 'developing child' is seen as incomplete, lacking in status, and relatively incompetent. The 'tribal child' is viewed as competent, part of an independent culture which can be studied in its own right, but not part of the same communicative group as the researcher. Both these constructions imply that children are unable to have the same status as adults as research subjects. The 'adult child' and the 'social child' do have that capacity; but whereas the former is seen as socially competent in ways comparable to an adult (as for instance in Alderson's work), the latter is seen as having different, though not necessarily inferior, social competencies. James suggests that none of these views is wholly wrong; but that the first three, although they have been fruitful of research insights, all have serious limitations. Inclining towards the 'social child' perspective, she suggests that one of its implications for research is that one may capitalise on the areas where children are more competent – for instance drawing and telling stories, where they are often more practised than adults who may be more comfortable with a traditional interview format.

Researchers have also challenged the view that information collected from children is somehow less reliable than that collected from adults. In fact this view has now been thoroughly evaluated in relation to the reliability of children as forensic witnesses, and found to be without much foundation. According to Dent, research has demonstrated that 'children as young as six years can be as reliable as adults when answering both objective and suggestive questions' (Dent and Flin 1992, p. 3). Her own research shows children, including children with learning disabilities, to be 'as reliable as adults when giving free recall or answering general questions, but less reliable when answering specific questions' (p. 8). Goodman and Schwartz-Kenney (1992) have shown that warmth and positive reinforcement increase children's accuracy and their resistance to leading questions.

Relating to children

The way in which an adult researcher relates to child subjects is an aspect of research where a choice must be made. One approach is the 'least adult' research identity proposed by Mandell (1991). In her research in kindergarten she joined in the children's activities in the sandpit and on the swings, constrained only by her size. Fine and Sandstrom (1988) and James (1995, 1998) argue that the 'least adult' approach is not the most effective way to do participant observation with children, since the very difference between adult researcher and child subject, combined with the ability to ask 'ignorant' questions, is a rich source of data that should not be lightly sacrificed. I would add that the very act of pretending to be a child may introduce an element of strangeness to the interaction that makes the purported naturalism, if that is the object, something of an illusion. In complete contrast is the approach of Opie (1993) to her playground observation, when she made no pretence to being anything other than an old fuddy-duddy; or Sluckin (1987) who in the same situation tried as far as possible to be invisible. Fine and Sandstrom (1988) argue from considerable experience that the most productive research stance is usually that of a friend who is unarguably an adult but without the authority or responsibilities of a parent, teacher or youth leader (although they admit that there probably is a residual responsibility of care, at least in extreme situations).

My own first experiences of interviewing children for this research caused me to think carefully about the process of establishing communication. For instance my interview with 'Joe' had seemed disappointing at the time; he was not very communicative, most of his responses were monosyllabic and their content generally non-committal. An example is the following exchange when I asked him about being invited to his planning meeting (which he had declined to attend).

Can we talk a bit about the planning meeting that happened today?
Yeah.
What did you think about being invited to the meeting?
Dunno.
Who was it who invited you, was it [social worker]?
Yeah.
Why do you think she invited you?
Dunno. Probably because it's my planning meeting.

It was tempting to think that the lack of response was due to lack of skill on the part of the interviewer; and indeed this may be partly so. However, on reflection it seemed that the way in which Joe handled this interview was very similar to the way in which he handled consultations about his future. This might be because of the sort of person he was, the developmental stage he was at, or what he had learned from his experiences as a child. However, it is also clear that there are characteristics of the situation he was in as the subject of this interview which were similar to his situation as a young person being consulted about plans for his care and which could also explain his response (or lack of it). He had not asked for the discussion to take place; the timing, the setting, the form and the agenda were all determined by the adults involved. Although on the face of it the subject of discussion was him, his future, his views, he was not necessarily interested in the subject as it had been defined by those adults. The apparent failure of the interview may therefore be revealing.[4]

On the other hand 'Neil' had a much more open manner and seemed easier to interview than Joe. Still, most of his responses were brief and lacked much animation; for instance in this passage early in the interview when asked about his admission to accommodation:

Does it look as if you'll be spending some time away from your family?
What do you think?
Dunno.
Whose idea was it that you should come to live away from home?
Dunno.

You don't know? Whose idea might it have been? Who decided that was what was going to happen?
Dunno.
So who told you that you were coming here?
My Mum.

However, there is a marked contrast in those sections of interview where Neil began talking about a subject that interested him, for example in this passage:

Do you see your Dad?
Yeah. I went to him...Saturday. I'm going to my Mum's this Saturday, and before I go to my Mum's I'll be playing football at ten o'clock Saturday.
Yeah? So you've got quite a busy life. Are you keen on football?
Yeah. I play for the school football team.
What position?
Centre defence.
It's quite important to keep things like that going at a time like this, isn't it, when you're not sure what else is going on?
Yeah. I don't miss anything off from, like, games or anything. I go Cubs Monday, Tuesday PE, Wednesday games, Thursday some activities sometimes ('cause we ain't choosed 'em yet) then PE, and Friday swimming, (um, and, um I'll go swimming today), what else have I got on Friday? That's it on Friday.

Not only are the answers longer, but they are also more reflective; when Neil is not sure of the answer he takes time to think and corrects himself; it is important to get it right.

The experience of doing these early interviews made me think that perhaps if one could get away from a question-and-answer format, and use methods that gave children more control over the interview process and content, they might be more forthcoming. For the second study Claire O'Kane and I developed a range of materials from different sources that enabled the interviews to take a rather different form. These methods proved very effective in enabling children to exercise control over their interviews and to say what they wanted to say, as we can see in the following extracts from my interview with 'Becky'.

I interviewed Becky in the living room of her home where she lived with her older sister. Becky and I sat on the floor – her sister was on a chair in the corner of the room. Becky was happy for the interview to be tape-recorded and helped to operate the machine. I showed her the interview materials and at my suggestion we started by working on the 'decision chart'. This involves the interviewer and the child in making a grid with significant decisions in the child's life on one axis and significant people on the other, so that the child can evaluate (using coloured stickered) which people have most say in each decision. Becky was very relaxed with the process and quickly took the initiative:

> *Right, let's draw some lines on there, shall we? Have you got a ruler?*
> Yeah, I've got loads of them. Do you want a pencil as well?
> *No, this is fine.*
> I had quite a lot of new school stuff for Christmas. [conversation with sister about this]
> *Very rough and ready this is. Should do the trick. How's that looking?*
> So we've got, 'time to be in', 'hairstyle', 'where I go', 'what friends I have', 'what clothes I wear', 'when to do my homework', 'where to live', 'bedtime', 'when to stay off school'...

Becky continued to direct the interview herself without the necessity for questions from me. Apart from the first and last, each move to a new decision-making topic was initiated by her. When Becky was sure of what she wanted to say she was able to despatch a subject quite crisply:

> What friends I have: that's mostly my decision. [Pause] [To sister] You have a bit of say in that [+] I have more say, though, cause I hang round more – people I hang round in the streets with, I either hang round there or go rollerblading with, and I hang around with my tidy[5] friends that's in school innit? Auntie V, she has a bit – she don't have much say; she has a bit but not much. Nannie and Gramp don't have no say with my friends. What clothes I wear: I have quite a lot and you do. [sister: 'I only advise you' 'Exactly, you advise me' 'I don't say don't wear it, you're not wearing it, do I?'] Auntie V; she's got no say in what I wear. Neither have Nanny and Grampa.

Becky was naturally talkative, which no doubt helped. 'Barry' was less so, but still the participatory approach seemed to make it easier for him to say what he thought. I interviewed him in his children's home with his key worker present (at Barry's request). Although he was keen to take part in the interview, initially his responses tended to the monosyllabic:

> *OK, so what happened when you were six?*
> My dad became ill and I went to live at my Nan's for a week.

Mm.
Shall I put my Nan?
All right; if you fill up that page we can do another one.
Yeah.
So Graham went with you to Nan's?
Yeah.
So that was when you were six – for a short time?
Yeah for a week.
Right.
Then I moved to Liz.

What the transcript does not reveal is that Barry was actually completing a 'time-line' while this conversation took place. He was fully engaged in the production of this account and, while not saying much, filled in the sheet assiduously. By later in the interview he was more confident and forthcoming. Reflecting on his 'decision chart', I asked 'do you think kids generally have enough say about things in their lives, or not enough, or too much?' He replied, 'Some of my friends, too much,' and explained this further:

> Like, me I'm told certain times for safety, and others they don't care what time they come in
> *It sounds as though it's important to know that people are concerned about you, and taking some control over your life?*
> Yeah
> *Yeah?*
> And I'm glad they're doing it.

Planning this research

My reading, and the experience of doing the earlier research, convinced me that I was right in wanting to get as much information as possible directly from children and to make the process of getting the information as 'child-friendly' as possible. It also led me to think more deeply about how to make the whole research process more accessible to children. I do not claim to have got any of this right; it has been a matter of learning as I went along. However, the progress that I have made has been due to the advice of the researchers I have mentioned as well as the experience of learning the hard way, and the insights of a colleague from a different background. I decided that I had to collect data from a variety of sources including policy statements, records, survey material, interviews and observations, but with a strong emphasis on gathering information directly from children, in order to find out what it is like for them to be having decisions taken about them and to be taking part in those decisions. In this section I describe how the research was planned.

The earlier research was carried out in an agency where I had worked for many years as a team leader and was now a policy adviser. This meant that I had working relationships and friendships that could help me in the process of getting access to research data. The original intention was to look at what happened when decisions were made about children in middle childhood who were at the point of admission to accommodation or change of placement. The plan was to observe meetings at which plans for children were made, to interview key participants, and in particular to interview children shortly after the meeting and again after an interval. In fact, even with the good relationships that I enjoyed, it was not possible to get access to cases at these crisis points. After three months I had interviewed two children, neither of whom had attended the meetings held to discuss their care, and concluded that a change of tack was needed if enough cases were to be obtained.

As part of the evaluation of a new system of planning and reviewing children's cases I agreed to undertake a study of participation in the decision-making process. It would include all cases and would encompass regular reviews as well as planning meetings. It was to be mainly a paper study, without direct observation of meetings, although it was agreed that a small number of interviews would also form part of the exercise. Teams were asked to send the minutes of every review and planning meeting over a three month period to me for an analysis of who attended these meetings. The initial response was poor, and the data collection period was eventually extended to six months. There was considerable variation in response between social work teams. The findings of this survey are summarised in the next chapter. At the conclusion of the survey two children and two social workers were interviewed; the results of these interviews are included in Chapters 9 and 10.

Although the success of the first study was limited, there was enough to convince me that the study of children's participation in decisions deserved further work. The research confirmed a number of my initial assumptions: that there was uncertainty about how best to include children in decision-making and about how to take account of their views; that the age series from eight to twelve included a significant transition in that children were very unlikely to be included in formal decision-making processes at age eight and very likely at age twelve; and that discovering children's views was not a simple or straightforward process. I now needed to get access to a larger number of children and to work with them in more depth.

I was given funding by the Nuffield Foundation to carry out a study in two local authorities in England and Wales. The objectives were to explore some of the ways in which children in middle childhood were being involved in decisions about their care, to explore children's perspectives on decision-making processes in conjunction with adult views of the same processes, to test different ways of discovering the views of children in this age group, and to identify obstacles to children's participation and suggest ways in which they might be overcome. In recruiting a research colleague I was fortunate in finding someone who had a great deal of experience of play and participatory activities with children and young people and who was able to bring to the research skills and knowledge in working in ways other than formal interviews, and a perspective on the research which was different from my own. These skills and this difference enhanced the research in all sorts of ways, and I must acknowledge the enormous contribution of Claire O'Kane in helping to give the work its final shape.

The research plan was to collect data on all children aged 8-12 who were looked after by the study authorities during a specified period, and then to study in more detail a small sample. The detailed study was to include direct observation of meetings, interviews with social workers, parents and carers, and interviews and discussions with children. Because of the problems found in the earlier study with formal interviews, I planned to develop different ways of gathering children's views including group discussions and games. I also hoped that it would be possible to avoid some of the problems encountered in the earlier study with identifying cases. It was expected that about 200 children would be included in the survey and 45 in the detailed study.

The survey was intended to get a general picture of children's involvement in decision-making and to begin to identify some of the factors which I conceptualised in terms of *background, context, process* and *outcome.*[6] The information from the quantitative survey was likely to be of interest in itself, since little information of this kind had been collected either in relation to this age group or since the implementation of the Children Act 1989. It would also guide the questions to be asked in the qualitative study, and in turn the qualitative findings of the detailed study would help to fill out, and perhaps to explain, some of the information obtained from the analysis of the first stage data.

The detailed study was intended to explore the perspectives of children and adults on the processes and issues involved in decision-making; to explore the meaning of what was going on and how it related to people's expectations of the decision-making process. This was to be the most substantial part of the project in the time and effort devoted to it. It would be of key importance in exploring some of my central research questions – what counts as effective participation, how much children expect to be involved, how adults deal with conflicts between children's wishes and their best interests, what are the advantages and disadvantages of different ways for adults to communicate with children in this age group. It included the more innovative elements of the research because of its focus on finding different ways of gathering children's views, and because of my determination to give children some control and influence over the research process.

Gradually the idea developed that the research would have a third stage, which would be the work I planned to do in disseminating the research, and especially in building on the findings and experience of the research to produce output that would be of use to those involved in the processes I was studying. Dissemination was very important to the funding body, and to me. My concern with children's participation in decisions grew out of my experience in practice, and it mattered to me that my research should have some visible benefits for practice, especially now that I was being given money to do it and that local authorities other than my own were apparently willing both to allow me to inconvenience their staff and to trust me with access to the children for whom they were responsible.

There was also a preparatory stage in which I arranged to meet young people with experience of the care system in order to help identify what questions to ask. Of course the perspective of an eighteen-year-old looking back on their earlier experience is not always the same as that of a ten-year-old in the thick of that experience (Shaw 1996). Nevertheless it may be closer than the perspective of an adult without any direct experience of being in state care or of being looked after by strangers.

Approaching the interviews

I wanted to ensure that the research methodology showed respect for children in the ways described earlier. First of all this meant designing the consent procedure to maximise children's choice to take part or not – a sensitive task because it involved limiting the extent to which adults were able to choose for the child. Any adult who has responsibility for the child's well-being may act as a gatekeeper for research: parents, carers, social workers and their managers, agency senior managers. I had to respect the position of these authority figures, but I also aimed to ensure that children who might want to take part were not unnecessarily excluded by these parental or quasi-parental figures. The principle I followed was that a child's participation should depend on active consent on the part of the child and passive consent on the part of adults. It was evident that difficulties in getting access to young children in foster care could limit our ability to construct a representative sample, and I decided to make a virtue of necessity by making consent the key determinant of inclusion.

In terms of interview methods the plan was to use a variety of methods rather than formal interview; it seemed likely that children might talk more freely if we used drawings, games and activities than if we questioned them. Children are often questioned by adults for a variety of reasons, and often to catch them out; children are rightly suspicious of adults' questions. In a way the process of questioning anyone can have a dictatorial aspect, especially if the questioner simply produces the questions without the other person necessarily having any idea of what is coming next and why. It was also important to give children as much choice as possible in the form and content of interviews, because the working assumption was that children's agendas would be different from adults' and this could not be tested if the agenda was predetermined.

For the interviews with parents and foster carers there were different issues associated with their own understanding of the research and their reasons for wanting or not wanting to take part. Some members of both groups had very definite things that they wanted to say to us – in a few cases this appeared to be their motivation for taking part. Others seemed defensive, as shown by their reluctance to take part at all or their 'caginess' when we did talk to them. Others – and these were probably the majority – were happy to take part and to respond to whatever questions we asked, sometimes with views that were already clearly established and sometimes with new reflections prompted by our questioning. In general, however, we did not find the need to do any specific preparation or groundwork for the interviews with these groups, beyond what we had already done in preparing them for their children's participation in the research.

In relation to social workers the complexities were greater. In doing research into an area such as social work practice it seems important to work with the grain of that practice and in a way that respects the genuine efforts of most practitioners to do a good job and the very substantial difficulties which lie in their way. As an experienced social worker and social work manager I was acutely aware of those efforts and those difficulties. However, I could not assume that the practitioners to whom I spoke would understand that I was aware. Some might regard me as an outsider from the ivory tower, clueless as to the realities of practice or wanting only to criticise. Others, including those whom I had met as students or as practice teachers, might perhaps assume that I was an insider or 'on their side'. It was important therefore to behave in such a way as to reassure doubters that I did have a clue and was not out to get them, and at the same time to reserve my ability to be critical or to ask naive questions. In other words, while wanting to work with the grain of practice, I wanted to avoid being incorporated into the system of practices and assumptions which I was studying.

One stance which helped, because I was used to taking it and it was familiar to many of those to whom I spoke, was that of the concerned questioner which I had often used in practice supervision in my days as a team leader. This stance I have found enables one to switch easily from knowing the score to being naive, because it is understood that part of a supervisor's role is to ask awkward questions about someone's practice and the assumptions underlying it, while at the same time making use of one's knowledge of the situation and context, and being supportive. The parallel should not be taken too far; my role was to find out the thinking underlying practice by asking and probing, not to modify it or to suggest alternatives (although of course, as reflective practitioners, many of those I interviewed did say that they had modified their approach as a result of thinking set in train by the research process).

Analysing the data

Lofland and Lofland, Glaser and Strauss, and others argue for the importance of combining data collection and analysis as much as possible. At times I felt that I was not doing this in the second stage of the research as much as I would have liked. The practical difficulties of arranging interviews meant that the process of setting them up and carrying them out demanded total concentration for a time. This meant that there was a limited amount of analysis during the conduct of the qualitative research: I and my colleague chatted after interviews and swapped notes, rough transcripts or actual tapes; we talked about the themes that emerged from this process, and this may have influenced our way of asking questions as the interviews progressed.

However, there had been considerable analysis and preparation before this stage of the research, and this had determined a number of questions which it seemed important to ask all respondents. In this respect the research was not following either a pure grounded theory model.[7] Hammersley and Atkinson (1995) suggest that we should not be too hard on ourselves:

> Fieldwork is a very demanding activity, and the processing of data is equally time-consuming. As a result, engaging in sustained data analysis alongside data collection is often very difficult. However, some level of reflexivity can and should be maintained, even if it is not possible to carry out much formal data analysis before the main fieldwork has been completed. Some reflection on the data collection process and what it is producing is essential if the research is not to drift along the line of least resistance and to face an analytical impasse in its final stages.
>
> (p. 206)

It is fair to say that this was achieved. In addition, of course, there was considerable reflection during the transition between stages one and two, and the emerging findings of stage one guided some of the questions asked in stage two. This is discussed further in the conclusion to Chapter 8.

'Reflexivity' of course means more than simply reflecting on the process of data collection. A number of authors especially in anthropology have emphasised the importance of what the researcher and the research process bring to what is studied; how what is studied is often in effect a research interaction rather than an event or setting 'out there'.[8] One of the defining characteristics of this particular research was that in some ways the research was precisely the same thing as what it studied. It *was* and it *examined* the process of adults discovering children's views; and in that it tried to give children choices about how to participate in the research, it also both *was* and *examined* the process of giving children choices about how to participate. How this worked out in practice will be one of the concluding themes. First we need to look at the overall findings of the research, and that is the purpose of the following three chapters.

8
Patterns of Participation

In this chapter I describe what was learned from the two pieces of research about the extent of participation by children in decisions about their care.

The first study

In all 116 forms were returned, covering 28 planning meetings and 88 reviews concerning 120 children. This was about half of what would have been expected if every review form had been returned. The average age of children for whom data were returned was just under twelve years, although there was some tendency for young people aged more than twelve years to be over-represented in the returns. The data were analysed to discover who participated in meetings about children. The total number of participants ranged from three to ten, except for one case where only the social worker was present. The average attendance was 5.85. This average did not vary substantially from one age-group to another, or between one team and another.

Children and young people were present at 62 per cent of their meetings. This proportion varied greatly with the child's age. Below the age of eight, children's direct participation was insignificant. Of children aged eight to twelve 50 per cent attended their own reviews, of those aged thirteen to fifteen more than 70 per cent, and at sixteen and over nearly 100 per cent. It appeared that some participation begins at seven or eight, and that a steady increase in the level of participation begins around eleven and continues through the adolescent years. The correlation between age and participation is strong enough to be the most striking aspect of these data. With a few exceptions there was a steady rise for each year of age in the proportion of children who were present at their meetings. Although there were wide differences between teams in the proportions of children who attended meetings, these variations appeared to be almost entirely explicable by variations in the age of children. Detailed analysis showed that when age was controlled for the differences between teams virtually disappeared.

Looking specifically at the eight to twelve age group, it is clear that this is the age at which participation in formal decision-making of this kind begins to happen. Not too much can be made of the increase from year to year within this group, because the numbers are extremely small. However, it is apparent that between the 0–7 age group where it is safe to predict that children will not attend meetings, and the 13–18 age group where it is increasingly safe to predict that they will, there lies a transitional group where decisions about participation appear to be being made on an individual basis. Clearly it is worth looking more closely at how these decisions are made and at what influences them.

In general participation in reviews appeared to follow a consistent pattern throughout the department, with little variation in the numbers of participants. A typical review meeting involved the social worker and her manager, a parent, a foster carer or residential care worker, and often one other professional – most commonly a teacher. It was unusual for any other relative to be present, and even more unusual for a child to have a friend at their review. It is possible that some children might prefer to have a close relative or friend at the meeting, rather than a schoolteacher or a psychologist. Conversations with staff suggested that the question of whom to invite to reviews was often decided without much reflection, and certainly without much thought about what might be the child's perception of their situation. Children's participation in reviews seemed to be an issue on which social workers had in effect been left to make their own policy.

The second study

The rest of this chapter is based on the survey of 225 cases which comprised the first stage of the second study. Information was gathered on all children aged at least eight and not more than twelve years who were looked after by the study authorities on 1 July 1996. It was collected using a structured pre-coded questionnaire. The first page collected information from administrative staff about the children's background (age, sex, ethnicity, health, legal status and reason for being looked after), and this was mainly done by post. The remainder of the schedule was used to gather information from social workers, mainly about the most recent decision-making meeting for each child: what sort of meeting, when it took place, who was invited and who attended, what work was done with the child before and after the meeting, whether and how the child took part. This information from social workers was gathered in face-to-face interview, with a few telephone interviews where this was necessary to complete the data.

It is important to distinguish between two different kinds of information which were collected in these interview schedules: *objective* information such as legal status, age, the number of people at a meeting or whether someone was invited, and *subjective* information such as the extent to which the child's views were communicated or the influence of the child's views on the decisions made. Whether the interviewer invited social workers to place their answers on a rating scale or simply recorded 'yes' and 'no' responses, these answers are clearly matters of judgement. This information seemed nevertheless to be important to collect because social workers' judgements are likely to be a major factor in determining how children participate, even where the specific content of those judgements may be a very shaky foundation for any general propositions about what happens to different children. Hill (1997) quotes a comment by Stone (1995) that the information she collected from social workers 'was useful precisely because, whatever its inadequacy, it represented the information on which decisions were actually based'. For instance, the fact that, as we shall see, most social workers asserted that individual children's views had considerable influence on the outcomes of decision-making processes deserves to be thought about, even if it suggests a whole set of questions about why they might think that, rather than telling us that it is 'true'. Where social workers were invited to give a specific rating, as in the assessment of children's contributions to the discussion at meetings, it may be that slightly more reliance may be placed on the content of those assessments; although it is still important to bear in mind that individuals may have their own personal benchmarks or expectations against which they make those assessments.

In what follows I set out the findings in terms of general frequencies before going on to look at what seem to be interesting relationships between the data. In doing so I will be discussing what might be the implications of the answers that were given, and what might be their meaning to our respondents. Throughout the account it will be important to distinguish between the more objective and subjective data as identified above, and I will draw attention to this distinction when necessary.

The children and their meetings

Of the 225 children 64 per cent were male and 36 per cent female. This reflects the higher proportion of boys in the care system at this age. The age distribution was extremely even, with between 39 and 45 children in each year cohort from eight to twelve. As defined by their social workers, 96 per cent were white and the remainder were of mixed parentage. In all 25 per cent had some form of ongoing health condition or disability, of which the most common were a learning disability (7 per cent of cases) and asthma (4 per cent). The children were the responsibility of 25 different social work teams and 110 individual social workers. Two-thirds were committed to the care of the local authority; the remainder were accommodated under section 20 except three who were on emergency protection orders and two who were placed for adoption. In 57 per cent of cases the main reason for being looked after was abuse or neglect. Most children (58 per cent) were placed in foster care with non-related carers; 21 per cent were fostered with relatives, 12 per cent lived with their parents, and seven per cent were in residential care.

Respondents were asked to identify the most recent decision-making meeting in each case. In 80 per cent of cases this was a review meeting, in nine per cent a planning meeting, and in another nine per cent some other form of meeting. In only two cases was the meeting a child protection case conference. In three quarters of cases between five and eight people were invited to the meeting. This included children themselves in 55 per cent of the cases, in addition to a further 6 per cent where the child was invited to part of the meeting; in 39 per cent of the cases children were not invited to their meeting at all, and in eight per cent the child was not even told that the meeting was taking place. Respondents were also asked whether planning between the agency and the family could be best characterised as partnership or conflict: in 47 per cent social workers felt that they were working in partnership with families, in only 13 per cent conflict, but with 39 per cent described as a mixture.

Respondents were asked about the kind of decisions taken at the meetings, the forms used to structure the meetings, and the child's satisfaction with their placement. Social workers identified 37 per cent of the meetings as being concerned with making significant decisions, 42 per cent as about maintaining the status quo and 21 per cent as a mixture. In 70 per cent of cases the social worker thought the child was living in a placement of their choice, and in 17 per cent not, with four per cent described as having mixed feelings. Not infrequently a rider was added to the effect that the child would really rather be living at home, but that aside was happy with the placement. The *Looking After Children* review forms were used in 60 per cent of the cases. All the agencies had begun using these forms in the year preceding the survey. This gave comparison groups in each area, since we were asking about meetings which had taken place in the six months or so preceding the survey. An additional set of questions added midway through the survey concerned the extent of difference between children's views and those of their carers, social workers or parents. Out of 127 cases in which these questions were asked, there were thought to be some significant differences of view between children and social workers in 23 per cent of cases, between children and parents in 38 per cent of cases, and between children and carers in 22 per cent of cases.

Work done with the children

According to their social workers a third of the children (32 per cent) had been consulted about who they thought should attend the meeting, and a smaller proportion had been given some choice about the time (23 per cent) and place (24 per cent). In many cases the meeting was planned taking into account the child's needs, in that meetings were held after school and in the carers' home, but the children had not actually been asked whether this suited them. In 52 per cent of cases, however, social workers said that children had been given an opportunity to help set the agenda. In 70 per cent of cases social workers thought that the purpose and structure of the meeting had been explained to the child, and in a further 17 per cent of cases 'to some extent'. In 12 per cent no explanation had been given. Some respondents commented that the child already knew this from attending previous meetings. The most common method of giving an explanation was direct verbal discussion with the child, and there was little sign of the use of alternative forms of communication such as games, drawings or activities.

The survey asked if children (a) had been told about their right of access to information kept about them and (b) had been given information about the complaints procedure. In most cases the answer was 'no' (60 per cent for information; 54 per cent for complaints) or 'don't know' (12 per cent; 7 per cent), although 37 per cent of children had apparently been told about the complaints procedure and 27 per cent about their right of access. In 48 per cent of cases reports were prepared in advance of the meeting and in 27 per cent the social worker read through these with the child. When asked how far they felt that they had found out what the child's wishes and feelings were before the meeting, 75 per cent of social workers answered positively. A further 19 per cent felt they had done so 'to some extent' and only four per cent answered 'not at all' (one per cent not known). The principal methods used to discover children's wishes were discussion with the child (88 per cent of cases), with the child's carers (63 per cent), and with members of the child's family (36 per cent). The *Looking After Children* consultation booklets were used in 28 per cent of cases, and in 26 per cent the child's views had been elicited at least in part through discussion with a teacher. However, activities had been used with children to facilitate communication in only 14 per cent of cases, and drawings in only 8 per cent.

In 43 per cent of cases social workers thought that children had been given a choice about how they participated in the meeting: whether they attended in person, spoke through a representative or sent a written or taped communication. However, we found little evidence of the latter methods actually being used. Some form of pre-meeting was held in 41 per cent of cases, giving children the opportunity to explore issues that might come up in the meeting (in another 26 per cent 'to some extent'). This meeting usually involved the child and social worker, and sometimes a foster carer or a parent. Very few children were offered the opportunity of having an independent advocate (8 per cent), or a friend or supporter of their choice to attend the meeting (12 per cent). Only two children (fewer than 1 per cent) had been offered the chance to attend an 'in care' group. Ten children had communication difficulties, and for six of these additional support had been available at the meeting. English was the first language of all of the children, and this was the language of all the meetings. In areas with a richer ethnic mix or a higher proportion of Welsh speakers language might have been more of an issue than it was.

Levels of participation

The majority of meetings (76 per cent) were attended by between 4 and 7 people. The most frequent attenders were social workers (97 per cent), followed by female foster carers (69 per cent); team managers (60 per cent); male foster carers (46 per cent); children themselves (46 per cent); mothers (38 per cent); foster care link workers and fostering officers (30 per cent); teachers (22 per cent); independent chairs

(20 per cent); senior social workers (17 per cent); and fathers (15 per cent). Apart from those included as foster carers, other relatives did not feature much. Brothers and sisters attended in 13 per cent of cases, and in some cases up to four brothers and sisters were present. Usually this was because more than one child in a family was being reviewed at the same meeting. Perhaps remarkably, solicitors were present at 13 per cent of the meetings; but in only one solitary instance did a friend of the child attend. The decision-making matters discussed included contact (68 per cent of cases), placement (66 per cent), education (54 per cent), health (38 per cent), legal status (30 per cent), leisure time (29 per cent), personal support issues (26 per cent), and financial considerations (11 per cent). Children actually attended the whole meeting in 36 per cent of cases, and part of it in 12 per cent. In 52 per cent of cases they did not attend at all. In spite of this social workers said that the child's views were communicated in 84 per cent of cases and 'to some extent' in a further 13 per cent of cases. Most often this was by the social worker (63 per cent) or the foster carer (50 per cent). The child communicated their views directly in 42 per cent of cases. In only two per cent of cases did social workers report that the child's views were not communicated.

Social workers were asked how they would characterise the child's involvement in the discussion at those meetings where they were present. The alternatives offered were: (a) the child freely contributed actively to the discussion; (b) the child contributed actively to the discussion when prompted; (c) the child gave brief answers when prompted; (d) the child didn't speak in the meeting; (e) n/a (the child wasn't present). The answers were (a) 21 per cent; (b) 12 per cent; (c) 12 per cent; (d) 3 per cent; (e) 51 per cent. This means that of those children who attended, 68 per cent were judged to have contributed actively, compared with 26 per cent who gave brief answers and only 6 per cent who did not speak. Social workers thought that 'the child's views were genuinely listened to' in 87 per cent of cases, and 'to some extent' in a further 8 per cent. Only in three per cent of cases did the social workers say that the child's views were not genuinely listened to. The influence of the child's views on the decisions made was described as 'a lot' in 57 per cent of cases, 'a little' in 32 per cent, and 'none' in 10 per cent of cases.

We were told that in 73 per cent of cases the social worker thought that the child was generally satisfied with the decisions made, and in 16 per cent of cases they were satisfied 'to some extent'. These are greater than the figures for parents' satisfaction (56 per cent and 17 per cent) but less than those for social workers (89 per cent and eight per cent). The child was given an opportunity to discuss what had happened after the meeting in 51 per cent of cases and 'to some extent' in a further 23 per cent of cases. This was normally through discussion with social workers or foster carers. In only 26 per cent of cases was the child given a record of the decisions made. In one area, where clerks were routinely present at reviews to take minutes, social workers seemed confused as to whether the child was given a record since they were not responsible for sending them out (and often they were distributed weeks or even months after the meeting).

Factors affecting children's participation[1]

The data were examined for relationships between variables, using cross-tabulations and comparing actual with expected frequencies. I concentrated on those relationships which were highlighted by my initial hypotheses; those between 'background' and 'context' factors and 'process' factors, and those between 'process' and 'outcome' factors. This analysis revealed some interesting differences, as well as some unexpected similarities, between groups of children and the ways in which they are involved in decision-making meetings.

Which children are invited to their meetings?

Three factors seem particularly important in predicting which children will be invited to their meetings: the child's age at the time of the meeting; whether the meeting is about making significant decisions or about maintaining the status quo; and whether the 'Looking After Children' review forms are used.

Within the age range covered by the study, there was a clear, and indeed very striking, relationship between increasing age and the likelihood of the child being invited to the meeting (see Table 8.1).

This relationship is consistent with that reported by Grimshaw and Sinclair (1997).[2] It is all the more striking because, when social workers discuss children's participation in meetings, they rarely offer age as a key factor in determining whether children are invited. This has been evident from this research as well as from earlier investigations (Thomas 1994, 1995). The biggest year-on-year increase is at age ten, which is also consistent with the earlier research.

In addition to the effect of being younger, children were also less likely to be invited to a meeting if the main purpose was to address significant decisions than if it was concerned with maintaining the

Table 8.1 Children invited to meetings at different ages

Child's age (in completed years)	Child invited to none of meeting		Child invited to all or part of meeting	
	No.	%	No.	%
8 or under	32	63	19	37
9	24	53	21	47
10	13	33	26	67
11	11	27	30	73
12 or over	7	15	39	85

$(N = 222; p < 0.0001)$

Table 8.2 Children's invitation to meetings related to purpose of meeting

Purpose of meeting	Child not invited		Invited to all or part	
	No.	%	No.	%
Maintain status quo	30	32	64	68
Mixed purpose	13	28	33	72
Significant decisions	44	53	39	47

$(N = 223; p < 0.005)$

status quo (see Table 8.2). The inclusion of the category 'mixed purpose' enables us to see that it was not the presence of significant decisions that was the critical factor, but their being the main purpose of the meeting.

The new '*Looking After Children*' forms seem to have a positive influence on children's involvement. In cases where the LAC forms were used children were more likely to be invited to all of their meeting (see Table 8.3). It is possible that this could be at least to some extent an effect of the newness of these materials, and it would be interesting to see whether the effect is maintained in a year or two.

In addition it appeared that children who were accommodated were more likely to be invited to their meetings than children on care orders (see Table 8.4).

Finally, there was a small difference in frequency of invitation between girls and boys, with 58 per cent of girls compared with 53 per cent of boys being invited to the whole meeting, but this is not statistically significant.

Table 8.3   Children invited before and after use of Looking After Children forms

Use of LAC review forms	Child invited to meeting		Child invited to part of meeting		Child not invited to meeting	
	No.	%	No.	%	No.	%
Forms used	87	64	8	6	40	30
Forms not used	35	40	6	7	47	53

$N = 223$; $p < 0.005$. *Note*: These data are based on only the second half of our sample, because the relevant question was added to the survey after it had started.

Table 8.4   Children invited to meetings according to legal status

Legal status of child	Child invited to meeting		Child invited to part of meeting		Child not invited to meeting	
	No.	%	No.	%	No.	%
Accommodation	40	67	2	3	18	30
Care order	82	52	10	6	66	42
Other legal status	0	0	2	40	3	60

$(N = 223$; $p < 0.005)$

Which children attend their meetings?

Clearly the biggest factor affecting whether children attend their meeting is whether they are invited or not. However, it also appears that there are variations in whether children who are invited decide to attend, which are associated both with their age and with the relationship between their family and the agency. Younger children were less likely to choose to attend their meeting when invited; 53 per cent of those children age ten years and under who were invited to the whole meeting actually attended all of it, compared with 81 per cent of the eleven and twelve year olds. Additionally, where the planning between the agency and the family had been marked by a degree of conflict, children were more likely to choose not to attend than when it was characterised by partnership. Initially I noticed a correlation between the partnership/conflict dimension and children's attendance, and thought that social workers might be protecting children from certain situations (see Table 8.5).

However, when I looked at how many children in each category were invited there appeared to be no significant difference (see Table 8.6).

I then looked again at children's attendance after selecting out the cases where they had not been invited, and found the strong correlation shown in Table 8.7.

Table 8.5   Children's attendance and relationship between family and agency

Family–agency relationship	Child not at meeting		Child at part of meeting		Child at all of meeting	
	No.	%	No.	%	No.	%
Partnership	47	45	10	10	47	45
Conflict or mixture	66	57	17	15	33	28

($N = 220$; $p < 0.05$)

Table 8.6   Children invited and relationship between family and agency

Family–agency relationship	Child not invited		Child invited to part		Child invited to all	
	No.	%	No.	%	No.	%
Partnership	37	36	8	8	59	57
Conflict or mixture	47	40	6	5	63	54

($N = 220$; $p < 0.6$)

Table 8.7   Children's attendance when invited and family–agency relationship

Family–agency relationship	Child not at meeting		Child at part of meeting		Child at all of meeting	
	No.	%	No.	%	No.	%
Partnership	10	15	10	15	47	70
Conflict or mixture	20	29	16	23	33	48

($N = 136$; $p < 0.05$)

Which children are given preparation and feedback?

Children who are invited to attend their meeting seem to get more support and information than children who are given no opportunity to attend. For instance, 52 per cent of children who were not invited had no form of pre-meeting with their social worker and 39 per cent were given no opportunity to discuss what had happened after the meeting. The comparative figures for children who were invited were 17 per cent in each instance. It appears, then, that children who attend meetings usually have some explicit preparation for doing so, and an opportunity, if not to reflect, at least to hear again the outcome of the meeting. On the other hand, children who do not attend the main event may be being left out of the whole process, including the explanation of what is happening.

Which children make the most active contribution?

As noted above, the majority of all children who were invited to attend their meetings were described by their social workers as having contributed actively (68 per cent). There did not appear to be any major differences between groups of children in this respect. There were some variations with sex, age and the context of planning. Only 64 per cent of boys contributed actively, compared with 79 per cent of girls; 62 per cent of under ten year olds contributed actively, compared with 71 per cent of eleven and twelve year olds; and 58 per cent contributed actively when the planning process was characterised by conflict, compared with 72 per cent for partnership cases and 65 per cent for those described as a 'mixture'. Apart from the difference between boys and girls, none of these differences appears to be statistically significant.

Which children have most influence on decisions?

As we saw above, social workers said that the overwhelming majority of children were genuinely listened to. This did not vary either with age or with their presence or absence at the meeting. Their influence on decisions did not vary with age either, although it did vary somewhat according to whether they were present at the meeting (see Table 8.8).

However, it appeared that the influence of children's views varied more dramatically according to whether those views were significantly different from those of their social workers. Children's views appeared to have less influence than usual when they disagreed with their social

Table 8.8   Influence of children's views and child's attendance at meeting

Child's attendance	Child's influence 'none'		Child's influence 'a little'		Child's influence 'a lot'	
	No.	%	No.	%	No.	%
None of meeting	17	15	40	34	57	49
Part of meeting	3	11	9	33	15	56
All of meeting	2	2	23	29	55	69

$(N=223; p<0.05)$

Table 8.9 Child's influence related to difference of view with social worker (as estimated by social workers.)

Difference in views between child and social worker?	Child's influence 'none' or 'a little'		Child's influence 'a lot'	
	No.	%	No.	%
'No' or 'don't know'	41	42	56	58
'Yes' or 'to some extent'	20	67	10	33

($N = 127$; $p < 0.02$)

workers (see Table 8.9). Of course, this is based on social workers' estimates of how much influence the children had and on social workers' opinions as to how far there was a difference of opinion; it may therefore be that the relationship is a self-maintaining one. However, social workers were certainly not saying in many cases 'the child disagreed with me and the child's views won the day'. Children's views were also thought to have less influence when they differed from those of their carers, but more influence than usual when they disagreed with their parents; however, these relationships were not statistically significant.

Implications of the survey findings

In general it would be premature to draw too many conclusions from the analysis presented here. It was implicit in the design of the research that the survey and the detailed study should support and illuminate each other. Nevertheless a number of things may be regarded as having been learned, or confirmed, from the survey. First, it is clear that age is a very important factor in predicting which children will be given the chance to take part in formal decision-making processes, although the precise way in which this operates remains to be explored. Second, it is apparent that other factors affect which children are invited to take part – the nature of the decisions to be taken, and even the forms and procedures used in the decision-making process – and it is probable that this effect is independent of age.

It is also fairly clear that whether children are invited or not is not the only determinant of whether they attend. Of course, not all invitations are equally inviting, and some children may be given more encouragement to attend than others. Nevertheless the strong correlation between parent–agency relationships and the frequency of children's attendance should not be explained away. It seems likely that some children will be more disposed to take part in formal decision-making than others, and also that some situations are more conducive to children taking part. The interaction of personal disposition and situational factors is worth exploring further.

Age also seems to play a part in whether children attend or not. A higher proportion of nine and ten year olds decline the invitation to attend than others. Of course, this may simply indicate that children who are invited for the first time often like to think it over and may be more likely to take up the invitation on a subsequent occasion; as always, it is important to be alive to the ways in which the effects of age may be social artefacts, as we saw in Chapter 2. Certainly the social workers' assessments of how active a part children play in meetings do not indicate any strong difference between older and younger children once they are there. It may of course be that social workers are basing their answers on differential expectations of active participation at different ages. Equally, it may be that the social workers, or the children, have correctly identified which children are likely to be able to contribute to a discussion of this kind and to benefit from it.

Much of this is speculation. It is in the nature of survey results that they often give us 'facts' which cannot readily be explained using only the data that accompany them. To make sense of them we have to use other methods of enquiry. None the less the survey data have produced some important questions which were not there before, and which demand some kind of answers.

1. *Why are so many children apparently being denied the opportunity to attend their reviews and planning meetings?* Given that a significant number of children choose not to attend when invited, or only to attend part of the meeting, could others not be given the choice too?
2. *Why is age such a strong predictor of whether children are invited to meetings?* Are there unwritten rules of thumb, or are social workers making judgements about children's ability to take part – judgements which may be unconsciously structured by reference to their age?
3. *If most of the children who attend their meetings appear to take an active part in the discussion, is it likely that this would also be true of those who currently do not attend?*
4. *Can the children who do not take part really have so much influence on the decisions made when they are not there?* We were told that virtually all children are listened to and have a lot of influence on decisions, regardless of whether or not they are present. Does this reflect reality, or are social workers giving a rosy view – or are their answers to this

question governed by limited expectations of the amount of say which children can have?

5. *How well can a child's views be mediated by a social worker or carer?* In a very large number of cases the child is not invited to the meeting but her or his views are reported by the social worker or carer. Independent advocacy is rarely considered, despite the fact that social workers and carers usually have their own views about what should happen which do not necessarily accord with the child's view. Is this fair or realistic, and how is the child's view mediated or interpreted?

6. *Why are children less likely to be invited to take part in significant decision-making matters?* It appears that children in this age group are more likely to be enabled to take part in the day-to-day issues, and less likely to be involved in the really important decisions. Is this because of a belief that adults know best and that children are not to be trusted to make really important decisions?

7. *Why are some children choosing not to attend?* Are they seeking to avoid conflict; bored by meetings; content to trust their social workers; or unwilling to accept their situation of being in care or accommodated?

8. *What are the expectations of children who do take part in meetings – do they enjoy or value the meetings or simply tolerate them?*

Many of these questions lend themselves to exploration using qualitative or ethnographic methods. In part this is because they are not yet well-formed questions, and relatively informal exploration of the social context may be necessary in order to refine them. This is the view of qualitative research as the handmaiden of quantitative methods, doing the groundwork which will eventually enable the proper edifice to be constructed. An alternative view is that these questions are fundamentally about meaning, and that we can only learn about meaning through interacting with subjects and coming to understand their point of view.

For instance, one of the objectives of the research was to begin to develop a typology of participation applicable to situations such as those under study. The 'ladder' of participation originally developed by Arnstein (1969), and modified for children by Hart (1992), can to some extent be adapted for our purposes, if one allows for the fact that it was developed in order to analyse and promote participation in collective and public decision-making, and that we are concerned here with individual and private decisions. However, additional problems can arise in applying these models to the data presented here. The first is that it is necessary to take account not simply of attendance at meetings but also of (a) the nature of the discussion which takes place and the effective ability of the child to take part in this, (b) the preparation and support which the child is given in attending and making their views known, and (c) the extent to which decisions are actually taken through this process rather than elsewhere. It could be useful to develop a grid which represents all these factors; but it is possible that a linear model such as a ladder will not do justice to the many ways in which the nature of participation can vary.

If one classifies cases according to whether the child was invited to a formal meeting or not (or only to part of it), whether he or she attended all, part or none of it, whether there was degree of preparation through discussion or an informal 'pre-meeting' and whether the child had an opportunity to discuss what had happened with someone after the meeting, we may find we have up to twenty categories into which at least some cases fall. Initially we hypothesised that those cases where children were not invited to the meeting, and where they received little information about what was going to happen or subsequently about what had happened, could be categorised into a number of sub-types within an overall category of *non-participation*; that cases where a child attended part of the meeting, or attended it all but had little preparation or follow-up, might be regarded as examples of *token participation*; and that only those cases where a child attended the whole meeting and was given explicit preparation and follow-up should be given the status of *full participation* (Thomas and O'Kane 1996).

However, ordering cases hierarchically in terms of 'levels' of participation began to seem increasingly arbitrary, in large part because of our lack of knowledge about the meaning of events for those involved, especially the children. This stage of research has been reliant on objective, but fairly crude, measures of participation combined with subjective opinions of social workers. Our initial classification depended on assumptions about the part played by explicit preparation and follow-up which may be unwarranted. We did not know how much preparation and feedback carers were undertaking. In some cases the child was not invited nor involved in a pre-meeting, but we were told that his/her views were communicated to the meeting and even that they had a lot of influence. In others it is possible that the child did not receive preparation because they did not need it, or that they made a positive choice not to take part in a formal decision-making meeting. It became clear that we could not develop this typology further, even as a working hypothesis, without the ethnographic evidence from the second stage of the research which is intended to enable us to learn more about the meaning of participation for those directly involved.

The aim of the detailed study was to explore as many of these questions as possible, in order to learn as much as possible about different kinds of participation and involvement; not only in formal decision-making but the informal kind too. Of necessity, the focus in the survey was on the formal processes represented by reviews and planning meetings. It is easier to ask questions about these than it is to find out about the informal processes of decision-making. In addition, the legal and policy framework in which decisions are made about children in state care emphasises such formal processes, as we saw in Chapter 6. It seems inevitable that any discussion or investigation of decision-making in care will concentrate on these processes. However, the plan in the detailed study was to compensate for this by looking also at what happens between meetings, and in everyday life.

9
Children's Views

It is time to present the findings of the qualitative research. In this chapter I concentrate on what children said; in the next on what adults said. The material comes from individual interviews and group discussions. It does not necessarily represent the 'opinions' of particular people who were interviewed, as though these are fixed and the job of research is to discover them; rather it represents ideas produced in the course of doing the research (see Holstein and Gubrium 1997). Sometimes a rough indication is given of how often a particular theme was mentioned or how strongly a view was put, in the way that 'qualitative' research so often speaks of quantities. Sometimes a view is quoted simply because someone expressed it and it seemed interesting. The material is organised and presented according to themes that emerged from the data.

Initial findings

In the first study I interviewed four children who were the subject of decision-making meetings during the study. The first two had not taken part in their meetings; their interviews were discussed briefly in Chapter 7. The other two, a boy aged twelve and a girl aged eleven, both had attended meetings held to discuss their care. The interviews were designed to explore the children's perspectives on decision-making processes. They followed a semi-structured format similar to that used in the earlier interviews.

The children were asked about their general understanding of the situation, of what decisions needed to be made, of who had views on what should happen. They were asked who they thought was making decisions, whether the people making decisions had talked to them, whether adults had listened to them or knew their wishes and feelings.

They were also asked whether they had talked their situation over with anyone else. They were asked what they had thought about being invited to the meeting, what they thought was the purpose of the meeting, who was in charge, whether they had a chance to say what they thought and wanted. They were asked whether it had been difficult to speak, whether they could think of anything that would make it easier, and whether it would help to have someone there to help them to speak. The children were also asked about their views of the decisions which had been taken, whether the decisions were what they wanted and whether they thought that adults had tried to decide what was best for them. They were asked in general about their views about how much say children should have in decisions, and what should happen when there is conflict between children's and adults' views.

Both children had attended their reviews prior to being interviewed. In each case this was not the first time they had attended a review meeting. The two children's perspectives on the review process were very different. One expected to remain in his placement, and did not think he faced major decisions or changes. For him the purpose of the review was 'to find out how I'm getting on ... at school and all that'. The other child wanted to go home. Her social worker and foster carer wanted her to go home, but her mother was resistant. For her the main purpose of the review was to make decisions about whether and when she would return home; but this purpose was impeded by her mother's power to block her return.

There were marked differences between the two children's attitudes to being at their reviews, which may or may not be related to these very different perspectives. One child claimed to feel very comfortable about attending his review, to have no prior feelings of anxiety, and to have no difficulty in speaking up for himself – although if he had wanted to say something especially sensitive he would have selected someone to speak to after the meeting. The other child was quite ambivalent about attending. 'I did want to come, but on the other hand I didn't as well.' She wanted to come 'to find out what I, what was going to happen to me.' Her reluctance was because 'it just didn't feel like I was supposed to be there ... I didn't feel like I was supposed to know what they were talking about.' She felt that she had not been able to say everything that she wanted to say because she was 'nervous in front of all the people.'

Both children said that adults should decide what was in a child's interests, even if that conflicted with the child's own wishes – but that this decision should be properly explained to the child. Their views differed as to how far this should change as they grew older. Both children appeared to be happy with the setting of the review. Both believed that the social worker's manager was the person in charge of the meeting and the one who set the agenda. One child was clear who this person was and what was her name; the other was not. This contrasted with the earlier interviews with two children who had not been involved in meetings, where there was much less sense of an understanding of the process, of who was taking decisions and of the reasons why things happened in the way they did; where neither child appeared to feel that he had a real part in the decision-making process, and both had a markedly fatalistic attitude to their futures.

How the interviews were done

The rest of this chapter is based on the interviews and group discussions with children that followed on from the initial survey in the second study. The 47 children interviewed were similar as a group to the survey population, although they were recruited largely on the basis of their willingness to take part.[1] Each child in the survey group received via their social worker a pack consisting of a leaflet or audiotape explaining the research, a set of activity sheets and a stamped addressed envelope. Some children asked to take part in the research when they received the packs, while others were recruited through follow-up calls to their social workers. Some social workers and carers were initially reluctant for children to take part because it might distress or unsettle them, or because 'they would not really understand', but in many cases these children were eventually included, partly because of the influence of the packs.

Each child was seen twice, except for a few children who only wished to be interviewed once. All the interviews were tape-recorded with the consent of the children and subsequently transcribed. Children were invited to choose either to be interviewed on their own or to be accompanied by a carer or friend; most chose to be on their own. There was no difficulty in being permitted to see children on their own. This contrasts with the experience of other researchers, and may reflect the fact that where children are looked after by local authorities it is relatively normal for social workers and other professionals to visit and interview children on their own (see Alderson 1994).

The interview questions were developed from those in the earlier study but took account of the feedback from young people who had been in care; the structure of the interviews was quite different. An interview guide was used to ensure that important questions were covered as far as possible, supported by a range of materials from which children could choose in order to explore the subjects that interested them. These were derived from materials used by social workers and guardians ad litem in direct work with children, and from techniques used in 'participatory rural appraisal' in developing countries (Striker and Kimmel 1979, Ryan and Walker 1993, Pretty *et al.* 1995). At the beginning of the interview the child was invited to look through the folder of materials so that they could choose whatever interested them at an appropriate stage in the meeting.[2]

The first interview was primarily focused on exploring with the child what kinds of decisions were made in her or his life that s/he thought were important or interesting, and who had a say in those decisions or helped to make them. A tool that children were encouraged to use because it proved so effective in exploring these issues was the 'decision chart', a grid constructed by interviewer and child together where the axes represented *decisions* in the child's life and *people* involved in those decisions. On it was plotted the child's evaluation of how much say each person had in each decision, represented by 'traffic light' stickers – red for 'no say', yellow for 'some', green for 'a lot'. Not only did the building of the chart stimulate children to talk about decisions in their lives, but the result was a record of what each child included that could be analysed quantitatively.

The second interview looked more at what was involved in being looked after by a local authority and especially at being involved in reviews and planning meetings. An activity that proved particularly useful in evaluating these processes was 'pots and beans' (O'Kane forthcoming). Children were given five jars which stood for 'how well I was prepared', 'how well I was supported', 'how much I spoke', 'how much they listened' and 'how much influence I had'. They were also given a pile of dried beans, and invited to put from one to three beans in each jar as their rating of that particular factor. A sixth, blank, jar which the child inevitably asked about was 'for how much you like meetings'. Like the decision chart, this activity both encouraged children to talk about issues and produced material that could be analysed quantitatively.

As well as a participatory approach and use of activity-based materials, another way to move beyond the formal 'interview' was to work with children in groups. Some children chose to be interviewed with a friend or relative, and brothers and sisters usually (though not always) preferred to be seen together. In addition the research included a series of activity days to give children the opportunity to explore issues further in a group. Thirty-six of the 47 children attended one of these days. Each day began with activities designed to help the group get to know each other, followed by exercises exploring decisions in children's lives, children's participation in different kinds of decisions and the processes involved in reviews and planning meetings. Again, one activity was particularly successful both in eliciting discussion and in producing material that could be analysed quantitatively. This was the 'diamond-ranking' of reasons for children to participate in decisions. The results of this are discussed at the end of the chapter.

Decisions that matter to children

Children were encouraged to use the interview materials to talk about whatever kind of decisions seemed significant to them in their lives. Most did so using the 'decision chart' which gave them the opportunity to identify decisions and people who were significant to them. The kinds of decisions they mentioned most often concerned 'where I go', 'what I do', 'school', 'play', 'contact with family', 'where I live', 'who my friends are', 'what time to come in', 'clothes' and 'food'; all these were mentioned by at least one child in three. Other common subjects were bedtime, sports, TV, activities, homework and housework, contact with siblings. A few talked about why they were in care, pocket money, staying with friends, how they behaved, who they talked to, hairstyle, use of the phone, having pets, holidays, going to church, music, being adopted, choice of social worker, and house decorations.

It is likely that many of these subjects would have been identified by a similar group of children living with their own families. However, topics like 'family contact' and perhaps 'where I live' seem to be particular to children who are looked after. There were also differences according to the children's legal status and the type of placement they were in: children who were accommodated mentioned decisions about 'where I live' more than those on care orders; children in foster placements out of their home area or in children's homes mentioned decisions about 'where I live' more often than those in local foster placements or living with parents or relatives; children living with relatives, and children in foster placements out of the area, mentioned family contact more often.

There were very marked gender differences in the topics children chose. Boys were much more likely to talk about sports, play, activities, times to come in and times to go to bed. Girls more often mentioned school, family contact, staying with friends and why they were in care.

There were similar differences between older and younger children, but these seem to be an effect of the greater proportion of boys in the 11–12 group and girls in the 8–10 group. However, regardless of gender older children were more likely to focus on decisions about where they lived and who their friends were, whilst younger ones talked more about play and television. It was clear from the subjects identified by children that they have their own 'agenda' in which everyday decisions such as where they go and who their friends are can be as important as long-term decisions about their future.

People involved in making decisions for children

Children generally seemed to think that adults they lived with and trusted should have most say in the day-to-day decisions that affect them. They did not want people who did not know them to be making decisions about them. Some wanted their absent parents to continue to play a part in decisions, and some had relatives who played active roles in their lives. A few mentioned brothers, sisters or friends who helped them make decisions, and teachers were frequently mentioned as having a say in children's lives. One group made a list that included 'grandad, granny, dad, mum, government, social worker, brother, council, president, boyfriends, girlfriends … God, Jesus, disciples, family, foster parents, my little brother and big brothers and sisters, teachers and police …' as being potentially involved in decisions about their lives. (See Table 9.1.)

Table 9.1 People who children mentioned most often

Person	Proportion of children mentioning
Self	100%
Social worker	87%
Foster mother	71%
Foster father	69%
Mother	60%
Teacher	44%
Father	29%
Grandmother	27%
Brother or sister	24%
Aunt	24%
Uncle	18%
Friend	16%

Parents' role in decision-making varied according to frequency of contact, the quality of the partnership with carers and social workers, and the parents' level of interest in their children's day-to-day lives. (Some children in the group were placed with their parents.) Children talked of parents as people who 'look after you', 'worry about you', 'speak up for you', 'are your friend', 'take you out', 'are interested in you', 'are nasty to you', 'don't care about anything, they just go down the pub and waste money.' Some children who did not see their parents could be very negative about them: 'He doesn't act a part in my life anymore because he lives somewhere else and I don't see him'; 'Leave them off it, it's a waste of card.' However, some children who were in regular contact with their parents still did not identify them as significant decision-makers in their lives. 'Whatever I do we don't involve them all the time, we just tell them.'

Foster carers were important people for many children. Most put their foster mother first on the list when they made their 'decision charts' – or second after themselves. Children said that their carers 'look after me and care for me'; make a lot of the day to day decisions; help arrange contact with your family; tell you what is and isn't allowed.

Residential workers seemed to occupy a position somewhere between those of the foster carer and the field social worker. For some children in residential care their keyworker was the most important figure, because of their relationship; for others it might be the head of home, because of their authority.

Social workers often acted as a mediator between foster carers and the child's parents, or between children and their parents. Some children did not see a need to see their social worker very often. Other children, and their carers, would have liked the social worker to visit more regularly and thought this would produce better communication and greater involvement in decision-making. Children described social workers as people who 'you can talk to'; who 'calm you down'; who sort out problems; who arrange meetings; who 'ask questions'; who 'look after you', care for you, help you and 'make sure you are happy'; who sort out contact with your family; who can make the decision for you to return home; who 'find you new places to live'; who help set rules and tell you what you can't do; who sort out conflicts; who speak for you in courts; who 'keep an eye on things'; who take you places and give you sweets; who give advice about your future.

A few children referred to their *brothers and sisters* as people who helped them with decisions. Usually this meant older brothers or sisters: 'My big sister helps me if like if my mother is drunk or something like that.' Sometimes children did not want to be overshadowed by brothers and sisters: 'Well I don't mind him having a little say for me but I like to say my own say as well.' Some children felt that they were responsible for their brothers and sisters, and sometimes this could be mutual: 'I've got my brother guarding me...and I look after him.' Surprisingly few children mentioned *friends* as people who help to make decisions about them. For some, this is because they do not reveal that they are children who are looked after: 'Most of my friends don't know I'm fostered. You know, it is the ones that I am really bothered with that I tell.' Friends were seen to share in decisions about play and activities; only occasionally did they advise on more momentous issues.

Other people mentioned by some children include: support workers, grandfathers, children's home workers, step-parents, and solicitors. Girls were slightly more likely to mention most family members, especially uncles and aunts; older children were more likely to mention friends. Children who were accommodated mentioned their fathers more often than those who were on care orders.

Children's experiences of decision-making

Children's lives are structured by *boundaries* of time and place set by adults; their daily lives marked by permission seeking, negotiations and rules. Many children felt restricted by adults whose words and regulations intruded at every turn: where they go, what they do, who they make friends with, what they wear. Others valued these boundaries; they felt that they were 'young' and they trusted adults to make decisions in their best interests. However, even when children appreciate boundaries within which they can be safe, they do not like to be treated unfairly or over-protectively, especially in comparison with their friends. Some said explicitly that they should be trusted more. Others described how they negotiate or plead with adults to push back the boundaries – to be able to stay out longer, go to bed later, venture further with their friends.

For some children a whole battery of adults seemed to join forces in setting boundaries for them. Others experienced different levels of restriction depending on who they were currently living with. Some children felt that they were not allowed to do anything:

> I'm not allowed to bring a lot of boys into the house; I'm not allowed to get dirty; I'm not allowed to go next door without saying; I'm not allowed to touch the telly; I'm not allowed to touch the phone...

When children are away from adults they have more freedom to make their own decisions:

> Yeah, just children. They can swear, they can do whatever they want. They can make dens. They can do whatever they want without their parents... Oh it is perfect, perfect, perfect, PERFECT.

Another theme was that of *control* and its converse, lack of control. It was clear that children's experience of the care system is often one in which they have little control. A few children said they had been in control of the decision to go into care, and seemed to have a greater sense of control over other decisions. Children's experiences in school are relatively highly controlled, with few opportunities for involvement in decision-making or negotiation of rules. At home adults used a variety of forms of discipline; 'grounding' was the most common. Some children had experienced physical punishment at home, but most were clear that their carers were not allowed to hit them, and approved of this.

Children identified *age* as a key variable in their lives. Legal age limits functioned to exclude them from settings and activities. Some adults prevented children from mixing with those who are much older or younger. Children said that adults did not explain things to them or trust them because they are 'too young'. Some cannot wait to be older and to be treated accordingly:

> A teenager, I like the sound of that – it appeals to me.

> I like the age sixteen... because you can be tarty and can do what you want. But if you are eight you can't.

Some children feel particularly young and small, in awe of adults' power:

> I am scared of my Mum really. I don't know why, but I am scared of her. So like she is a grown up and I am like a ten year old.

Children were given more opportunities for involvement as they grew older; many said they began to take part in decisions from age seven or eight, whilst some saw the move to secondary school as a time when they were expected to take more responsibility.

Children reported that their autonomy varied in different *settings* or aspects of their lives. *School* was seen as a place where they had relatively little power. Rules are made by adults; children commonly have little choice about what subjects they take or what they wear. One eight-year-old spoke eloquently of a myriad of rules: 'Oh rules, rules. They have got loads of rules in school. You must put your litter in the bin. You must be quiet when the teacher signs your form. You have got to be quiet. You have to be good or you get a yellow card.' A few children said they had more freedom and independence in secondary school than in primary school. For others break and dinner times were islands of freedom where they had some say about how they spent their time. Only a few schools had any system of pupil representation and few children had heard of a school council. Some children obviously felt frustrated by their lack of decision-making power, and talked about the need for more 'pupil power' within schools. Children had varying degrees of choice about which school they would attend, and sometimes a child or young person's choice of secondary school was overridden by adults.

Many children said clearly that their *choice of friends* was up to them, but others said that adults influenced them to make friends with children who are well behaved or 'a good influence'. Many expressed strong views about difficulties when they want to stay at friends' houses, because most authorities expected the friends' parents to be 'police-checked'. Many felt that this was unfair, and that their carers should be allowed to make these decisions.[3] Children talked about how decisions were made about times to be in. Most did not mind coming in at a specified time if they thought it was reasonable and comparable to their friends. Times varied with children's age, the time of year, where the child was going and who would be with them, and whether it was a school night; most children appeared to regard these as fair considerations. Whilst carers had most influence over these matters, social workers were sometimes involved by children if they wanted to negotiate change, or by carers if they needed support.

Some children were actively involved in choosing *what to wear*, others less so. For many the most important thing was to have clothes with the right labels. Likewise some were consulted about what they ate, but others were expected to eat what they were given. Adults had different rules about allowing children free access to *food*. Many children were not involved in buying or cooking of food. Adults regulated children's use of *television*; what programmes they watched, how much they watched and how late they watched. However, children also made a lot of their own choices. Some children were not allowed to watch programmes which contained violence or bad language. Whilst some children thought it a good idea for adults to stop them watching programmes that might give them nightmares, others thought they could judge for themselves.

Many children talked about the decision to come into *care* or accommodation. Some were able to explain why it had happened, but others did not know or could not understand. The majority had little say in the decision, and some felt that they had been 'put there' by their parents. Even children who were actively involved in the initial contact with social services often felt that they had no control over the actual decision to go into care.

Generally, children reported a wide range of experiences of involvement in decision-making. They reported being given more say in decisions as they got older and gained confidence, or as adults became less protective. Some children found decisions difficult if they had too much choice, or not enough information about their options and the likely outcomes. Some had been involved in placement moves and felt that they had some degree of choice, whilst others had a different experience:

> The very first time I went, they didn't let me visit or anything, they just took me there. This time I visited, but I didn't really want to come here. They just made me come.

Some found it easier to become involved in decisions after they accepted that they would not be returning to their parents:

> We were different then because we wanted to go back, it has changed now. Well I've let it go now.

Children needed to feel in control of their lives to move forwards:

> Getting my life in one piece, that's what's given me the confidence.

Children who had *family meetings* or mealtime discussions often found them useful, especially if they were made to be fun:

> We are all messing around, then someone says, 'Open the meeting.' Then at the end we bang the table with a fork and say, 'Meeting is closed.'

Some children saw themselves as quick to *understand*:

> Some people take longer to understand what is going on. Like I knew when I was six ... as soon as I moved here. I was like 'Oh I have got the idea now'.

Others did not understand things because they had not been explained to them. Where children were given clear and full explanations they were more able to understand what was going on. Lack of explanation or understanding could increase children's fears; for example, a child was afraid to say in his review meeting that he liked his foster placement, because 'I felt as if I was being taken away from my mother and I'd never see her again.' Children found that adults explained more as they got older, with the perverse effect that children who were regarded as less able to understand sometimes had to work more things out for themselves:

> I would say I was quite young when I started to understand, but later on I grew up, people explained to me what was going to happen to me.

In general children said very clearly that adults do not *listen* to them, or not so attentively as they listen to other adults: they ignore them or leave them out of conversations; they interrupt, override, or redefine what they say. They gave several reasons why adults fail to listen: because 'they think you are too young to express yourself', 'you are a child so you don't know nothing', or 'you are lying'; because adults 'don't understand the sorts of things that worry children', 'don't care', 'like to show off and show that they are bigger', 'think they know better than us and that they can rule us', 'think they have got more rights', or are 'basically just ignorant'. When children are not listened to they may 'get fed up', 'give up and get depressed', or 'develop a bad attitude'. Children identified particular adults who were the exception in that they would actively listen, encourage them to speak and offer support. This might be a parent, a foster carer, a relative, a grown up friend, a social worker or even a researcher. Teachers were often singled out as particularly bad at listening to children.

Children were less likely than adults to talk about *power* explicitly, but often expressed themselves as lacking power both in everyday life and in more momentous decisions. Some were strongly aware that they had rights, but others appeared to feel quite overwhelmed by adult power. Some children said that their voice was heard and they were taken seriously. Others had needed to negotiate in order to have a say; or get older; or choose who to talk to. Some children were happy to share decision-making, while others felt that they were not heard when it counted, or if heard were not allowed to have what they wanted (but see the discussion below under 'Reasons why children should have a say'). One girl said that she would do things differently if she were the adult. Some children felt that they were able to lead decision-making, at least in certain areas; for others it was a shared process, whilst others thought they had little say or that what they said made no difference. Some were fairly happy about that, but for others it was a real cause for complaint. Children said that some adults listen to them more and give them more choice.

Children in general understood adult concerns for their *safety*, but some thought it was exaggerated and suspected that adults' concerns were mixed with self-preservation. Children objected less to measures for their physical protection than to attempts to protect them from ideas or images: one group objected vociferously to the film rating system. Those over ten years sometimes suggested that concerns with safety were more appropriately addressed to younger children. Children sometimes distinguished between 'big' and 'little' decisions.[4] Some children thought that they should have a lot of say in 'little' decisions, but more adult input in the bigger decisions. There were some difficult decisions that children preferred adults to make for them. One said,

I like them making the decisions about when I go to my Mum and Dad's, because I find that difficult.

Another said he preferred adults to decide about 'putting the dogs and cats and animals down.'

The process of participation

Children seemed to communicate best with people with whom they had good relationships. They were more able to contribute to decision-making processes if they had been prepared and given time to think about things, and perhaps a chance to write something down; but they did not like to be asked the same questions over and over again. Children expressed a need for support, and sometimes to be actively encouraged to speak up. They particularly needed support and encouragement in situations where they had something difficult or negative to express, and this sometimes meant adults offering to express their views for them. For many children it was important to be given a choice as to how and how much they participated in a decision-making process, and to have a clear understanding of the process; it helped if there was room for negotiation, an element of compromise, and perceived fairness. Explanation at every stage of the process – what is happening, why, how, what the options are – appears fundamental to genuine involvement by children, especially when it is not possible to do what they want.

Many children expressed a preference for one-to-one communication rather than talking to a group of adults. For some face-to-face communication was important, although when someone was less familiar indirect communication could be easier – for instance by telephone. Some children had difficulty communicating verbally or directly and might need to use other forms of communication such as drama, writing, or drawing. Many children clearly find it very boring to 'just sit there and talk', and activity-based communication made it easier for them to talk about issues that concerned them. Children preferred to talk to people who were friendly, informally dressed and who talked calmly and nicely. They did not like adults who were aggressive or authoritarian, or who 'stare'. They did not want to take part when they felt judged or scrutinised.

Many of the things that children said about decision-making might have been said by any child living in a modern 'Western' society. Much of what they said about communicating with adults would be likely to apply to a variety of social settings. However, much of what the children talked about in this research was specific to the business of 'being in care' and 'having a social worker'. A major focus of the first stage of this research was on what happens in planning and review meetings for children who are looked after, and this was a theme that returned in the interviews and group discussions with children.

Reviews and planning meetings

Some children described reviews as occasions when people check up if you're happy; for others they were occasions when people make decisions about you or plan your future. For some children what is distinctive about them is that 'people ask you questions', whilst others had no clear idea of what a review is about (including some who had attended reviews). Many children could list the people who attended their reviews, although they might be unsure who some people were and particularly who was in charge of the meeting. Some children felt themselves to be at the centre of the review meeting, whilst others felt on the fringes. Children variously described reviews as 'boring', 'scary', 'frightening', 'horrible', 'upsetting', 'stressful', 'nerve-racking', 'intimidating', 'embarrassing'; or as 'exciting', 'fine', 'lovely' and 'OK'. The most commonly used word was 'boring'. Some of the things that children said make reviews particularly difficult were: everyone sitting looking at you; everyone talking about you; people interrupting you; people not listening; having to speak up in front of a lot of adults; having your teacher there. Children who enjoyed reviews often seemed to be those who liked being the centre of attention or who were able to laugh and joke.

Some children always attended their reviews, either because they wanted to or because they felt they were expected to. Some had very positive reasons for going to their reviews: 'it is all about you', 'if things aren't right you can change it', 'it's my life, I want to know what is going on'. Others went mainly to find out more about what was going on or to know what was being said about them. Some were proud that they had never missed a meeting. Others had never attended, usually because they had not been invited but sometimes out of choice – because they would rather be doing something else, to avoid conflict, to avoid a particular person, or because they were happy for someone else to speak for them. Some children decided whether to go when they knew what was going to be talked about. A few children saw their reviews mainly as a chance to have contact with parents or relatives.

In the 'pots and beans' exercise (described at the beginning of this chapter) all the children who had attended reviews were asked to indicate how well *prepared* they were for the meeting, how well *supported* they were, how much they *spoke*, how much they were *listened* to, and how much *influence* they had. They were also asked to say how much they *liked meetings*. This technique was helpful in stimulating discussion, as the following paragraphs show. It also produced numerical data which could be aggregated, and Figure 9.1 shows the aggregated scores for each 'pot'.

Children's experiences of *preparation* for reviews were very mixed. Most of them thought it important to be well prepared – although a few worried more if they knew what was coming up, or even claimed to enjoy the uncertainty of not knowing! Some were prepared by a visit from their social worker before the meeting; others were not. Some children felt well *supported* at their reviews by carers, social workers or other professionals, or by their parents and family members. Others would have liked more support, and a few felt very unsupported and isolated. Some wanted particular people to support them, while others were happy to accept support from a range of adults. Children who felt they could rely on someone for support were more likely to attend and speak for themselves. Many children said they did not *speak* much because they 'just go to listen', because they 'don't have a lot to say',

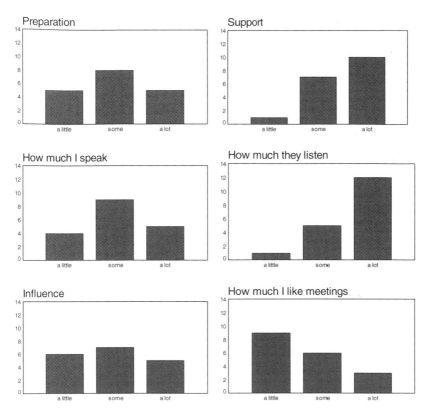

Figure 9.1 How children rated their review meetings ('pots and beans')

or because that is 'just how I am'. Social workers said how difficult it is for some children to speak up because of shyness, or too much emotion, or perhaps because they want to please adults. Other children found it easier to speak freely, especially as they get older.

Most children felt that adults really *listen* to them: 'They all wanted to hear what I had to say and they were interested'; 'They stop everything and listen to what I have got to say'; 'They think I am really special.' A few, however, felt they were not listened to: 'I think they are saying, in their mind they ain't going to listen to me because they think they know what I am about to say, which they don't'; 'It is hard because I don't speak very loud, so people can't hear me.' A few felt they had no *influence* on decisions, and a few said they had a lot. Most, however, thought they had a moderate amount of influence. Most children did not *like* meetings. Mainly this was because 'they are boring', but in some cases it was because people might be 'cruel' or 'nasty'. A few children actively liked meetings: 'I like meetings because I get to say what I want to say and they get to know what my views are.'

Some children thought it important to speak for themselves; others preferred to have someone to say difficult things for them. Very few children had any experience of independent advocates. Few children had been invited to take a friend to their meeting, although the Department of Health guidance (Department of Health 1991a, 8.15) appears to suggest this. Some children would welcome the chance to do this because their friend could 'back them up'. Others would be reluctant to let a friend know so much of their private business.

Children expressed feelings of being left out or puzzled when they were not included in a meeting: 'It is not very nice', 'You wonder what they are talking about', 'I feel left out when they don't explain more.' Others were more resigned: 'It is for our benefit', 'I probably would have got bored anyway', 'They might start talking about...and I don't want to hear about that.' Children were aware of being excluded from school meetings which might be attended by their social worker.

Many children said that they became more confident in taking part as they got older, and some said that they understood more. However, children also said that they were given more preparation, explanation and time to think about things when they were older, and it may be that some apparent effects of age are a result of changes in adults'. expectations of children. One child put it directly: 'they talked to [the foster carer] instead of me...probably because they thought they could get more of a straight answer out of her.' Although eight- and nine-year-olds were often thought unable to understand things that are discussed at reviews, many of their comments showed a remarkably accurate understanding of what was going on.

Children who were given a choice of how to participate seemed to benefit and value this. Some liked to write things down beforehand, perhaps by using the 'Looking After Children' consultation booklets – which might also be a substitute for attending the meeting. Some liked to drift in and out of the meeting, and others valued the fact that they did not have to answer every question put to them. However, some children felt that they were expected to go, even though they might prefer not to. All children thought they should be given the choice of whether to go or stay away.

Children who had been given a choice about who was to be at their meeting clearly valued this. Some children were confident that they could exclude anyone from 'their' meeting – except the social worker – although in most cases they do not want to, or feel that 'it would be rude'. A few children had chosen not to have their school-teacher at the meeting, and others said they would object if it was suggested that a teacher should be there. Some children were given an opportunity to include a particular person. Many children, however, were given no choice either to include or exclude; and many did not even know who was going to be at their meeting. In general children thought that a review should be a meeting with a small group of people who knew them well. Many did not want teachers there; some did not want their parents, or occasionally their carers; many did not want 'strangers', and one did not want a particular team manager who had upset him previously with an intrusive question.

Many children were not consulted about the time or place of the meeting, although the Department of Health guidance recommends that they should be. Social workers usually seemed to decide these matters, although usually with some thought as to what would suit the child and the carers. In practice this often meant after school in the foster home. In many cases this seemed to be the right choice, although that is perhaps an assumption which could be checked more often. There was an overwhelming feeling among children that the agenda for the meeting was predetermined, either by social workers or by some rules and regulations to which children are not privy. Subjects for discussion often appeared to drop from the sky as far as children are concerned. On the occasions where children had some influence over the agenda, it seemed to be easier for them to contribute. As we saw, children are often more interested in day-to-day matters than in 'big' decisions. However, they often only bring up their own concerns with active prompting from adults.

It is an unusual experience for a child to be alone with a group of adults. Some children found it very strange, and would perhaps have liked other children there. Others did not mind or enjoyed the experience. Some children found the language of meetings difficult to understand, although not as often as we expected. It is clear that many people are making a real effort to conduct meetings in a language that children can understand; and perhaps that some children have a good grasp of social work jargon! Although children often stayed away from meetings where there was conflict, many others attended. For some the effect of the conflict could be distressing. Children fiercely resented occasions when the review was used to focus on negative aspects of their own behaviour, sometimes including episodes which they thought were over and done with.

Children talked about things that made meetings harder: not knowing who's going to be there; difficult questions; being interrupted; being embarrassed; when people shout; not knowing what people are going to say. When asked what would make meetings easier, children talked about:

- preparation: knowing who will be there and what will be said, being involved in planning the meeting, having time to think about things;
- support and familiarity: knowing everyone who's there, someone you trust sitting by you, having the meeting in your own home;
- informality: more activities, 'food and toys, turn it into a tea party!'

Some children had rich ideas for how meetings could be improved. Mostly these were to do with getting away from simply 'sitting round talking', and introducing activity and things that are fun.

Working with social services

Children clearly want as normal a life as possible, and want to be able to get on with their lives without unnecessary intrusion from social services. Many children in stable placements call their foster carers 'Mum' and 'Dad' and clearly enjoy the feeling of being in 'a real family': 'They are really like my real mum and dad. And A. is like a real brother to me.' 'I'd like to have a proper mother and father, someone to say Mam and Dad then'. They also want to be able to do the same things as their friends: 'Why do I need a social worker, I've got you, why can't I have a normal life, why do you have to have my friends checked if I want to sleep over?'

Children had a good deal to say about their social workers, and about their ideal social worker: someone who is easy to talk to and who understands and explains things well; someone who listens to what you have got to say and doesn't butt in; who understands what you feel and your view of things. Personal style is important: 'the way they talk, not strict or boring, generally happy', 'a sense of humour', 'friendly', 'doesn't lose their temper', and even 'fashionable'. They must be helpful – give you time to think about decisions, sort things out, 'get you good foster parents' – and caring – 'has time for us', 'kind', 'calms us down', 'like a friend', 'generous'. Some children wanted an advocate who is willing to say difficult things on your behalf, someone you can trust, who is fair and doesn't take sides.

10
Adults' Views

This chapter is based on the views expressed by adults in the course of the two research studies. In the initial study two social workers were interviewed by telephone. Both were responsible for children who were in the study, including children who were present at their meetings and others who were not. They were asked about their view of the most important elements in making decisions, about how much say they thought children should have, and about what had happened in a particular case and why. It was obvious that both workers had thought carefully about how to involve children in decisions, and that they favoured including children in meetings wherever this would be helpful or positive for them. It was also clear that there were often particular reasons for not inviting children. These might have to do with the child's own capacities; for instance, a child with a learning disability might not be included when his age would otherwise indicate it. Alternatively it might reflect the circumstances of the case; for instance, there might be factors in a decision which could not be discussed openly with the child because of a need to protect their feelings or those of adults.

It appeared that thought would normally be given to including a child in meetings from the age of eight or nine, and invitations would be virtually automatic from age eleven or twelve. However, respondents also said that many children were anxious about attending meetings and should not be compelled or pressurised. There was a feeling that the usual form of a review or planning meeting might of itself be inimical to children's participation, and that greater participation might only be possible if the meetings themselves were made more 'child-friendly'. There appeared to be little use of advocacy, and staff had not considered asking children who they thought should take part in meetings to discuss them. These perceptions were supported by informal discussions with team leaders.

Both workers interviewed placed a high value on gaining the cooperation of both children and parents in whatever plans were made. Rather than anyone's view of a child's best interests having overriding weight, it appeared that the decision-making process was seen as being one of negotiation, compromise and the mobilisation of consent; and that this process was seen as one which included the child, whether or not the child was present at the meeting.

In the main study a much larger number of adults were seen; not only social workers but the carers and parents of the 47 children. The rest of this chapter is based on what was said by these people seen during the intensive stage of the study (and to a lesser extent on comments made by a larger number of social workers during the survey stage). Each child's social worker and main carer were interviewed. The latter might be a foster carer (or couple), a key worker in a residential home, or a parent or relative with whom the child was living. In 15 cases a non-resident parent was also interviewed. Interviews used a simple guide that began by asking about how much say children should have in decisions about their lives, and went on to cover: what kind of participation was desirable and how this was affected by factors such as age, what could be done to encourage participation and how well processes like review meetings did this, and how respondents handled conflicts between a child's wishes and their 'best interests'. Interviews followed the flow of what interviewees said, rather than dealing with points in any particular order. Interviews usually lasted 45–60 minutes and were tape-recorded.

The context of decision-making for children

Adults talked about changes in society that had affected children's lives: unemployment and poverty, drug abuse, greater awareness of violence and sexual abuse, and increased road traffic, making adults fearful and restricting children's autonomy. Others expressed a sense that children are growing up more quickly, experimenting with sex, drugs and alcohol at a younger age. Opposite views were expressed, sometimes by the same people: things had become harder for children, or easier; they were more exposed to danger, or more protected. These accounts are not necessarily as contradictory as they seem; they may express different aspects of the same complex reality, or the reality for different children. Some suggested that children have little experience of decision-making because their parents take decisions without consulting them, and that children in general are more capable of talking about their views and feelings than they are given credit for.

In comparing children who are 'looked after' with other children, some respondents emphasised ways in which their situations are similar, and spoke of the need to 'normalise' the lives of children in care or accommodation as much as possible. Others drew attention to important differences in children's situations; different sorts of decisions have to be made, in different sorts of ways. Still others pointed to differences in children themselves; for instance many children in care have been abused and may therefore be less able to take a part in decisions or, conversely, more in need of a sense of control over their lives. I discuss these different perspectives further in the next chapter. Many adults remarked on changes in the care system over the last twenty years. In the past children were not consulted, things were 'done to them', reviews were 'a paper exercise'. There was little partnership with parents and little involvement of children; indeed, it was rare for children to be spoken to on their own. Many thought that children are now listened to more and included in decision-making more. Reviews are now more child-centred and also more concerned with consultation and negotiation. The Children Act was seen as influential in making children part of the process. The United Nations Convention on the Rights of the Child, on the other hand, was not much mentioned as a factor in encouraging change. Some suggested that change has been for the better, in that things are 'out in the open' rather than 'hidden behind closed doors'. A few felt that change had gone too far and that children now have too much power.

Experiences of decision-making: key themes

Power was clearly an important dimension for many of our respondents, although not necessarily one on which they agreed. Adults were struck by the powerlessness of children; although a few parents and carers saw children as being powerful – they can no longer be punished and lack respect for their elders. Foster carers sometimes saw themselves as powerless in relation to children and weak in relation to social workers or parents. Social workers were generally said to have a lot of power – perhaps too much – by themselves, by carers and by parents, as well as by children. The social services hierarchy was seen by many as an important source of power, as were the courts.

There seem to be two adult views of *boundaries*. One speaks of the need to maintain credibility by being strict; the other emphasises negotiation, and that rules should be a compromise agreed between adults and children. For some a key consideration is the difference between individual children: with some children it is especially important to say what you mean, while others 'know their limitations – where they can go, what they can do.' Others try to deal in the same way with all children. In foster care the female carer is generally regarded as 'the boss'; male carers are described as being around the home less or showing less interest in children's day to day activities, although they too may set some boundaries.

Control was seen as a particular issue for children who are looked after. As one carer put it, 'you have got someone coming in and putting a child from here to there, but they have got no control about it at all, and all these feelings they have got, there is nothing they can do about it. It is a dreadful situation to be in.' Some children were seen as having less *understanding* because of learning difficulties. Adults identified *age* as a key variable in children's lives. Legal age limits impinge on children's lives, excluding them from settings and activities. Many adults prevent children from mixing with those who are much older or younger.

Families had different ways of making decisions. In some the adults simply decided, or ad-hoc consultation took place. Others had discussions around the meal table, or more formal 'family meetings', as one foster carer explained: 'If there is a major problem we have a meeting with the whole family and everybody says their view. We say we decide as a family what should happen'. Families also had different ways of making their rules known; some foster carers explained the rules of the house to children when they arrived, whilst others let them work it out for themselves. Some social workers felt that clear explanation was important and encouraged discussion of rules in the initial planning meeting. Children who have experienced a number of moves may have lived by many different sets of rules.

Factors affecting when children have a say

Many factors seemed to influence the way that children are included in decision-making. These could be classified into factors relating to children, factors relating to adults, and factors relating to situations.

Individual differences between children included their personality, their level of confidence, their maturity; their awareness, their intelligence, their ability to trust, and their emotional stability. Children were seen variously as placid, assertive or attention-seeking, strong willed or 'easily led', talkative, sociable or quiet. Some children seemed to be born communicators, while others who initially seemed quiet might become talkative in their attempt to be heard. There was some indication that girls tend to speak out more than boys. Many adults identified children's understanding and maturity as significant factors, but often found it painfully difficult to articulate clearly how they assessed these. Obvious benchmarks were noticeable by their absence; however, people mentioned getting to know the child and indicators such as their ability to think through the consequences of actions, how they had learnt from previous experiences and their level of distress.

Many adults identified age as a key factor, as did children. (Particular views about the age at which children should be included in decisions varied widely. Many adults and a few children said that children from five upwards could be included; many children and some adults thought that six to seven or eight to nine was the critical age. A few children and adults identified ten to eleven years as a significant age, as children move to secondary school. A minority of children and adults suggested that the key point was later, at fourteen, sixteen or even eighteen. Sixteen was certainly seen as a significant age for freedom by many, and some adults feared that when children reached sixteen they would do what they wanted regardless of what adults said.)

Many adults commented on how past experiences can affect children's ability to take part in decisions; but views on this differed. Some said that children learn from difficulties to become both more knowledgeable and more resilient, and are able to take part at an earlier age. Others saw children as damaged and disempowered by their experiences so that that they find it hard to make decisions. Rejection and abuse can diminish children's confidence and self-esteem, or they may put up protective blocks or deny reality. When children had faced difficult circumstances, many adults felt it was especially important to include them in order to help them regain control. These differences are discussed further in the next chapter.

Factors relating to adults seemed particularly important in affecting whether and how children were included; especially adults' attitudes, beliefs and values, but also their skills in communicating with children. Some adults were very positive about the value of including children as much as possible as a matter of right, whilst others were more cautious either because of what they saw as dangers to children or because of their own accountability. Some thought that children had too much say and were too powerful. Welsby's (1996b) typology of attitudes was further developed in the course of this research and is discussed in the next chapter.

Factors in the situation that were seen as important included the level of security and stability which children may need in order to explore new options, and whether there is open conflict between adults, which some thought was a reason for excluding children from decision-making processes. However, others said that children have already lived with conflict and it is important to include them, giving adequate preparation and if necessary excluding the parents or holding separate meetings.

Disability is as much a feature of the situation as it is of the child. Some adults saw it as very difficult to involve children with learning difficulties, and tended to exclude them from the process. Others went to great efforts to overcome barriers and include all children. Many children with disabilities seemed very adept at finding other ways of making themselves understood. Determined efforts to find more creative ways of explaining and communicating with individuals with differing abilities seemed to pay dividends.

In general there appeared to be wide differences between different settings as to how much children were involved. These differences can be seen in terms of the prevailing culture; each living place has its own set of rules, boundaries, ways of caring. Where there is an atmosphere of open communication, trust and co-operation, children seem more likely to be involved in decisions.

Finally, some adults felt that children at this age can be involved in 'little' decisions such as what they wear or where they go, but not the really 'big' decisions such as where they live. Some were wary of imposing 'heavy' decisions on children. Others thought that children should be involved in all decisions, but that adults need to provide more guidance and have more influence in the really important decisions.

Weight given to children's views

Associated with the question of what factors affect children's inclusion in decision-making is the question of how much weight their views have in those processes. In talking to children and adults about this, it appeared that children's influence varied with several other factors: how well the child's voice is heard; the degree of consensus between children's and adults' views; how much influence other people have on decisions; how far adults want or need to keep control; the age of the child; the kind of decision at issue; the strength of any perceived or presumed risk to the child.

Some adults pointed out that children's words cannot always be taken at face value and that they don't always know what is best for them. For many it seemed that adults tend to focus on the long term and children on more immediate issues. Many adults referred to children wanting 'to please mother' or 'say what dad would want', saying what was expected of them, answering questions they didn't actually understand rather than be awkward, not wanting to hurt someone, having 'torn' or 'divided loyalties'. This could create difficulties for adults who want to know what children 'really' think or feel.

Adults differed over how much influence children have, or should have, on decisions. Some said very strongly that children's views should lead; others thought children's views were only one factor to be considered, while some thought that children really had very little influence, often because of concerns about safety. For some the process of negotiation and explanation was most important. Some made the point, however, that children may have to be allowed to try something that adults know will fail, in order for them to accept the fact. It could be easier to respond to the child's voice if it fitted with adult perceptions of the child's best interests. Where the child's wishes were in conflict with the parents', for example, the social worker's position could be uncomfortable. Some adults talked of the importance of making sure that the child is heard even if the decision is not what they want; others went to great lengths to take account of children's wishes. Adults commented both on individual differences and on differences between teams and agencies. It was clear that accountability could be a problem both for carers and for social workers, who can feel reluctant to take apparently reasonable risks because of their organisational accountability.

One of the most difficult questions for many of those we spoke to was how to choose between what a child wants and what adults think is in the child's best interests. For social workers the dilemma could be acute. Some were unambiguously for giving precedence to the child's voice, at least in the examples which they gave. For others it was important to listen to the child as much as possible, but the child's voice had then to be weighed against other factors, and sometimes the child had to be overruled in the interests of his or her welfare. Some adults identified situations where the balance between giving the child control and looking after their safety was especially fine. For many the important thing was to explain properly to the child why they could not have the decision they wanted, and if possible to give them control over other aspects of the process. This issue is discussed further in the next chapter.

Adults expressed a great deal of concern with children's safety. Parents and carers tended to be preoccupied with dangers outside the home, and especially with children 'who can't see danger'. Social workers were more concerned with dangers from parents and others with whom children might be living. In either case a concern with safety was often seen as a particularly strong reason for disregarding a child's wishes. For others it was less clear:

> If a child can't go home because of their own safety, how far do you take that? I think we have to take risks but they should be minimum. I think if we listen to the child there's going to be risks and what better have we got to offer them…sometimes the choices are two evils isn't it?

There were a number of different ways in which children and adults dealt with conflict between their views of what should happen: *direct action* ('When you asked to go down the park and I said no, it's too late, what did you do? You went down anyway'); *compromise* ('So normally if we can't decide, we'll go somewhere else'); *discussion and explanation* ('It's teaching them how to deal with conflict as well, how to discuss with one another – this is my view, this is your view'); *siding with the child* ('If there's conflict between him and the carers I go for him, it's the bottom line'); or *having it out* ('With a number of them it's necessary to have that major confrontation, otherwise…they think they've won, and they think they can do it again').

The process of participation

Some adults talked about participation in decision-making as a *process*. For many children the process can be as important as the outcome; indeed for some being involved in the process was the most important thing. It was clear that genuine participation by children requires an investment in time, especially for preparation and support. It was also evident that the process is dynamic over time; people learn continually how to take part in decisions, negotiate and take responsibility, and children can gain in skill and confidence as a result of taking part and as a result of having more sense of control over their lives. Adults' perceptions of children affect the way they explain things to them, and so affect how much children understand and are able to take part, or whether they have the opportunity at all. There were signs of a growing recognition that children can be included at a younger age.

Reviews and planning meetings

Like children, some adults saw reviews as occasions for checking that all is well, whilst for others they are decision-making meetings.[1] Respondents commented on how much reviews have changed in recent years, especially since the Children Act 1989 and more recently the introduction of the 'Looking After Children' materials. In general foster carers, parents and children all seemed to feel more included than in the past. Although some parents and carers saw reviews as boring, repetitive and predictable, others welcomed them as a chance 'to thrash out issues'. Social workers' comments were often very negative. Many felt that review meetings were an unsatisfactory way of involving children in decisions: 'not enjoyable', 'a hollow exercise', 'a refined torture', 'a flawed tool', 'a paper exercise'.

Opinions differed about which children should be invited to reviews. Some adults and children thought that children should be invited when they were old enough to understand, which might be from age seven, eight, nine or ten. Others thought that all children should be invited: 'it should be up to you' (child); 'ultimately they have all got the right to be at their own meeting' (social worker). Some social workers suggested that children should not be invited if the experience was likely to cause them distress or if their attendance would be pointless; carers and parents sometimes saw children as getting in the way of adult discussion. Some adults thought there were occasions when it might be better for children not to be present for part of a meeting, to avoid distress or boredom. However, sometimes it seemed that these might actually be the most important parts of the meeting. Some social workers and carers had been surprised at what younger children were able to understand when they were given a chance. A carer suggested that it would be better if meetings could start with the matters that the child considered most important.

Social workers and foster carers generally regarded preparation as important, and some clearly saw it as essential and set aside time for it. Others assumed that children who had been to reviews previously would know what to expect, and only gave time to preparatory work if there were major issues coming up. Some had found the 'Looking

After Children' consultation booklets useful in preparing children for reviews; others preferred to use more active or informal methods.

Social workers used a range of strategies to minimise the effect of open conflict on children, including preparatory work with children or parents and in some cases separate meetings. Several workers pointed out that for some children conflict is the reality of life and there is little to be gained by pretending it does not exist. Carers also mentioned intimidating language and formal dress as adding difficulties. Some social workers longed for a more natural setting in which to make decisions, something closer to ordinary family life: 'have the meeting around the kitchen table...at ten past eight in the morning over dippy eggs and orange juice.' Many people emphasised that reviews are only part of the story and that what happens before and after the meeting is often more important.

Social workers and carers often found themselves speaking on behalf of children. Many clearly see this as their responsibility and take it seriously; some social workers were sure that they were the best person to do this. However, others saw problems with this process. Social workers and carers usually have their own views of what is best for a child, and if these are different from the child's view it can be difficult to do justice to both. As one carer said, 'We like to think people are honest and really putting across that child's point of view, but if she's saying something to me and I didn't want to hear it, would I then say the truth to somebody else?' Others were wary of putting words into children's mouths.

An alternative way of providing mediation is through advocacy. Very few children had been offered independent advocates, and most social workers would not know where to get access to one. Opinions differed about the value of an independent service, but where people had experience of such a service they tended to speak very positively of it. It may be particularly useful in situations of conflict, where we found that children often tend to stay away from meetings at present. Social workers and carers made similar comments to those made by children about the advantages and disadvantages of inviting friends to meetings.

There were a variety of different methods of chairing reviews. In some areas team managers chaired their own reviews, while in others there were 'independent' chairs from another area, or a specialist reviewing officer. All systems seemed to have their strengths and weaknesses, and often what seemed most important was the skill shown by the individual chair in preparing for the meeting, in introducing everyone, in keeping the focus on the child and in dealing with conflict.

For children to participate effectively it does seem to be extremely important that they should be familiar with everyone at the meeting. There was also great variation in how minutes and records were produced, and in whether children received copies of them. (Some children commented that they would not want minutes in any case, but it is by no means always clear that they have the option.)

A number of people made comments about the 'Looking After Children' system; views were mixed. Many people had clearly found the Assessment and Action Records useful, although others found hem perplexing. The LAC review forms provided a structure which many people valued, although others thought they were too rigid. They certainly appeared to have increased children's attendance, as the survey findings indicated. The consultation booklets were widely used and some children found them helpful. However, the positive effect seemed to have worn off quickly in some cases and a number of children were finding them dull and repetitive; as one social worker said, 'it can become like homework!' Carers and parents tended to make more negative comments about the Looking After Children materials than social workers or children.

There was much less mention of planning meetings than of reviews, and some apparent confusion between the two. Where planning meetings were identified, children were as likely to be invited to them as they were to reviews. In some areas planning meetings were used more as a focus for day-to-day decision-making and setting out roles and responsibilities. Where the meetings were limited to people whom they knew well, children could be more involved in the process. Children were less likely to be invited to core group meetings, case conferences or school meetings than they were to reviews or planning meetings. Some adults commented that it could be harder to involve children in child protection case conferences because of the number of people involved, with the result that the child's voice might have little weight in the important decisions which were being taken.

From comments in interviews it appeared that adults generally thought children had relatively little influence on what was decided in meetings, although in the initial survey social workers had credited children with a lot of influence.

Working with social services

When people talked about the interaction between families and social services a major preoccupation was with issues of normality. Some carers, particularly in long term placements or with relatives, did not want any involvement at all with social services. They saw social workers and review meetings as an intrusion on their daily lives: 'I wish they'd sort of push out of it and stop telling us to do this and that because I really think it's up to [us] to get on as a family' (relative carer).

This meant that social workers faced a dilemma. As one said,

> I don't know whether there's a way round it really, because we can't say we're not going to ever come and see you, because we have a responsibility to do that; but I think you have to accept that they've got their own lives and they don't want social workers breathing down their neck all the time.

Residence orders may be one way of handing over more responsibility to carers where children are settled in long-term placements. However, it seemed they were rarely considered and even then not pursued – often because of the presumed financial implications. As one foster carer put it,

> The whole system is geared to short-term care ... I think once the plan has been made that the child is going to be in care long-term then there should be a different set of regulations ... and a large part of that should be normalising their lives as much as they can.

People had sharp things to say about 'the system'. A frequent criticism was the lack of suitable placements or limited choice of placements for children, together with comments that children have to move for financial or bureaucratic reasons, not because it is in their interests. 'I think sometimes we should be sued for what we do to kids, how we move them around and sometimes it's no more than because it's convenient to someone.' People also suggested that the care system can make children feel powerless. A social worker said 'Their first experience of the care system is one of powerlessness', and a carer spoke of children who are 'very passive, and they just go anywhere ... they become acclimatised to a system that shunts them around.'

Another frequent criticism was that pressures of work do not allow social workers to spend enough time with children to build relationships, to communicate effectively, and to involve children genuinely in the decision-making process. Social workers argued that if they are to find new ways of involving children the system must become more flexible. They complained that they were 'swamped' with paperwork and that this made it very hard to spend time with children: 'All the documents are intended to be helpful and many of them are, but there is just far too much of it all.' Carers and children said that both carers and social workers are too accountable, that the system is too protective, and that children are not able to enjoy normal lives. One foster carer acknowledged fears of abuse, but commented 'if the will was there to make these kids' lives more normal...I don't think it will happen, everybody is about watching your backs so they don't get in trouble.' Another social worker said 'I think what they've ended up with is something which is almost too mechanistic...it's over-controlling and doesn't leave any room for the creative professional.'

Most agencies seemed to lack a complaints system which was really child-friendly, although some workers had tried to explain to children what they should do if they were not happy about something. In a few cases where children had tried to use the complaints system it had not got them very far, as one carer reported: 'What they were complaining about was actually quite significant things...the continual fobbing off we have is amazing.' In contrast, another thought that if 'the normal moans and groans all adolescents have...are taken as complaints, as they sometimes are, I think it doesn't serve children.' Some children, carers and social workers argued for creating opportunities for children to meet to share information and support each other, as well as to help adults understand what issues are important to children.

Reasons why children should have a say

Adults gave many of the same reasons why children should take part in decisions as did children. Some also mentioned children's right to have a say, and the greater sense of self-worth that can come from children having more control over their lives. Some saw disadvantages in involving children: raising expectations and disappointing them, adults losing control over outcomes, children putting themselves in danger, taking advantage and losing respect for adults, or being upset and traumatised by the content of discussions. However, most adults felt that it was important to involve children and to give them a say in decisions that affect their lives. One social worker said, 'Most departments haven't seen it as an issue of empowerment, rather they have just seen it as an issue of making a decision...Empowerment isn't about getting what you want; it's about taking children along in the process.'

When the 'diamond-ranking' exercise (pp. 151–2) was repeated with social workers, who were asked in groups to rank the statements as they thought children would, several groups put 'to get what I want' firmly at the top of the list. This may illustrate an adult fantasy about the effects of giving children a greater voice.

Concluding comments

There is a problem about the presentation and interpretation of extensive qualitative data, which is fundamentally a problem of the arbitrariness of selection. One way of dealing with this is to select boldly on the basis of the author's own theoretical concerns. This strategy is often effective, but it can ask a lot of the reader in trusting the author's judgement and objectivity. Another approach is to try to give as full a representation as possible of the data so that the reader can both see what is presented in context and make his or her own selection of what is significant, representative or 'interesting'.[2] Yet another is to find ways to give research subjects themselves a direct voice in the selection and interpretation of data.[3]

I have used a combination of these approaches. In this chapter and the preceding one I have tried to give a broad picture of the sort of things that were said by research subjects and of the ideas they produced – about the initial themes of the research and about other issues that were salient for them. As I have said, this is necessarily selective but I have tried to make it as full as I can and to reflect a range of experiences, attitudes and opinions. Elsewhere I have looked more closely at how the individual interviews were done and how 'data' were constructed from that process.[4] In the concluding chapters I try to make some more theoretical inroads into the data, by discussing ways of using the research material to construct typologies which may help to understand what happens about children's participation in decisions, and by reconsidering some basic theoretical questions raised or illuminated by the findings of the research. I also indicate some ways in which the research can inform practice.

11
Making Sense of the Research

In this chapter I want to look at what can be learned from the research described in this book. First of all, we should return to the questions that followed the review of the survey findings in Chapter 8, to see if any answers are suggested by the findings of the detailed study.

1. *Why are so many children apparently being denied the opportunity to attend their reviews and planning meetings?* It seems clear that there are a number of different reasons why children are not invited to take part in decision-making meetings. The attitude, personality and confidence of the child sometimes make a difference, and the stability of the placement is also important in that children in unstable situations seem less likely to be included. However, the most important factors are often to do with the attitudes of the adults involved. Where adults – particularly social workers and carers, but also managers – are positively committed to the value of including children as much as possible in decisions, then children are more likely to be invited to take part in formal decision-making meetings as well as in the day-to-day processes of sorting things out.

2. *Why is age such a strong predictor of whether children are invited to meetings?* It appears that adults make assumptions about children based on their age which are not fully explicit, but which have the effect of limiting children's participation in a number of ways. First, social workers say that they judge children's understanding and competence as individuals, but they seem unable to give clear accounts of how those assessments are made, and their results seem to correlate closely with age. It seems likely that differences in children's experience and their ability to handle abstractions, which also correlate with age, may be affecting the selection process. Second, many of our respondents believed that younger children had a less clear or

realistic idea of their own interests. Although this does not necessarily justify excluding them from discussion, it may be a reason why they are often not invited to those meetings which are arranged principally to consider major decisions.[1] Third, the format of decision-making meetings is often seen as inimical to younger children's participation, and it may be that they are not invited because it is assumed that they would not enjoy the experience or would be upset by it.

3. *If most of the children who attend their meetings appear to take an active part in the discussion, is it likely that this would also be true of those who currently do not attend?* Most of the children seen in this research were well able to express their views, and to understand their often complex situations, in ways that would have enabled them to take an active part in any well-managed discussion. This applies to those who did not attend their meetings as well as to those who did. When the children met in groups there was no obvious difference between attenders and non-attenders in their ability to take part in discussion.

4. *Can the children who do not take part really have so much influence on the decisions made when they are not there?* When social workers reported that most children had a lot of influence on decisions regardless of whether they were present at meetings, they were applying a subjective judgement of what constituted 'a lot' rather than 'a little'. None the less it was remarkable that so many of them said that this was the case. Having initially been rather sceptical about this finding, I am inclined now to think that children's influence was probably being overstated in cases where they were present as well as those where they were not. It is clear that for many the process of working with children to discover their thoughts and explain the options to them is extremely important. If this process is successful then a child may have considerable influence notwithstanding her or his absence from the formal decision-making meeting. If it is lacking, then the child's participation in the meeting may make little difference to the outcome. In the detailed study, the children who had attended their meetings generally said that they did not have a lot of influence on decisions.

5. *How well can a child's views be mediated by a social worker or carer?* Despite the above, it is clear from the interviews that many children who attended their meetings really value the opportunity to put their own views directly, and would not have been satisfied with someone else speaking for them. It is likely that some social workers

and carers are very good at expressing children's views on their behalf, and there is a case for offering this as an option to every child. However, enough adults were uncomfortable with the idea of having to voice the child's views as well as their own to support the argument that independent advocacy should also be available routinely to children who are not able or willing to speak for themselves in decision-making fora.

6. *Why are children less likely to be invited to take part in significant decision-making matters? Is this because of a belief that adults know best and that children are not to be trusted to make really important decisions?* There is considerable evidence in the interview material to support this hypothesis. It would be interesting to use an objective measure of adult attitudes in enough cases to examine whether these were linked with children's inclusion or exclusion from particular kinds of meetings.

7. *Why are some children choosing not to attend? Are they seeking to avoid conflict; bored by meetings; content to trust their social workers; or unwilling to accept their situation of being in care or accommodated?* It appears that all these explanations apply in some cases. However, being bored by meetings in general, and not liking the way in which these particular meetings are arranged, seem to be particularly important reasons for children's voluntary absence. An additional factor which emerged from the qualitative research is that children sometimes base their decision whether to attend on who else is going to be at the meeting.

8. *What are the expectations of children who do take part in meetings – do they enjoy or value the meetings or simply tolerate them?* The interviews revealed a very wide variation both of expectations and of attitudes, from children who look forward to 'their' reviews and enjoy holding the centre stage, to those who attend reluctantly or resentfully and who may be hurt by the experience or disappointed by the outcome. It is clear that the quality of the experience can be very different for different children, for reasons which are only partly in their control.

In such ways the qualitative phase of the research was able to answer some of the questions, and develop some of the hypotheses, that were produced in the quantitative phase. There are still important unanswered questions, further exploration of which could usefully include both quantitative and qualitative elements. Objective measures of adult attitudes to children's participation, and of beliefs about the significance of age and understanding, could be used to explore the connection between these attitudes and beliefs and children's actual participation. Further evaluation of children's influence on decisions would also need to include an objective element, but in the context of ethnographic work based on observation of the whole process of decision-making before, during and after a meeting.

Constructing typologies

This was conceived and planned as exploratory research; it was never expected to produce definitive statements of cause and effect, or of the relative weight of different factors in producing effective participation. However, an important contribution that exploratory research can make to our understanding is in helping us to identify patterns and enabling us to give names to social phenomena. In reviewing what was said by children and adults in relation to some of the key themes of the research, a number of classifications or typologies began to emerge.

Children's attitudes to their involvement

For instance, when we look at the kind of things individual children say about their involvement in decision-making it is possible to discern several distinct attitudes to the question of how much say children can expect to have. These may be called the 'assertive', 'dissatisfied', 'submissive', 'reasonable' and 'avoidant' positions.

The *assertive* position holds that children should have a say, and children taking this stance would expect to get a say. Few children talked explicitly about rights, but those who did were in this group. On the other hand a child holding the *dissatisfied* position would say that children should have more say than they do, and perhaps that 'it's not fair'. The *submissive* position is that 'we don't need much say' or that 'adults know best'. The *reasonable* position is different in that it talks about compromise; children expect to be heard at times, but also to listen to the adults' point of view, and they also think it right that adults should make some decisions without consulting them. Finally, there was a small *avoidant* group who appeared to find decision-making with adults difficult. Children in this group would often say 'I don't mind' when asked directly about how much say they should have.

Adult attitudes to children's involvement

When we look at what adults said or implied about children's involvement in decisions and the reasons for including or excluding them, it is clear that there are a number of different attitudes in operation. Welsby's (1996b) typology of 'clinical', 'bureaucratic' and 'value-based' approaches to involving children proved useful in analysing the research. The *clinical* approach focuses on the child as in need of treatment. Decisions about including children in decisions are therefore likely to revolve around their emotional capacity or incapacity and their vulnerability to distress. In practice this approach often leads to the exclusion of children on the basis that they 'are not ready', 'would not understand' or might make a regrettable decision. However, there were also examples of very sensitive work to engage children being done within the context of the clinical approach. The *bureaucratic* approach as described by Welsby centres on fulfilling organisational and procedural requirements in relation to decision-making, which may leave little space for effective children's participation or sensitive communication with children. In the research we found two sub-variants of this attitude. One was espoused by social workers who said they would like to involve children more in decisions but that regrettably bureaucracy got in the way of doing so; either because the procedures were inflexible or because the demands of their other responsibilities made it impossible to find the time. The other was represented by workers who were actually involving children more than they had done in the past, or more than they would have done of their own accord, precisely because it was seen as a procedural requirement.

The *value-based* approach is promoted by Welsby as one which regards children's involvement in decisions as a positive good in itself, either because it is a right of children or because it leads to better decisions, better practice and better outcomes. One of the more pleasing aspects of carrying out the research was in finding many social workers and carers who sincerely held this position, and who really appeared to do their best to promote children's understanding and involvement in decisions and to 'empower' them. At the same time we found it necessary to develop the classification with the inclusion of a fourth category, which we initially called 'manipulative' but which I now call 'cynical'. The *cynical* approach is characterised by one or more of the following assertions or assumptions: that children have too much say already; that they do not know what is best for them; that they want power without responsibility; that they are manipulative; that they are 'spoiled'. Such views were expressed vociferously by a couple of foster carers who felt that a girl was 'running rings round everyone' by refusing to go home, but were clearly held in varying degrees by a number of the adults who spoke to us.[2]

Adult attitudes to the inclusion of children with special needs

A second typology of adult views relates specifically to the inclusion of children with disabilities in decision-making but may also have a more general application. In looking at what people said, especially about attempts to include children with a variety of learning and communication problems, it became clear that there was a distinction between those who focused on the child's capacities or lack of them, and those who focused on adults' skills or attitudes. There was a separate distinction to be made between whether people were positive or negative about the likelihood of children being successfully included. This gives us a matrix as shown in Figure 11.1.

	Focus on child	**Focus on adult**
Positive attitude	'this child can find ways to make herself understood'	'with creativity and determination we can include her'
Negative attitude	'her disabilities are too profound to include her'	'I just can't see any way to find out what she thinks'

Figure 11.1 Matrix of attitudes to participation by children with disabilities

Views of the effects of adverse experiences

A further area in which a typology seemed to lie waiting to be found was in relation to what people thought were the key differences between children who were looked after and other children, particularly in relation to the effect of their previous experiences. These we may call the 'damaged', 'resilient' and 'special need' positions. The *damaged* position suggests that children in the care system have typically had experiences which have traumatised them emotionally, made it harder for them to trust people, or damaged their confidence in themselves. The impact of this on their ability to take part in decision-making is seen to be largely negative. The *resilient* position, in contrast, suggests that children may have learned from their adverse experiences, grown up more quickly as a result of having had to face change or loss or to take more responsibility for themselves, become 'streetwise', and therefore be more able to take part in decisions. The third position argues that children in the care system have a *special need* to be included, to be given power and autonomy, because they are relatively alone in the world and will 'need to stand up for themselves more'.

Using the typologies

The attitudes identified in these classifications are not necessarily to be identified with particular individuals. Views change over time or in reaction to circumstances, and the same person can say contradictory things. First and foremost they represent possible ways of thinking about the data, and because they are typologies of attitudes – because this research was as much as anything about attitudes – they also represent ways in which the 'subjects' of the research may think about their situation. In this way the typologies open up a set of possible connections between formal theories of children's rights or child development and the ideas in practice which people use to negotiate, and to live in, the situations which we have studied. For instance, the 'clinical' and 'value-based' positions on children's participation can be quickly found in a glance through some of the literature referred to in earlier chapters; as can the 'resilient' or 'damaged' readings of the effects of early adverse experience on children's ability to take part. All this can be explored simply by thinking about the different perspectives that have been identified and drawing out their implications.

However, it is also possible in reviewing the interview transcripts and summaries to categorise our respondents according to the positions which each one predominantly expresses. When this was done, for instance, with children and the adults caring for them, it was then possible to look at the relationships between the two sets of attitudes as views held by particular individuals. A chi-squared test showed that the association between particular child attitudes and carer attitudes was significant at $p > 0.1$. The strongest association appeared to be between children who were identified as 'assertive' or 'dissatisfied' and carers identified as 'clinical' or 'value-based'. Of the *dissatisfied* children 5 were with 'clinical' carers, against an expected value of 2, and only 1 with a 'value-based' carer against an expected value of 5. When it came to the *assertive* children, none was with a 'clinical' carer (expected value 1.8), but 8 were with 'value-based' ones (expected value 4.6).

It is not possible on the basis of the research to be over-confident about this relationship, let alone suggest a specific causal connection. It is not hard to see how the carer's approach to children's participation might be reflected in the child's attitude. At the same time it is likely that some children are relatively easier or harder to include because of their attitude. In this study there often seemed to be a mutually supportive relationship between carers who encouraged children's involvement and children who expected to play an active part in decisions.

Likewise the combination of a carer who found reasons to exclude a child 'for their own good', and a child who felt unjustly excluded, was a pattern that sometimes seemed to have its own repetitive momentum.

The ladder of participation

The other piece of typological work to be done is in relation to the different kinds of participation. I suggested in Chapter 8 that a 'ladder' was too linear to encompass the multidimensional character of children's participation in decisions about their lives. What might be an alternative?

The 'ladder of participation', as originally conceived by Arnstein and later adapted by Hart for children, was designed with collective participation in public or semi-public decisions in mind (Arnstein 1969, Hart 1992). The modification of Arnstein's model by Thoburn et al. (1995) was intended to apply to processes of individual decision-making in which children and their families might be involved, such as a child protection case conference. Grimshaw and Sinclair (1997) used the same version of the ladder in order to evaluate participation by children and their parents in reviews and planning meetings. They did this by marking the 'highest' point on the ladder that an individual was observed to reach in a particular meeting, acknowledging that this was a rough and ready way to evaluate participation.

The problem with all these frameworks when applied to children's participation in continuing and complex decisions about their lives is that they assume that one person's participation can be ranked unequivocally as more or less significant or substantial than another's. They operate as if participation is *something* that one can simply have more or less of. What we have seen in this research is that the kind of participation I am interested in is more complicated than that. If we look simply at the formal decision-making meeting, we need to take account not just of how much a child says in the meeting and how much notice is taken of what s/he says by the other participants, but also of how well the child understands the issues at stake, the options available and the reasons why certain decisions have already been taken. We need to take account of how much choice the child has over the time and place of the meeting, the subjects for discussion and the people who have been invited. We need to consider whether the child has been given a free choice whether or not to attend, and whether s/he has been offered alternative ways to participate or to be represented. We need to know whether the child understands the context in which the meeting is held and the power which the meeting has, and whether the child knows how to challenge the decisions which have been taken or to complain about the service provided. If we want our classification to apply to the child's participation in informal and everyday decision-making processes too, then it must become still more complicated.

Is a child who attends a meeting because s/he is told that s/he must, and then takes a very active part in the discussion, higher or lower on the ladder of participation than one who attends as a free choice but then says nothing? Is a child who takes a very active part in dealing with all the matters on the agenda, but who does not realise that she could have asked for other things to be discussed, a 'participant' or is she merely being 'consulted'? What about a child who has a great deal of say in everyday decisions at home but is excluded from the major planning for the future, compared with one who is carefully included in formal decision-making with a great deal of support but who has very little say in what happens from day to day?

The 'climbing wall'

Our conceptualisation of participation needs to include all these dimensions if it is to grasp the reality of what participation is like for children. It is possible to think in terms of a *grid* or *matrix* that allows categories to be located on two axes, or of a *web* or *network* that allows our idea of participation to develop in more than one direction. In explaining the research to practitioners Claire O'Kane and I used the images of *bridges* and *barriers* to participation; but these are more helpful in thinking about what facilitates participation than in analysing what it is. However, the idea of a *wall* – not as an obstacle or boundary but as a construction – may have some potential. A wall can extend both laterally and vertically, and within limits it can also extend unevenly at different points. We can identify different aspects of involvement in decision-making as bricks or pillars in the wall, and extend them differentially. The aspects I would suggest as being of key importance are:

- the *choice* which the child has over his or her participation
- the *information* which s/he has about the situation and her or his rights
- the *control* which s/he has over the decision-making process
- the *voice* which s/he has in any discussion

- the *support* which s/he has in speaking up
- the degree of *autonomy* which s/he has to make decisions independently

This enables us to acknowledge that one child's involvement in the decision-making process may be strong in some respects and weak in others. By analogy with the 'ladder' we may call it the 'climbing wall', with more than one route up it. The illustration in Figure 11.2 represents a child who speaks up for herself a great deal, gets a moderate level of support and enjoys a moderate degree both of choice and of freedom, but does not really understand what is going on and has little control over the process of decision-making.

It will be seen that this way of measuring participation does enable us to take account of more than one aspect of the process. It could of course be made more complex, for instance by adding sections relating specifically to everyday decision-making and others relating specifically to formal processes. It would also be possible to identify obvious or commonly recurring patterns or configurations and give them names, in the same way that the rungs of the 'ladder of participation' have names.

I do not put this forward as a replacement for the 'ladder of participation', which still has enormous value as a way of identifying dramatically how seriously individuals are included in the decision-making process. However, it does seem to represent a useful alternative if we want to look more closely at what is involved in giving children an effective part in decisions. This is especially so when we consider that some children are vocal, assertive, and may only need the information

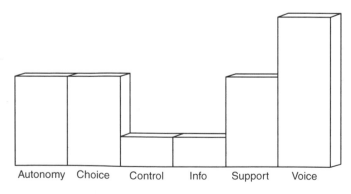

Figure 11.2 The 'climbing wall' of participation

and the opportunity to exercise their right to be heard, while others are shy or emotionally bruised and may need much support and coaxing before they can have enough trust in themselves or others to take a full part. For this is another striking discovery from this research about adults listening to children: that with some children it really is little more than a matter of turning on the tap, while with others it is more like mining for gold. This applies both to the practitioner and to the researcher, as we saw in the previous chapter.

Communicating with children

The last comment is related to one of the main theoretical themes of this research. I have referred earlier to what we might call its *doubly reflexive* nature. As with any ethnographic research, part of what was being studied was the interaction between researcher and subject. In addition, however, an explicit object of this research was the interaction between adult and child and especially between social worker and child, which has many points of connection with the relationship between adult researcher and child subject. Working in a participatory way, using methods of communication that are 'child-friendly', is methodologically sound and enables the resolution of some difficult ethical problems in research, and arguably in social work practice too (see Thomas and O'Kane 1998b and forthcoming).[3]

Both from the process of doing the research and from what people said in interview, we learned a lot about what sort of things make communication between adults and children satisfactory – and what sort of things get in the way. The key points seem to be that children can communicate more effectively in the context of trusting relationships; that time and patience are often needed to discover what children think and want, and that they will not necessarily be ready to talk at the times that adults find convenient; that children need preparation and support in order to take part in decision-making meetings; that they need choice as to how, and how far, they participate in any decision-making process, and a say in what subjects are discussed; and finally that many children find it very boring when people 'just sit there and talk', and they prefer communication based on activity. Many of these are points made by Kroll (1995) and Thurgood (1990) and referred to in Chapter 6; they were strongly confirmed by the evidence of this research.

Children do communicate differently from adults. My son, then aged eight, was watching me transcribing an interview onto the computer.

After watching the screen for a few moments he asked, 'Who's "*f.c.*"?'. I said, 'A foster carer.' He said, 'I thought it was a grownup; when it's a child talking it's just short lines, but here it's in big chunks.' The research confirmed that children often experience adults as 'going on' about things, when their own preference is usually for short utterances. It also confirmed that children have a suspicion of adults asking questions, which is probably well-founded. Adults ask children a lot of questions, and often the motive is in some sense ulterior. Perhaps the adult knows the answer and wants to find out whether the child knows it; or they may be trying to find out whether the child has done something wrong, or if they know who is to blame for something. At any rate it is often a good strategy for children to avoid answering adults' questions, or to avoid situations in which they are likely to be asked.

Much of this may seem obvious, but it seems that it is often forgotten by busy professionals, or else the knowledge is excluded by the system within which they work. When I began my field research I thought, 'I am a researcher interviewing children and I need to use interview schedules to ask them questions,' completely excluding all the knowledge and skill in communicating with children about sensitive issues that I had developed in my practice as a social worker. It was only after I reflected on why this approach was not working – and coincidentally had to rediscover some of those skills when I began working as a guardian *ad litem* – that I realised that the skills could be translated from one setting to another. The irony is that I and my colleague then found ourselves telling social workers about better ways to communicate with children on the basis of our experience as researchers, when much of the material we had used came from social work sources. One problem seems to be that 'direct work' skills are compartmentalised in certain areas of social work practice and shut out of others. Where structured assessment, prescribed supervisory activities or complex decision-making procedures are dominant, then work which is intimate, informal and relatively heedless of time constraints may not easily find a place. This applies especially to the review meeting, which is constructed in formal ways that seem inimical to relaxed communication with children.

Children's wishes and children's interests[4]

Another key question in theory and in practice relates to conflict between a child's wishes and feelings and their 'best interests'. Chapter 5 looked at this issue in theoretical terms. The research enables us to put some flesh on that discussion. It confirmed that both adults and children did experience a degree of conflict between what children wanted for themselves and what adults thought was in their best interests, and that this conflict was not always easy to resolve. Chapter 8 referred to the evidence from social workers in the initial survey of levels of disagreement between what children wanted and what parents, carers and social workers thought should happen. In the course of the survey social workers made further comments about situations where there was a conflict between children's wishes and adult views of their best interests, and in the detailed study both children and adults talked in more depth about conflict between what a child wanted, or thought was best for her or him, and what adults thought was in his or her interests. All of these comments referred to one of four situations: differences over placement, differences over contact, differences over school and differences over leisure.

Differences over placement almost without exception involved a conflict between a child's wish to return to live with her or his family, and the view of social workers, carers or others that this would be against the child's interests. For instance, a boy of eight wanted to be at home, and the social worker commented that he 'doesn't understand the implications of the care order'. Another boy of ten wanted to go home, but 'they can't cope with him and they abuse him.' A girl of ten wanted to go home, but there were concerns about the conflict between her parents. Two girls of eleven and nine had not settled in foster care and were 'continually asking to go home' even though their mother was not able to look after them. There was just one case where the disagreement was not over return home: a boy of twelve wanted to remain in the children's home where he was temporarily placed, rather than be fostered again; he had been told that his request would be considered but was unlikely to be accepted.

Differences over contact fell into two categories. In one the child wanted more contact than the social worker or the carer thought advisable. A boy of twelve wanted more frequent contact to be arranged with his mother. The objection in this case was that 'she lets him down and he gets upset.' Another child's social worker commented that she 'would want to see mother every week' if she were consulted – which presumably she was not. In the other type of case children wanted less contact than was proposed. One group of children were not wanting contact with their grandparents although the adults thought it would be in their best interests. In another case contact was resumed by the local authority when, according to the foster carer, the children 'don't really want it.'

Differences over school were generally about choice of school or change of school. A boy of ten with a learning disability wanted to go to a mainstream school with his friends, but his grandparents who cared for him thought he should go to a special school. The social worker was concerned at 'his limited understanding of the prospects.' Another boy of eleven, in foster care, did not want to go to Catholic school as his mother wished. In this case the social worker referred the case to a special needs advisor who supported the child's view. A girl of ten wanted to change schools because she was 'picked on', but the adults involved with her thought a move would not help.

Differences over leisure time were generally about freedom versus safety, or about what was age-appropriate. A girl of eleven with learning difficulties wanted to go off with a sixteen-year-old friend, and her carer thought this inappropriate. A boy of twelve wanted to go with a friend to a leisure centre in town, returning after dark. A boy aged eleven, with some learning difficulties, wanted to go fishing on his own. A girl of eight wanted to go playing with friends where she would need to negotiate main roads. Her mother was worried and commented 'she's always thought she's older than what she is.' (The same child also wanted to watch TV programmes which her mother thought unsuitable.) In contrast, an older girl was believed to be going out of her children's home to meet a pimp.

Ways of resolving the conflict

Clearly these cases were resolved in a variety of different ways. How they were resolved appeared to reflect sometimes the issues that were at stake, occasionally the assertiveness of children, but most of all the attitudes of the adults involved. Some social workers and carers were very clear about their responsibility on occasion to override the child's wishes in the interests of their welfare:

> You have to base your decisions on what is realistically in the child's interests as well. Particularly with the little boy that I have got, I mean if he had his way as he feels it he would want to see his mum every week. Yet each visit he has he is just totally destructive after it. So that would be the point at which we would have to say 'No, that is not in your interests'.

Others were less confident of their own ability to make the right decision, or more willing to allow the child a substantial role in the process:

> She was stating very clearly where she wanted to be, who she wanted to live with, and as it worked out it was a good decision. I think we would have had far more trouble management-wise if we tried to impose a decision that she didn't want. We would have all sorts of difficulties trying to detain her.

Still others emphasised the importance of a balance between protecting children from harm and allowing them to learn by taking risks:

> To an extent you can let them do what they want and they learn by their own mistakes – for me to turn round and basically tell her no, it'll have to be something that I seriously don't believe is right.

Where it was seen to be necessary to override a child's own wishes, many adults stressed the importance of explanation:

> With the younger child it's getting down to their level and explaining the reasons why and doing it in whatever way is best for them. It's not always easy, because a lot of the time children don't see why they need to be protected, and that's a very tricky area to have to explain, and they still might say I don't think this is fair; but as long as they've got some understanding as to why it's having to happen…

Children's responses to issues of conflict also varied, and the typology related earlier in this chapter is clearly relevant here. Some were remarkably trusting in adults:

> They care about you. You think 'Oh, why are they telling me off?' and they care about you – they want you to do what is best.

Others could see that their own viewpoint was not the only one. 'Barry' who said:

> If I had the opportunity I'd pack my bags now, but, not my choice. I'd like to go home now.

also said

> But they've got to have my safety and my brother's safety – that's not a very good idea, going home.[5]

Others were more ready to challenge adults' claim to know what was best. One child said emphatically:

They didn't care what I thought, it was about what they thought. What they thought was best for me. I could say what is best for me as well, like you could as well. You could say what is best for you. I don't need – well I do need sometimes – but most of the time I don't need people to say what is best for me.

Children often seemed more ready to accept adults' decisions when they were made with their physical safety in mind, and less so when they were based on some vaguer concept of their best interests. Nowhere was there more hostility to adult 'protection' than when a group of children talked about film classification; they said firmly that they could decide for themselves whether the content of a film was something which they could handle.

An exercise which we did with several groups of children was to ask them to rank in order of importance a number of reasons that individual children had given us for being involved in decision-making. Consistently at the top of the list they put 'to let me have my say' or 'to be supported'; and at the bottom they put 'to get what I want' or 'to help adults make good decisions'. It was very clear from these results, and from the comments the children made in subsequent discussion, that what they wanted was above all the opportunity to take part in dialogue with adults, not for either themselves or the adults to determine the outcome. Interestingly, when we repeated the exercise with groups of social workers and asked them to rank the statements as they thought children would, several groups put 'to get what I want' firmly at the top of the list. If this illustrates a recurring adult fantasy about children's participation, it is one which may get in the way of listening to children. As Roche (1995) puts it:

It need not be a question of adult imposition versus child autonomy: rather a matter of acknowledging the interconnectedness of our lives, of no longer seeing the relationships that children have with significant adults as naturally and necessarily hierarchic. We, as adults, might also benefit from dialogue with children in confronting our dilemmas.

(pp. 286–7)

In reporting the research to practitioners we used an exercise involving three fictional scenarios based on the kinds of cases summarised above: a boy of ten on a care order following physical abuse by his stepfather, who is asking to go back to a neglectful mother now that his stepfather has left; a girl of eight in long-term foster care who is asking to see her mother more often, although her foster carers feel that it should be less often because her mother often lets her down at the last minute; and a girl of twelve in a children's home who wants to stay overnight with a friend whose parents have convictions for using illegal drugs. Participants in the workshops were asked to reflect briefly on each scenario and then to arrange themselves physically along a line on the floor which represents a continuum from doing what the child wants to imposing the adult view of their interests, to indicate their initial reaction to the scenario as presented.

It was remarkable how different groups of social workers formed very similar clusters in response to the three cases. In the first two scenarios participants ranged themselves along the full length of the continuum, but with a very pronounced bulge at the end which represented doing what the child wanted. In discussion when participants were pushed to justify their stance, it seemed that the 'bulge' represented a mixture of three distinct viewpoints: first, that what the child wanted happened to be the right thing anyway; second, that it appeared to be the right thing, partly because it was what the child wanted; third, that there were serious doubts about this course of action which were outweighed by the positive value attached to following the child's wishes. The overall pattern, however, was repeated in a wide variety of settings. For most participants, following the child's wishes did not mean simply doing as they asked. Rather it meant taking on the children's aims as objectives, and planning to achieve them in a way that protected the child from any 'collateral damage'.

In the third scenario the pattern was rather different. Most participants positioned themselves at the opposite end of the line, indicating that they would be likely to prevent the child in this case from doing what she wanted. It was interesting that people who had been prepared to give a lot of weight to the wishes of younger children in the face of concerns about their long-term welfare, were actually more restrictive in the case of an older child where the risk was primarily that of scandal. When pressed, participants often admitted that they were thinking as much of their own interests as of the child's. Mnookin made the point many years ago that 'many decisions are made because of organisational considerations' but 'justified under the vague rubric of best interests' (1976, pp. 273–4).

Understanding, competence and participation

Schofield and Thoburn (1996) argue against those who imply that it is a question of 'balancing' the child's wishes and feelings against her or his best interests. They contend that good practice consists in bringing the two together:

> Implicit in the idea of balance is a presumption that 'welfare' is a specific route [*sic*] to be weighed against the specific wishes and feelings of the child. As soon as we look at an individual case, this apparent clarity evaporates. It is likely that we are deciding between a range of options, each of which will meet some but not all of a child's needs and some but not all of her wishes.
>
> (p. 18)

In the case examples which they give

> The process of decision-making becomes in some senses more of a partnership in which it is acknowledged that the young person has some of the power and that a good outcome for the child depends on the child having a major stake in the decision. The role of children here is not simply based on the idea that these are competent children who should therefore have the right to make their own decisions. We would argue that these children continue to be in need of caring and support and are looking to adults whom they trust to help them make difficult decisions. To that extent both the young person and the professional involved take some degree of responsibility for the decision – and for the risks.
>
> (pp. 24–5)

Schofield and Thoburn refer to Lansdown's suggestion, as they put it,

> that decision-making involving children needs to be linked to an assessment of the competence of the child in relation to a particular decision. It is her view that if a child lacks the competence to understand the implications of a decision then the parent should still only override the child if to do so is necessary to protect the child or to promote his or her best interests. If the child is competent, then the parent should only override the child if failure to do so would result in serious harm.
>
> (p. 23; see Lansdown 1995)

The important point, they suggest, is that competence should be assessed *in relation to a particular decision:*

> We would argue that making a clear dividing line between competent and non-competent children would not be helpful in child protection practice. The decisions involved and the circumstances of the children and their families are so complex that the role of any individual child in relation to any particular decision has to rely on a sensitive and careful process of negotiation with the child concerned and perhaps, in the most difficult situations, adjudication by the court. The role of the child cannot be determined by reference to a simple formula or check-list. We would be concerned that placing children into an either/or category may actually be unhelpful in labelling many children as non-competent and reducing their role in proceedings.
>
> (pp. 25–6)

This approach to the issue of conflict between children's 'wishes and feelings' and their 'best interests' is, I would argue, a constructive and helpful one. Combined with Eekelaar's concept of 'dynamic self-determinism', it offers a conceptual path through what we found to be a genuinely tricky problem in practice (Eekelaar 1994; see Chapter 5 above). In particular it adds the crucial element of *dialogue* that seemed to be missing from Eekelaar's account. However, I argued in Chapter 5 that Eekelaar's formulation does not provide a complete solution, and even with the addition of Schofield and Thoburn's insights there are still areas of difficulty. One potential flaw is that tests of competence may have to be applied by the same adults who are deciding whether to make a choice for the child. In Chapter 5 I quoted Seymour's suggestion that an entitlement for older children 'to have their actual capacities determined, rather than being subject to presumptions based on their ages,' is unlikely to lead to very radical changes in practice; because 'the tendency will be to assess this capacity by reference to what is thought to be in the child's best interests.' A similar view was expressed more plainly in relation to the Children Act 1989 by a foster carer who said: 'So really it's, they can make decisions as long as they don't disagree with the adult views and perceptions of what's going on; because if they do then obviously they don't understand the situation.' When we asked social workers how they decided whether to include children in a decision–making meeting, their replies frequently made reference to assessing the child's ability to understand. However, when we asked them how they made such an assessment their answers tended to be muddled and incoherent. It does appear that it is difficult in practice to assess a child's understanding of the issues involved in a decision without the circularity suggested by Seymour and our informant.

There are instances when the contest is clear-cut, when a child can say: I understand your concern for my safety or long-term welfare, but I am frankly more interested in being happy doing what I want to do now and in being with the people I feel close to. One trouble with discussions of children's competence is that there is often an unspoken assumption that, where children use different criteria for making choices, those are necessarily defective or at least inferior to adult criteria. But adults do not have a monopoly of wisdom, and as Mnookin (1983) points out, the balance between present and future happiness may not be obvious.

Does one look at the problem from a short or long-term perspective, each of which may throw up different answers. Conditions which make a child happy at seven or ten may have adverse consequences at age 30. Should the judge decide what will make the child happy in the next year? Or at 30? Or at 70? Does the judge look at the problem by picturing the child as an adult looking back? How is happiness at one age to be compared with happiness at another?

(p. 10)

An unfortunately memorable experience for me some years ago was to be involved in a case where a girl with a long-standing problem of absence from school (and a mother with agoraphobia) was forcibly taken to a residential school far from home, although she had recently been told that she had a form of cancer which might mean that she had only a few months to live. Clearly the girl's view, that how she spent her time now was more important than her future prospects, was one with a rational basis – perhaps more rational than that of the psychiatrists and social workers who insisted on taking her away.

Clearly there will always be situations where the conflict between different perspectives is very hard to resolve. In such situations it is arguable that considerable weight *ought* to be given to the child's own view, if only on the basis that, as so many of them put it, 'it's my life.' In this way we may begin to make a presumption of competence, rather than of incompetence, in deciding how much weight to give to children's views; just as in deciding whether to include a child in a decision–making process we must make a presumption of competence, and look for a process of communication that will elicit and augment the child's actual competence, rather than submit them to 'tests' of competence or look for reasons to exclude them.

A related difficulty with the flexible approach advocated in different ways by Schofield and Thoburn and by is Eekelaar is that in general it risks making children's participation too dependent on the inclinations, sensitivity and skills of adults. Eekelaar is of course right that it is not simply a matter of asking the child to give their view of a complex situation, but that subtle and sensitive work may be needed to elicit the child's wishes and feelings in their proper context. Cantwell and Scott (1995) emphasise the importance of taking account of the emotional context of children's wishes and feelings, and of working with them in a process which includes explanation and reassurance, rather than simply asking a child to make a choice. On the other hand, children's rights to participation cannot be solely dependent on the quality of professional work; sometimes children *want* to make choices, and need to know that they have the right to do so. Schofield and Thoburn (1996, p. 26) quote Scarman to the effect that 'rights may be better protected by professional standards than by "*a priori* lines of division between capacity and lack of capacity".' However, they also say that 'children should have the right of access to advocates or complaints procedures when they feel that decisions have not taken their views into account' (ibid.). This is an extremely important qualification, and without it our modified dynamic self-determinism is seriously incomplete.

Finally there is always the need to be prepared to take risks, or to let the child take risks. As Musgrove put it long ago, 'protective measures are a two edged device; while they may signify concern for the welfare of the young they also define them as a separate, non-adult population, inhabiting a less than adult world' (Musgrove 1964, p. 58; cited in Hockey and James 1993). Or, as a foster carer put it to us:

> People say they're in the best interests of the child but if they never talk to the children – there's a lot of these adults who think they know best, and the children have no say in it do they? So are we really deciding what's in their better interest, it's our best interest for them really.

Using the research in practice

An important objective of the research was to inform social work and care practice with children. The third stage of the research included ongoing work with a group of children to produce an audiotape from the research, and a series of feedback meetings with staff in the participating agencies to begin to report on the findings and to clarify some of their practice implications. This work was part of the research in that findings and conclusions were being tested through further discussion with the main groups from whom data had been gathered. It also represented the beginnings of the process of wider dissemination; and in the process of doing this work materials were developed and tested to help both children and those who work with them with some of the issues identified in the research. These materials include:

a) A user-friendly summary of the research, written in such a way as to be readable for children and adults who want a lively picture of the research, but with more detail available for those who are interested (Thomas and O'Kane 1998a).

b) The audiotape 'Voices with Volume' produced with a group of eight children, who helped to select and read quotations from the qualitative research grouped around a series of themes (Thomas, O'Kane and McNeill 1998).

c) A training pack based on the exercises and materials used in our feedback sessions (Thomas, Phillipson, O'Kane and Davies 1999).

d) A set of picture topic cards to help children and those working with them to discuss issues and prepare for meetings. This is intended to complement the 'consultation booklets' provided as part of the 'Looking After Children' package, which many users find insufficiently flexible. Associated with it is a set of sentence completion cards.

e) A board game about reviews and planning meetings called 'Success', devised by Claire O'Kane in collaboration with a group of the children.

It was an irony of the research project that on the one hand the research methods used were in part based on techniques developed in social work practice and training, yet on the other hand some of these techniques were found to be relatively little known or used in current practice. Rather than use more imaginative or creative ways to communicate and work with children to elicit their views, the tendency was often to use routine verbal questioning methods and to apply preformed, adult-designed processes of discussion and decision–making. There frequently appeared to be a lack of confidence in undertaking direct work with children, and a feeling that agencies and official procedures made little space for such work. At the same time there often seemed to be a wish to improve this aspect of practice, and the dissemination of practice and training materials developed from the research has been an attempt to support that process.

In many ways the most powerful lesson from the research for practice has been to do with the variety and the individuality of children and their situations, and therefore the need for flexibility in fitting systems and procedures to them. A fundamental point is that it is not satisfactory to exclude a child from a decision–making process because 'they would not understand' or 'they would not be able to cope', without first asking how the process could be modified in order to make it accessible to them. Linked with this are a presumption of participation, a presumption of competence, choice for children in whether and how to participate, and the offer of independent support or advocacy. Finally and perhaps most importantly, a secure place must be established in social work practice for direct work with children. It must be recognised and supported instead of being undermined by an emphasis on formal assessment or, as at least one social worker put it, 'swamped by paperwork'.

12
Children's Decisions and Children's Place

In this concluding chapter I want to return to some earlier themes in the book, with further reflections on children's participation in decisions in care and in the family, and some thoughts on rights, on competence, and on children's place in the world.

Developing formal decision-making processes

The attempt to give children who are 'looked after' a greater voice in decisions about their lives has clearly had some success. Many more children are attending meetings to discuss their care, and at a younger age. In some cases they are taking an active part in those discussions and appreciate the chance to be included. However, there are also problems with the way in which they are being involved. Most children find the meetings boring and some find them very unpleasant. They often feel insufficiently prepared to take part, and they are hardly ever given the chance of independent advice or representation. If progress in involving children is to continue there must be change both in what happens before and after decision-making meetings and in the way that the meetings themselves are organised. There needs to be greater flexibility in making the process accessible and responsive to the ways in which children like to communicate, and in tailoring the process to the needs of individual children.

As Grimshaw and Sinclair note in relation to the greater presence of young people at reviews,

> the routine fact of their attendance should not be taken as a sign of participation. There is a sense in which their attendance has become an administrative norm rather than something that has led to

changes in the meeting format.... Further thought needs to be given to new ways in which young people can be given a more central, informed and comfortable role in the review process.

(1997, p. 167)

They also said:

The review process seems governed by the assumption that, with some exceptions, attenders approach meetings on a reasonably equal footing and that fair and open discussion can be generated with little prompting. The avoidance of undue formality in discussions seems to be intended to support that approach. But it is one thing to remove artificial barriers to communication; it is quite another to promote discussion in ways that maximise calm and knowledgeable participation by children and parents.... For young people the meeting can never be simply a business-like discussion about 'what to do', no matter how informally this is discussed. To them, it is often more about the underlying question of 'What kind of person am I?' or 'What kind of person do others think I am?' Meetings are successful only if they find ways of recognising the unique position of young people who attend.

(1997, p. 166)

Another way to look at it is this. The relative formality of the 'official' decision-making arrangements, and their lack of connection with the everyday texture of children's lives or with the ways in which children and families are used to resolving issues, make it hard for children to engage fully with them. Changing this depends on making the process more child-friendly in two ways. First, getting the process right *around* the meeting – which means key adults making relationships with children, spending time getting to know their concerns, explaining what is happening and what the options are, and giving support through the meeting and feedback afterwards. A lot of this is being done, and where it is done children's participation seems to be more successful. Second, getting the process right at the meeting itself – introducing more flexibility in arrangements, using methods of discussion that are more in tune with children's ways of expressing themselves and dealing with things, opening up the process to children's own agendas and concerns. This is more of a challenge, but there are some signs that it may be beginning to happen.

The location of decision-making

Sinclair and Grimshaw (1997) suggest that the review should be redefined as a continuing process rather than a single meeting, a process that may incorporate a series of discussions between different people. They point out that the Department of Health guidance (1991a) appears to edge towards such a view, but then to withdraw. The benefits for children's involvement of losing the obsession with the single meeting as constituting a review are potentially considerable. The process could be opened up to more relaxed styles of communication and to discussions at times and places that children might find more comfortable; and some of the problems caused by conflict and misunderstanding could be avoided.

However, there may be a danger that if reviews are separated out in this way then children will find themselves excluded from the process at just the point where important decisions are likely to be taken. It is therefore important that efforts are made to make every part of the process accessible to children. I would argue that this includes making the process open to children's own agendas; to their definitions of what is important, what needs to be decided, what is at issue. Ryburn (1991) has pointed out that many care planning meetings proceed as if the participants believed (a) that social workers must know better than clients what is in the clients' interests and (b) that adults must know better than children what is in the children's interests. Once stated, such assumptions are hard to sustain.

In this respect adults, including professionals, may need to think carefully about where their own interests lie. One view is that there is a community of interest in the successful outcome of decision-making processes and in the pursuit of the 'best interests' of children. On this view it is also in both children's and adults' interests that the process of decision-making should be agreeable, even enjoyable. It may be that in making, for instance, care review meetings 'child-friendly' we may also make them 'people-friendly'; no one likes to be bored, embarrassed or mystified. The other view is that children's and adults' interests are in some way opposed, and that the outcomes that children might achieve if they were to be successfully empowered are outcomes that adults would strive to avoid. On this reading adults may want to keep the process of decision-making securely in their control and relatively inaccessible to children. The issue then becomes one of power, and concepts from political theory and political sociology become highly relevant to an understanding of what is going on: for instance, power itself, representation and participation. In a seminal piece of work at the end of the 1960s, Bachrach and Baratz (1970) developed the concept of *nondecision-making*. Taking Schattschneider's (1960) notion of 'mobilization of bias' which they define as 'a set of predominant values, beliefs, myths, rituals, and institutional procedures ("rules of the game") that operate systematically and consistently to the benefit of certain persons and groups at the expense of others', they argue that 'the primary method for sustaining a given mobilization of bias is nondecision-making' (Bachrach and Baratz 1970, pp. 43–4).

Bachrach and Baratz focus on 'nondecisions' imposed through the direct use of power including force, or through the intentional use of rules and procedures to suppress dissent and challenge. In less obviously political contexts such as the one we are dealing with, it may be that subtler processes are at work, in which the conventional arrangements for making decisions serve to exclude certain issues or to *take for granted* certain aspects of the situation, without anyone really thinking about it.[1] The effect will still be to maintain the status quo, and therefore – according to an interests-based analysis – to serve the interests of those who are gainers from the status quo – in this case adults. Interests are complex things, however, and it may be that for any party the status quo is meeting some needs and failing to satisfy others.

Bachrach and Baratz's focus is also on 'key issues' that involve 'a demand for enduring transformation in both the manner in which values are allocated in the polity in question and the value-allocation itself' (1970, p. 48). However, there may be more than one way in which we can use the concept of nondecisions to help understand what happens when children are invited to take part in decisions about their 'welfare'. Nondecisions could include issues excluded from the planning process because they are resolved elsewhere – perhaps without participation; it could also include things that are taken for granted in families and not subject to discussion or negotiation. We can explore how specific issues which children would want to raise are intentionally excluded from the decision-making arena, as an example of adult oppression of children. Alternatively we can look at how a range of issues which children might want to raise are simply not seen by the decision-making process, with the result that its focus is narrower and its outcomes less beneficial than they might otherwise be. In a sense one is a class analysis, the other a liberal one which assumes that all parties want the same ends. It may be that both analyses have their uses.

Rights and relationships

Although 'manipulation' is a term often applied by the powerful to the powerless, it is arguable that it is more correctly applicable in reverse. At any rate it can be extremely easy for adults to manipulate children. It is important that alongside an approach to planning and reviewing that emphasises relationships and forms of communication that are sensitive and enjoyable, there is also a greater stress on children's rights to participate, to have the support of friends or advocates, and to challenge decisions with which they do not agree. There can be a tension in work to involve vulnerable children in difficult or complex decisions, between an approach based on sensitive casework and the building of relationships of trust, and one based on children knowing their rights and being encouraged to use them. In my view there is no fundamental contradiction between the two; on the contrary, a combination of both approaches is needed if we are to empower children to take an effective part in the planning of their lives.

It is interesting to compare children's involvement in formal decision-making processes and what goes on in families. In Chapter 5 we saw how the state is reluctant to adopt policies which might risk undermining conventional power relationships in families, and I suggested that one problem with increasing the involvement of children in decisions when they are in state care may be that it represents a challenge to such relationships. However, the reality now appears more complex. Family decision-making processes are characterised by informality and intimacy. People know each other well and have many opportunities for casual conversation alongside other activities. On the other hand, rules and expectations vary from one household to another and these differences may not be made explicit. We found that children's autonomy and their ability to have a say were highly dependent on the values, skills and 'style' of the adults in the household – especially foster mothers. In contrast, the social services system uses decision-making processes which are relatively formal and impersonal. The key process is the planning or review meeting, which is usually a gathering of between four and seven people who are not always well known to each other or to the child. The agenda for the meeting is to some extent pre-determined, and the time for discussion is structured and limited. On the other hand there is often a degree of clarity about the purpose of the meeting and who should be there, and children may be aware that they have a right to take part and to challenge the decisions that are made.

Many of the children seen in this research were aware that they had a right to have their voice heard by those in charge of their care. Some of them knew how to challenge decisions they did not agree with or to make a complaint about their treatment, although these were a minority. None the less, compared to the majority of children living with their own families, they had a high level of awareness of their own rights and of the limits on adults' power over them. For instance, they knew that their carers were not allowed to hit them. It may be that the key to empowering children in the care system lies in the successful interweaving of an approach based on rights with one based on care and relationship. If the strength of family decision-making lies in the ability to take opportunities for discussion at times that suit those involved, including the child, and in the use of relationships of intimacy and trust, and the strength of official processes can be in their clarity and accountability and in the awareness of rights, perhaps there is some scope for synthesising the best of both processes. Perhaps review meetings really could be held around the breakfast table; and perhaps children living in families, whether foster families or 'natural' families, could be made more aware of their right to have a say.[2] In this way life for children who are 'looked after' may become a bit more like life can be for children in their own families, when it works well. At the same time, perhaps this 'disadvantaged' group can provide a model for progress towards citizenship for other children.

Children in most of the world have no legal right to take part in decision-making within families, although there are some exceptions.[3] It is even debatable whether the United Nations Convention implies any such right, referring explicitly as it does only to judicial and administrative proceedings. The Scarman judgement refers to a child's increasing ability to determine his or her own destiny, but does not speak directly of the right to express a view before reaching the stage of autonomy – although it is arguable that it implies such a right.[4] Lansdown (1994, 1995) has argued that children ought to have a right to a say in decisions in families, such as the decision to move house. My research into children's participation in decisions when they are in the care of the state exposes the illogicality and impracticality of giving children the right to take part in decisions about where they should live, and not giving them the same right to take part in decisions about their everyday lives. Experience in Scandinavia seems to show that requiring parents to consult children before making decisions that affect them does not lead to aggressive policing of families or to litigiousness among children – any more than does the outlawing of corporal punishment. What it can perhaps do is establish a benchmark or a social standard, and give children a message about what they are entitled to expect. It is intrusive, from the point of view of defenders of family privacy; but we saw in Chapter 5 that the state does have a legitimate interest in how children are treated in families, and that it makes sense to see parental authority as a trust rather than as an automatic right.

We have also seen that children *learn* to take part in decisions, rather than simply acquiring the ability at a predetermined age. Our research therefore lends support to the view that the family can be a school of democracy (see Elshtain 1989). Pateman (1970) has shown how participation underpins real democracy, and demonstrates the value of participation in political and industrial settings in giving a sense of efficacy and in political socialisation – aside from the fact that it may produce better decisions. To return to the question I asked in the introduction: if children cannot be heard in decisions about their own lives, what hope is there of them being heard in decisions about social, economic and political purposes? There are those who would argue that they do not have a place in all these decisions, either because they are incompetent or because they simply have no place in certain kinds of discussion – nothing of value to contribute. I want therefore to conclude with some reflections first on competence and then on citizenship.

Situating children's competence

In Chapter 3 I discussed children's cognitive and social competence in terms of a psychological discourse based on testing and comparison. There is also a sociological discourse in which the different reading of children's social competence offered by Solberg (1990), James (1993, 1995) and others has begun to stimulate a real exploration of the nature of competence and how it is constructed. In their introduction to a recent collection, Hutchby and Moran-Ellis (1998) describe competence as an *achievement* of children, as *situated* and as *negotiated*. They put forward 'a picture of childhood as a dynamic arena of social activity involving struggles for power, contested meanings and negotiated relationships, rather than the linear picture of development and maturation made popular by traditional sociology and developmental psychology' (p. 9). Their fundamental argument is that

> the social competence of children is to be seen as a *practical achievement*: that is, it is not something which is accorded to children by

adults, like a right, and can thus be redefined or removed. Rather, social competence is seen as something children work at possessing in their own right, the display of which is an active, agentic achievement. But it is an achievement that is bounded by structural features of the milieux in which children live their lives.

(p. 16)

Christensen (1998) shows how competence is negotiated in the specific context of children's use of medication. Children who have to use powerful medication on a regular basis may achieve a definition of themselves as competent, in a way that distinguishes them from other children who continue to be seen as unable to be trusted with responsibility for handling medication. This echoes Solberg's (1990) account of how 'bigness' is negotiated in Norwegian families (see Chapter 2).

'Competence' of course may present itself in many different ways. Silverman et al. (1998) show how adolescents' silence and unresponsiveness in parent-teacher interviews can be understood as a highly competent strategy for 'avoiding implication in the collaboratively accomplished adult moral universe' (p. 220). Hutchby and Moran-Ellis say that 'competence cannot be separated from the structural contexts in which it is displayed or negotiated' (p. 16). This echoes ideas put forward by Lee (1998). Starting from Jenks' idea of the *ambiguity* of childhood, Lee argues that this ambiguity arises from the search for a *generalised* answer to the question whether children are the same as adults or different, and that it is more productive to look for *situated* accounts of what children are like. He applies this to the instance of a court deciding whether a child is competent to give evidence, where he suggests that 'a mythical image of "maturity" as a stable, general property is necessary to tack the credibility of the court together' (p. 7). This allows us 'to efface the sociality of evidential practices and to ward off the creeping suspicion that they are rather more arbitrary, situated and ultimately less reliable, than we would like to think' (p. 8).[5]

This sociological account of competence has points of contact with some of the ideas found in my review of psychological theory and research, particularly those of Vygotsky, Merleau-Ponty, and Richards and Light.[6] It also strongly echoes some of my own findings, where both in the process of doing research with children and in the information collected about decision-making processes it appeared that children's 'competence' depended largely on how these social processes were understood and managed by the adults and children involved.

Children who had the experience of (and practice in) taking part in decisions were more 'competent'; children who had good information and honest explanations were more 'competent'; children who were able to communicate in ways that they found congenial were more 'competent'; and children whom adults believed to be competent were more 'competent'. Competence is much less a property of the child, and much more a specific feature of a particular interaction. The implications for policy of taking this different view of competence are not trivial. If we accept that children, like other members of society, should be able to participate as much as they can in decisions that affect them, the fundamental question in practice becomes, not *whether* a particular child or class of children is competent to take part in particular decision-making processes, but rather *how* those processes can be designed so as to elicit and enable children's competence. Underlying this must be the recognition of the child's *right* to take part: as Verhellen puts it, 'the recognition of self-determination in children is essential in order to make them more competent and vice versa' (1992, p. 81).

Children and citizenship

I referred much earlier to Qvortrup's argument that children have been excluded from the *oikos*, in part because the *oikos* has been redefined in such a way that it excludes children. This is a development of arguments he made previously about the economic value of children and children's work.[7] The implication of Qvortrup's argument, and that of Oldman referred to earlier, is that children's value to society in the sense of their economic activity is unrecognised. If the 'problem' of childhood is that children are not seen as contributors, are perceived by themselves and by adults as dependent and recipient rather than independent and contributing, then Qvortrup's argument is that this is based on a fundamental misunderstanding of the place of children in the political economy. A further implication is that a view of society that fails to see children's substantial contribution is seriously incomplete and even fundamentally flawed.

This echoes two other readings of the relationship between children and adults that I want to weave into this final discussion. One is John O'Neill's exploration of citizenship, in which he argues that a *social contract* view of society which tends to exclude children also tends to exclude much important social activity in the area of welfare and caring for each other, and that a *social covenant* is a better expression of the relatedness of people and their claims to a part in society. O'Neill's argument is underdeveloped in relation to the part children can play in a 'covenant' society, and from some of his remarks I suspect that he is resisting its full implications for children's lives (O'Neill 1998 and discussion at conference). The other reading is Minow's (1986) intervention in the rights debate, in which she suggests that a reason why adult rights may not easily fit children is because the account of adult rights used is a mistaken one.[8] Minow argues that a stress on the rights of an individual against society leaves out all the ways in which our interests are connected and bound up with each other, and that an account of rights that includes this connectedness will have less difficulty in accommodating both adults and children.[9] What is implicit in both these arguments is that social contract theory has perhaps developed in order to answer a question – 'Why should I not do exactly as I want?' – that is less interesting and important than other questions – like 'How can we live together?' Just as our exploration of the conflict between children's rights and their best interests suggested that an apparent irreconcilability could perhaps be finessed by a use of dialogue, understanding and relationship, so do O'Neill's covenant and Minow's 'rights for the next generation' seek a new synthesis of the apparent conflict between individual freedom as a risky business and childhood as a time of dependency.

So is there a form of citizenship that can include children, and is it perhaps a better form of citizenship because it is inclusive? Cockburn (1998) has begun the attempt to modify Marshall's account of citizenship to one that can accommodate children. In principle the concept has real potential for an understanding of how children might find a place in the polity that reflects their real place in the economy; but as Lorenz (1998) has argued, a great deal of work has to be done to make it a working reality. On the one hand, children's needs for guidance and protection do not disappear because they are given rights. On the other, history offers few examples of powerful groups giving up power without a struggle – even when they are shown that they could benefit thereby – and many examples of them justifying their power by reference to the needs, the dependence, and the incompetence of those subject to them. I would argue that the attempt to bring children into the polity as active participants is an important one and worth making; that it depends in part on challenging their privatisation in the family; but that it may depend also on extending the informality and person-specificity of family activity to a wider social world.

Final comments

We have moved from considering the relationships between children and adults at an individual level to considering them at a societal level. In my earlier discussion of methodology in terms of Layder's 'research map', I suggested in effect that this microsociological research needed to be located in a macrosociological framework. Qvortrup (1990, 1998) and Alanen (1995, 1998) have convincingly argued that the concentration on ethnography in the 'new paradigm' needs to be supported by a development of 'macro' research and theory. In this respect it is again interesting to think about the differences and similarities between children looked after by the state and other children. We have noted how children looked after are subject to multiple 'parenting', with all that implies not only in instability and unpredictability but also in the complexity of decision-making processes; and we have also noted how, in the United Kingdom at least, they do have legal rights to take part in decision-making that are denied to children who remain in their own families. We have seen how children looked after by the state are different from other children in that they are often from especially disadvantaged backgrounds. They are also in a peripheral or marginal situation as children who are not securely located in a family, in a society which takes 'the family' as normal.[10] Although an explicit aim of state care since the war has been to 'normalise' their situation, it remains a stigmatised one.

In some ways, then, studying children who are 'looked after' has the appeal and the drawbacks of the extreme case, and is open to questions of how representative they are of children in general. The problem with this perspective, as I said in the introduction to this book, is that it assumes a concept of 'children in general' which is highly suspect. The children who took part in my research are representative of themselves and worthy of study in their own right. They are also highly representative of children aged eight to twelve who are looked after by local authorities in England and Wales.[11] How far they are representative of other children is in some ways a secondary question. However, as children living in families or in the care of adults, and negotiating the multiple transitions between domestic and more public settings, they have a great deal in common with most other children living in Britain and similar countries. Children and their situations vary in a multitude of ways, and the differences between children who are 'looked after' and those who are not represent only one dimension of this variation.

Although my research began by looking at what happens in the process of planning and making decisions for children in the care system, it has led us to more general questions about how decisions are made in families and about the relationships between adults and children. There is a need now for ethnographic research that tracks more closely the processes of negotiation, discussion and decision-making both in families and in official settings.[12] In a time when decisions about children's welfare are highly contested both in public and in private arenas, and when everyone seems to have a view on what is in children's interests, it is even more important that children's own voices are included effectively in those debates. When the patterns of children's everyday lives are changing dramatically, it is important to understand how those patterns are determined and what part children have to play in the process. At a time when politicians are proposing to introduce curfews for children – in other words are suggesting that it might be an offence for a child simply to be in a 'public' place at the wrong time – the question of what is a child's place, in the world and in the family, is one that deserves our attention. If we are to understand these things better, we need theories and research that are based on respect for what children themselves might have to say.

Notes

Chapter 2

1 The English translation was originally published by Jonathan Cape in 1962, but all page references here are to the Penguin edition. 'Idea' is actually 'sentiment' in the original.

2 A similar observation is made by Mount (1982).

3 Le Roy Ladurie (1980) also provides evidence for the regard which parents had for their children in the middle ages: 'it was usual for mothers to nurse their own babies in Montaillou, as in similar villages. ... the birth of a child could become a matter of care and anxiety. But, culturally and emotionally, it was still felt as a fundamental happiness' (pp. 208–9).

4 In this he received considerable support from Plumb (1975). Plumb makes a great deal of the fact that in the eighteenth century books began to be produced for the entertainment of children. As with Mount's comment on painting, this may of course tell us as much about the development of publishing as about the development of childhood.

5 Qvortrup (1998) recently put it more robustly: 'Although several righteous and fussy historians have attempted to kill Ariès by showing – probably correctly – that he failed to take on board a lot of differences between families and children, they are likely to soon end up in oblivion, while Ariès survives because he had a fruitful methodological point.'

6 Kennedy (1998) has recently suggested that de Mause's categories may be more useful if applied within historical periods rather than across them, recognising that elements of different types of parent–child relationship can be co-present.

7 'What is being postulated for the late sixteenth and early seventeenth centuries is a society in which a majority of the individuals who composed it found it very difficult to establish close emotional ties to any person. Children were often neglected, brutally treated, and even killed; many adults treated each other with suspicion and hostility; affect was low, and hard to find. To an anthropologist, there would be nothing very surprising about such a society, which closely resembles the Mundugumor in New Guinea in the twentieth century, as described by Margaret Mead. The lack of a unique mother figure in the first two years of life, the constant loss of close relatives, siblings, parents, nurses and friends through premature death, the physical imprisonment of the infant in tight swaddling-clothes in early months, and the deliberate breaking of the child's will all contributed to a "psychic numbing" which created many adults whose primary responses to others were at best a calculating indifference and at worst a mixture of suspicion and hostility, tyranny and submission, alienation and rage' (Stone 1979, p. 80).

8 Shorter's faith in modernity and expertise, and his contempt for ordinary mothers, are remarkable: 'Now by the late eighteenth century, parents knew, at least in a sort of abstract way, that letting new-born children stew in their own excrement or feeding them pap from the second month onwards were

harmful practices. For the network of medical personnel in Europe had by this time extended sufficiently to put interested mothers within earshot of sensible advice' (1977, p. 203). This is presumably the 'sensible' medical advice that at that time included fulminations against masturbation (and surgery to prevent it), or in our own century rigid feeding schedules and recommendations to start toilet training within weeks of birth. See Plumb (1975), Hardyment (1983).

9   For a devastating critique both of Stone's methods and of his view of English history, see the review by Macfarlane (1979).

10   See also Laslett and Wall (1972), Laslett (1983). More balanced accounts are also to be found in Goody (1983), Herlihy (1985), and Houlbrooke (1984), although Houlbrooke was disadvantaged by being unaware of Pollock's work.

11   Interpretation can be a very personal business. Where Stone takes the sending of children away from home as evidence of lack of care, Laslett sees the opposite: 'This is one of the few glimpses we can get into the quality of the emotional life of the family at this time, for it shows that parents may have been unwilling to submit children of their own to the discipline of work at home' (p. 13). Many years earlier Hartley and Elliot (1928) surveyed the fourteenth-century English records and concluded: 'Beyond the usual "schoolchild" records and the inevitable birch-rods, throughout this century, we have found nothing but gentleness for children' (p. 29). Other historians have looked at the same evidence and found nothing but brutality.

12   A few references occur again and again in discussions of the history of childhood. One is to Susannah Wesley's advice to 'break his will betimes', although it is sometimes attributed to John Wesley; see Newson and Newson (1974) for an accurate quotation. Another is the story of John, the 'marshal of England', whose young son was hostage to King Stephen and threatened with execution. '"What recks it me of the child," replied the good nobleman, "have I not still the anvils and the hammers wherewith to forge finer ones?"' (source on this occasion Bloch 1965, p. 135). Most commentators cite this as incontrovertible evidence of the callousness and lack of feeling of the period. Shahar, however, offers a completely different interpretation of this story, suggesting that both sides knew that the child would not be executed and that the whole incident was an exercise in bravado (Shahar 1990, pp. 119–20; Shahar's interpretation follows that of Duby in *Guillaume le Marechal*).

13   Though not necessarily beginning with the well-off. Many schools were established for poor children and subsequently colonized by the better off (see Pinchbeck and Hewitt, 1969).

14   Skolnick (1975) suggests that 'The major contrasts between premodern societies and our own focus on the middle-aged child – the seven-to-twelve-year-old. In a worldwide and historical perspective, our culture is decidedly unusual in that children of this age are not involved in productive work' (p. 65).

15   Le Roy Ladurie (1980) comments 'From birth to two years of age the documents refer to a child as *infans*, or more usually *filius* or *filia*. From two to twelve years, the word *puer* was applied generally. Towards thirteen or fourteen at the latest, the records switch to the term *adolescens* or *juvenis*' (p. 215).

This coincided with employment (in the family or as apprentice) and with the age of reason.

16 Shahar adds: 'The childhood of those destined to become knights was brief, in the sense that their professional training began in childhood and they became involved at a very early age in the activities of the adults of their social group. However, contemporary opinion was not only aware of the "childish" nature of children, but also distinguished between young men who had just completed their training and adult knights, and this distinction finds expression in literature' (p. 212). See also Bloch (1965).

17 This connects in an uncanny way with Piaget's stage of 'concrete operations', despite the fact that Piaget's conception has been criticised as being culturally specific (see next chapter). It is hard to escape the conclusion that there is something that happens during the process of maturation to which these very different historical settings are responding in their different ways.

18 Qvortrup (1998) has talked of the Greek 'oikos' which united household and wider economy having now become separated, producing children's consequent detachment from the economy.

19 Of course, some of the rights in question were only granted to most adults in the nineteenth century.

20 The period beyond twelve or fourteen, variously described as 'youth' or 'adolescence', was seen in the middle ages as distinct both from childhood and from adulthood, and the extent to which people in this age group could exercise adult rights was extremely variable. For instance in medieval Tuscany, according to Shahar, emancipation sometimes took place as early as twelve although the legal age of majority was twenty five (Shahar 1990, pp. 226–8; see also Ariès 1979). This of course echoes the position in contemporary Britain where a young person can marry and be employed in full time work at 16, but is not fully entitled to social security benefits until 25.

21 The Children Act 1989, Section 105(1): '"child" means ... a person under the age of eighteen.' United Nations (1989), Article 1: 'For the purposes of the present Convention, a child means every human being below the age of eighteen years unless, under the law applicable to the child, majority is attained earlier.'

22 Whereas historical accounts of childhood sometimes have an underlying purpose of showing our own practices in a flattering light, cross-cultural studies often seem to have the opposite purpose of offering an example of a better way of rearing children than that followed in the modern affluent West; for example, Turnbull (1984), Liedloff (1975). Both are popular accounts, the first by a professional anthropologist, the second not. Both are also based on a fairly jaundiced view of Western child-rearing: Turnbull uses his own emotionally frozen upper-class English upbringing as a comparison, while Liedloff appears to believe that whatever idiocies are written in baby-care manuals are followed slavishly by Western mothers: 'It may be the current fashion to let the baby cry until its heart is broken ... or as one recent school of thought had it, to leave the baby in an emotional vacuum, untouched except for absolute necessity and then never shown any facial expression, no pleasure, no smiles, no admiration, only a blank stare. Whatever it is, the young mothers read and obey ... '. (p. 32).

23 Benedict in her study of Pueblo Indians praised the permissiveness of Zuni parents and maintained that as a result Zuni children were rarely disobedient. However, a Chinese anthropologist studied the same people and reported that responsibility for discipline in this matrilineal society is widely shared, so that children may find themselves being reprimanded or mocked for misconduct by any adult in the village: (Li 1937, cited in Farb 1971). The Zuni eventually became rather tired of being visited by anthropologists (Giddens 1993).

24 Brazelton 1977; Kagan 1977; Ainsworth 1977; LeVine 1977.

25 Hallden (1991) looked at the implicit psychological concepts used by a group of rural working-class parents in Sweden, and again found that the dominant perspective on child development was one of an individual unfolding. Coexisting with this there was also a sub-dominant view of 'the child as project', requiring parents to prepare the child for the demands of the world.

26 'Out of the vast amount of scientific data of recent years, two facts stand out in clear relief. One is that the foundations of human personality are laid in early childhood; the second, that the chief molder of personality thus becomes the family' (Bossard and Boll 1966, p. 67).

27 See also Dreitzel (1973).

28 They also connect it with the understanding of the ways in which the modern Western framing of childhood is exported to contexts in the 'developing' world where its lack of fit with political and economic and cultural realities may produce considerable discomfort (Ennew 1986; Boyden 1990).

Chapter 3

1 This is not necessarily so, although the common equation of developmental psychology with child psychology tends to imply that it is (see Burman 1994). It is perfectly possible to study developmental changes throughout the life course without artificially separating childhood and adulthood; and the differences between children, and the differences between adults, may sometimes be more interesting than what divides one from the other.

2 Shotter (1974) describes human development as 'intended' and argues that this characteristic distinguishes it from development in other animals.

3 Some (though not all) of the recent criticisms of Piaget had been made many years previously by Isaacs (1930).

4 See for instance Hirschfeld and Gelman (1994). These theories have been supported by studies of information-processing in which sophisticated computer programmes are used to model the operation of the brain in response to inputs over time.

5 'To some people it seems that cognitive developmental research in the US has been measuring years of schooling, using age as its proxy variable.' Laboratory of Comparative Human Cognition, quoted in Rogoff et al. (1984).

6 Skolnick (1976), in discussing changes in the five-to-seven period, suggests a link with the myelinization of many areas of the brain, which increases speed of mental functioning.

7 Rose (1976) suggests that the brain continues to develop well into adult life, and that the changes during childhood and adolescence to some extent match the Piagetian stages. More recently Gazzaniga (1992) has related the establishment of the cerebral cortex by age three to the beginning of development of a theory of mind. Although the cortex is basically established at this stage, 'up into the teens, new cortical networks are being generated' (p. 60). Gazzaniga suggests that the physical development of the brain is partly directed by the brain's own electrical activity, and gives the example of stereopsis, where the brain requires environmental inputs of a particular kind to develop in a particular way. However, he argues that the 'evidence is meager' for any direct effect of learning or experience in changing brain organisation. Sacks (1995) takes the contrary view. Case et al. (1988) have attempted to restate the Piagetian framework in terms which take account of more recent research and in particular of domain theory. The attempt is not totally convincing; much of what they say is either questionable or obvious, and the overall scheme is probably far more rigid than the evidence warrants. Chandler and Chapman (1991) argue that many of the disputes around stages of acquisition of competence are a result of confusion about what is competence and what are the criteria for competence.

8 Campbell and Olson (1990) are sceptical of some of the 'demonstrations' of early conceptual abilities, and suggest that by removing much of the difficulty from a task they may prevent it from being a real test of thinking. However, they admit to being 'jaundiced', and a more balanced account of what is left of the 'move to operational thinking' is given by Meadows (1993).

9 In fact it has been argued that it is the demands of social interaction, rather than those of technical achievement, which have provided the evolutionary impetus for the growth in capacity of the human brain; Bruner (1972), Gazzaniga (1992).

10 Ainsworth later added a fourth category of *disorganised* attachment, but it has since been shown that these cases are better understood as disorganised examples of one of the other patterns (Bowlby 1988). See, however, the criticisms of attachment research made for example by Schaffer (1989, 1991).

11 Elsewhere she has argued that parental responsiveness to the child is the key factor in producing obedience (Ainsworth, Bell and Stayton 1974).

12 Harré (1974) has argued that the 'attachment mode' is actually a passing phase of no significance for adult life; that what is striking about adult social interaction is how little it has to do with emotional bonds, and how much with ritual; and that in essence there are two worlds of childhood, the 'autonomous' world of attachment and a 'precursor' world of play and negotiation which has much greater similarity with adult patterns. Almost certainly he overstates the case, but it is an important argument.

13 For an alternative view see Schieffelin and Ochs (1983), Pye (1986).

14 Rogers (1978) suggests that this awareness begins much earlier than has been thought. He discusses changes in the perception of others in terms of *attribution theory*, and suggests that the tendency of young children not to describe others in 'dispositional' terms is to do with the causal analysis of behaviour and an understanding of *intention*, and is related to difficulty in processing complex information. He also argues that Piaget's study of

understanding of intentions and consequences is based on confusing examples; with a different design Rogers (1978) and others have produced judgements in terms of intention from five- and six-year-olds. They appear to be less good at judging others' intentions, especially adults, and expect adults to make judgements in terms of consequences – which may of course be highly rational!

15 A study by Bannister and Agnew suggested that children aged nine had much clearer ideas of themselves as personalities than did five-year-olds. The research was based on getting children to talk about themselves, and then asking them four months later to identify the statements which they had made and to explain how they selected them. The older children were more accurate and used different strategies, based on the psychological appropriateness of the statements. Rosenberg studied self-concept across a wider age-range, from eight to eighteen. A sample of children were interviewed about their view of themselves, and the answers appeared to divide into broad categories which corresponded to the ages of the children. Younger children described themselves in terms of 'objective facts, overt achievements, manifested preferences, possessions, physical attributes, and membership categories ... characteristics that could potentially be described by others.' Older children begin to use descriptions of traits of character, followed later by interpersonal characteristics, while those in later adolescence are more likely to talk about their internal world. Source: Harter (1983).

16 In many parts of the world, of course, children of this age are economically self-supporting, in the sense that their direct economic contribution is at least equal to their consumption.

17 See in particular Freud (1973), Klein (1975), Fairbairn (1952). Psychoanalytical accounts have tended to be based on clinical experience rather than experimental work, and have for this reason been subject to some scepticism. However, there may be more than one way of being scientific, and the explanatory or heuristic value of such approaches is sometimes attested in practice.

18 Miller (1987a) has used clinical and observed material to argue that the concentration on 'psychic reality' or 'phantasy' ignores the reality of what happens to children, which is frequently if not universally abusive or damaging.

19 Bruner (1992) has pointed out how the entire thrust of contemporary psychological investigations of teaching and learning is premised on the desirability of producing enquiring, challenging minds, which 'society' generally might regard as less than desirable.

20 The concepts of external and internal locus of control of reinforcement are explained, and the early research reviewed, in Rotter (1966). Measures have been developed which appear to have a high degree of reliability and validity, and variations along a continuum from high internal to high external locus of control appear to relate both to situational factors and to characteristics of personality. Rotter suggests that both extremes can be regarded as pathological, but that an internal locus of control is associated with more successful functioning and in general appears to be adaptive to the demands of modern Western culture. For a more recent summary, see Maccoby (1980). For a recent application of the distinction to well-being in

adolescence, see also Winefield et al. (1992). See also the learning theories of Bandura (1977) and Seligman's (1975) concept of 'learned helplessness'.

21   See also Furth (1978), McGurk and Glachan (1988).

22   Stevens interprets this in Piagetian terms, although a Vygotskyan analysis might be more appropriate: 'The expansion of ideas was rapid, given the right stimulus' (p. 95).

23   See also Tulkin and Konner (1973), Cazden (1970).

24   But a robust child-centred approach of the kind outlined so beautifully by Donaldson (1978), rather than the vapid variety caricatured with depressing regularity by current political commentators on education.

25   Fahlberg (1994) in the wisest of her wise books, tells the story of a girl who before coming into care had the responsibility for caring for her younger sister. A key task for her new carers was to enable her to hand over that responsibility to them but in a way which showed that they valued what she had done and what she had learned from it, and indeed what she had to teach them about the younger child's needs.

26   There is another account of 'competence' and its meaning to be found in recent sociological discussions, which starts with quite different assumptions from the psychological account, although it echoes for example Light, Vygotsky and Merleau-Ponty. I refer to this account again in Chapter 12.

Chapter 4

1   Not 'a slogan in search of a definition', as it is sometimes quoted to rather different effect. Rodham's own subsequent career has had its ups and downs, but her phrase lives on.

2   The text of the 1959 UN Declaration is given in Aiken and LaFollette (1980) and in Newell (1991), pp. 182–3. As Young (1980) points out, 'even the acknowledgement of all the rights set forth in the *UN Declaration* would not be incompatible with the prerogative parents typically have to determine what will serve the best interests of their children, excepting those occasions where even "parental rights" are set aside in favour of the state and its appointed agencies. Worse still, however, accepting the *UN Declaration* or like at its face value would provide support for such present realities as: children (and youths) being restricted as legal agents, being compelled to attend schools, having little or no freedom of travel or association of their own devising, having little choice over the fundamentals of their life styles and, within some limits, albeit rather broad ones, being dealt with by parents and other parties in ways that would in adult affairs constitute actionable assaults' (p. 179).

3   Wringe (1996) argues that the social contract implies that there must be some benefit to an individual from membership of society and that therefore 'if there are any rights at all, then there are also welfare rights, so that those rights claimed in Articles 6, 24 and 26–29 of the 1989 Convention on Children's Rights are not mere appeals to charity but are entitled to the same urgency of implementation as those others which claim protection from oppression and abuse' (p. 22).

4   It is also linked with the arguments of Gilligan (1982, 1990) referred to in Chapter 3.

5 Palmeri writes that 'interfering with a child's liberty should be as serious a matter as interfering with an adult's liberty' (1980, p. 113).

6 We often argue on the assumption that adult rights hinge on the ability to choose to do harm to ourselves without interference. In fact this ability is limited in all kinds of ways in most if not all societies. Suicide is forbidden and actively prevented; seatbelts and crash helmets are required by law; dangerous working conditions are outlawed (see reference to Franklin later in this chapter). Most of us would probably seek to prevent a friend – or a stranger – from throwing themselves over a cliff, by force if necessary, even though they were rational and lucid.

7 Cohen's philosophical justification for giving full adult rights to children is better formulated than the arguments of Holt and Farson, although he probably relies too much on the proposal of a system of 'child agents' to overcome the practical objections. Houlgate (1980) also uses utilitarianism as a foundation for children having equal rights, mainly in relation to the criminal justice system.

8 Elsewhere (Worsfold 1980) he argues that the fact that children may make mistaken decisions is part of the inevitable price to be paid for giving them rights.

9 Locke, *Second Treatise of Government* (cited in Feinberg, 1980).

10 In recent years two British authors have attempted comprehensive reviews of the arguments for children's rights; Archard (1993) and Wringe (1981). I have relied heavily on Archard's account in this chapter and made little use of Wringe's, not so much because Archard is more up to date as because he has a clearer position and better logic. Wringe has some useful arguments – he gives cogent arguments for not equating rights with powers, duties or claims, argues convincingly that rights may be justifiably overruled and still remain as rights, points out that different sorts of rights can have different implications, and that moral rights are *not* parasitic on legal rights but 'may be both characterised and justified independently' (p. 45). He distinguishes helpfully between rights as liberties, claim rights of freedom, rights of participation, special rights based on transactions, roles and relationships, and welfare rights, and argues that if children do not have rights of liberty they cannot 'in any meaningful sense' have other rights. However, he takes a number of positions which seem at odds with his overall stance on children's rights, and he begs the question over age and reasonableness. Archard is more consistent and follows through his arguments better.

11 See also Wolfson (1992) who analyses justifications of rights based on 'project interests' and 'welfare interests' and concludes that neither is sufficient but both are necessary to a conception of rights.

12 In addition the example of 'street children' in many modern cities shows how children as young as seven or eight can be economically independent, even though they may lack legal rights or other benefits.

13 Archard objects to grounding children's right to vote on the fact that their interests are affected by the laws. He points out that this would include other groups, such as foreigners; and that it does not circumvent the competency argument because some measure of competence is required in order to promote ones interests effectively.

14 The reference is to Joint Working Party on Pregnant Schoolgirls and School-girl Mothers (1979).

15 See also Kitzinger (1990).

16 He gives the example of laws governing safety at work, although the laws requiring road users to wear seat-belts or crash-helmets might provide a more telling illustration.

17 A similar argument is used by Wolfson (1992) who suggests that an emphasis on 'welfare interests' should gradually give way to a stress on 'project interests'. In this way she attempts to provide a basis for an operational synthesis between rights and best interests. See the next chapter for further discussion.

18 Articles 19, 27, 28; Articles 15, 14, 13 and 12. Freeman argues that 'The ideological conflict between those who see children's rights in welfare terms and those who wish to promote a child's self-determination is still present in the Convention' (1992, p. 5). See Johnson (1992) and Marshall (1997) for discussions of how the two kinds of rights were articulated in the drafting process.

Chapter 5

1 Earlier they write: 'In many ways, the presumption of ownership, or at least of possession, is at the core of the liberal conception of the family and of parenthood. Imagine that a child is born in a hospital and is abducted from the nursery. When, a few hours, or days later, the child is found and returned to the parents, this is because he or she is regarded as "their" child. The baby is not the child of the "state", to be placed in a community nursery until the genitors, or perhaps others who might make better parents, are entrusted with caring for him or her. The baby is regarded as *belonging* to the parents' (p. 20.) They contrast this conventional view of the position of bio-logical parents with the status of adoptive parents who are subject to vetting; but the position of adoptive parents, once they have adopted, is precisely the same.

2 Lawyers tend to expect these concepts to fit a legal form, which may account for some mutual incomprehension between them and philosophers.

3 A similar view is expressed by the Department of Health in its introduction to the Children Act 1989: 'The Act uses the phrase "**parental responsibility**" to sum up the collection of duties, rights and authority which a parent has in respect of his [*sic*] child. That choice of words emphasises that the duty to care for the child and to raise him to moral, physical and emotional health is the fundamental task of parenthood and the only justification for the authority it confers' (Department of Health 1989b, p. 1).

4 Papadopoulos (1996) has shown how in Greece a strong cultural belief in the importance of 'the family' can coexist with minimal support for actual chil-dren in families.

5 The (often adverse) comparison of assumptions about state support for families in the UK and US with those in much of continental Europe is an abiding theme in discussions of family policy. Cannan (1992) looked at the develop-ment of family centres in Britain and how a service targeted at families who are not coping, and provided only as long as they are not coping, has grown at the

expense of – even on the ruins of – more general day care provision. In France, on the other hand, there appears to be an acceptance that ordinary families will need and expect a range of provision including day care in order to enable them to live normally. In Britain, she suggests, 'there is a long tradition of British individualism which opposes the family and the state, and limits state intervention to families with pathologies' (p. 142). She opposes this to European ideas of social *integration* which have the support of the Christian Democratic tradition as well as of the left, and gives as an example the shift whereby 'in most European countries the former welfare emphasis in daycare has given way to more open access since the 1970s' (p. 148).

6 For example, a recent comprehensive overview of policies toward children and families, numbering twenty contributors and four hundred pages, fails to mention children's rights, children's views, or anything that recognises children's subjectivity; Zigler, Kagan and Hall (1996). The comment in the Cleveland report that 'the child is a person and not an object of concern' (Butler-Sloss 1988) is often quoted, deservedly.

7 Since the 1970s there has been a discernible shift away from a universalist approach to child welfare. Cannan (1992) suggests that 'the relationship between the family and the state which was drawn in the late 1940s establishment of the welfare state may have been a strange interlude in the development of British social policy' (p. 144). Since then policy has reverted to a selective approach, with all that that means in terms of stigmatised service provision. As we shall see when we come to look at the 1989 Children Act, it possible to see some recent legislation as an attempt to hang on to elements of a universalist approach against all the odds.

8 Frost (1990) points out that 'rolling back the state' actually increases the need for intervention to protect children. In effect, he says, non-intervention and intervention are two sides of the same policy coin: 'the government, which has made a virtue of rolling back state support and coterminously boosting the independence of "the family", has also presided over the largest number of place of safety orders ever taken' (p. 38).

9 See also Ukviller (1979) who is firmly committed to parental autonomy in the face of arguments based on children's best interests.

10 None the less the argument that 'best interest' alone should not be a doorway for state intervention in families without some additional threshold is widely accepted. In England and Wales the Review of Child Care Law noted that 'taken to its logical conclusion, a simple "best interests" test would permit the state to intervene whenever it could show that the alternative arrangements proposed would serve the children's welfare better than those proposed by their parents ... it is important in a free society to maintain the rich diversity of lifestyles which is secured by permitting families a large measure of autonomy in the way in which they bring up their children.' (Quoted in Parker 1994.)

11 Elshtain (1989) questions whether there is a conflict between authority and obedience in the family and a democratic society. (Since Locke it has often been assumed that there is no connection between the two frameworks, but this seems too convenient.) Elshtain initially puts forward a strong case for parental authority: 'Family relations could not exist without family

authority, and these relations remain the best basis we know for creating human beings with a developed capacity to give authoritative allegiance to the background presumptions and principles of democratic society as adults' (1989, p. 63). However, she finds this position unsatisfactory because it contains a number of arbitrary elements – the recognition of only certain kinds of family, a valuing of obedience that begs the question. She attempts to modify the model to take account of ambiguities, but with only limited success.

12   On the other hand Carney (1992) takes issue with Seymour and argues for a broader view of the state's responsibilities based on social rights of citizenship.

13   The concept of socialisation appears to contain both of these assumptions in some measure, and one of the many things which that concept obscures is the need to pick the two assumptions apart in order to understand them more fully.

14   Where reference is made to the views of children, parents or significant others it is in this context. There is an interesting contrast between Section 1 of the 1989 Act, which makes the child's welfare the paramount consideration in court proceedings, and Section 22, which directs a local authority to promote the welfare of a child looked after by it. In Section 1 the court is instructed to make use of a checklist of factors to be considered in determining what is in a child's interests. The first item mentioned on the list is 'the wishes and feelings of the child'. The clear intention is that the child's wishes and feelings are to be regarded as evidence of what is in the child's interests, whether directly – in that the child's wish may straightforwardly indicate the disposal to be preferred; or indirectly – in that, for instance, the fact that a child has certain feelings may point to ways in which his or her needs are or are not being met by the current situation. In Section 22 the local authority is required to ascertain the child's wishes and feelings and to give them due consideration having regard to the child's understanding. It is not clear from the context whether the intention is that this should inform consideration of what is best for the child's welfare, on the lines of Section 1, or whether it is required because it is assumed to be positively in a child's interests to have notice taken of his or her wishes and feelings. The distinction is subtle, but may be important.

15   This is Mnookin's account of the research. Macfarlane's own account also refers to particular categories of deficit which did predictably produce poor long-term outcomes, such as 'the loss of the warm, supporting parent during the preschool years, with no adequate substitute,' or 'homes of unequivocal pathology where irrational pressures made integrations impossible' (McFarlane 1964, p. 122). However, these examples do not vitiate Mnookin's argument.

16   Mnookin uses 'least detrimental' and 'best interests' as alternative standards appropriate to different legal settings, but argues that both are subject to uncertainty both as to predictions and as to values.

17   For an illuminating discussion of the areas of conflict between universal standards of 'best interests' and different cultural formations, see the contributions collected by Alston (1994). Roche (1995) also makes a useful contribution to this debate.

18 See Newson and Newson (1974), p. 328. (Also mentioned in Chapter 2 above.)
19 See Wolf (1992).
20 Eekelaar also shows how the origins of parental responsibility lie in parental interests. Referring to Graveson's 1953 monograph *Status in the Common Law*, he relates: 'Graveson, it seems, conceived the status of infancy as (apparently always) grounded in the law's special solicitude for the well-being of children. How quickly we forget! In 1765 Blackstone explained the legal disabilities of married women as being "for the most part intended for her protection and benefit. So great a favourite is the female sex of the laws of England".' Eekelaar (1994), p. 44. The point, of course, is that legal protections are often erected to compensate for legally constructed disabilities.
21 See Goldstein, Freud and Solnit (1973, 1980), Mnookin (1976, 1983). Eekelaar's suggested rules are more extensive, because he allows more knowledge about the benefits and hazards of particular disposals for children's welfare.
22 Donegan (1993) quotes a leading representative of directors of social services as suggesting that 'the pendulum has swung too far in favour of the rights of the child'.

Chapter 6

1 This way of thinking about children often seems pervasive. The Department of Health guidance on preparation for leaving care says: 'There are three broad aspects to preparation for leaving care:

enabling young people to build and maintain relationships with others
    (both general and sexual relationships);
enabling young people to develop their self-esteem;
teaching practical and financial skills and knowledge.'

The following text is all about training children and doing things to them; despite the talk of 'enabling' there is very little sense of autonomy or exploration (Department of Health 1991a, p. 95).
2 Dingwall and Eekelaar (1988) argue that there was no real extension after the nineteenth century, either in legal definitions or in numbers, but this seems a perverse reading in that in legal terms the changes are arguably quite marked. As for numbers, they do not give figures for any period before 1951 but suggest that the large increases that have been quoted for the period since then are artefacts. Packman's figures suggest that the 1951 total was 14 per cent above that in 1949. Parker (1990) shows a consistent decline in numbers throughout the inter-war period.
3 It is likely that in many cases the same children were finding themselves in the system but for ostensibly different reasons, or without proper legal sanction. However, it also seems likely that the overt purpose of admission, and how the child is defined, affects what happens subsequently.
4 There were exceptions; Parker (1990) points out that the system was sometimes reluctant to relinquish older children because of the economic value of their labour.

5 Not that children always resented that differentiation as much as is sometimes imagined; see for instance the reminiscences of Jessie Harvey of Swansea in Grenfell-Hill (1996), pp. 120–4.

6 This is not to say that everything changed in practice following 1948. As Parker (1990) points out, 'tradition, habit and the pressure of other matters' meant that children continued to 'languish' in the system and to lose contact with their families (p. 36).

7 There continued to be some expectation that foster children would work for their keep right up until the middle of this century; see Hitchman (1966).

8 Parker (1990) shows how the tension between high standards and 'less eligibility' was a real problem for Poor Law officials following the expansion of boarding out in the 1870s and 1880s.

9 In addition, case law established more than once that even the High Court could not direct the local authority in its exercise of its functions of caring for a child.

10 See also Thomas and Beckett (1994).

11 Children Act 1975, section 3. Case law later established that this duty applied even when a local authority was taking a strategic decision to close a children's home; there was an obligation to ascertain and take account of the views of the children directly affected by the proposed decision.

12 Vernon and Fruin's account of supervision in social work agencies is not wholly consistent with my own experience around the same time. When I began to supervise social workers in 1978 there was a clear expectation that supervision would include a process of taking stock and of overall caseload management, as well as discussing those cases defined as critical or urgent. The description of planning in relation to individual cases as being largely reactive is somewhat more familiar, although there were certainly exceptions.

13 Again, this does not entirely accord with my own experience. I remember some careful discussions as to whether in a particular case it would be better to receive a child into care under section one of the 1948 Children Act (section 2 of the 1980 Child Care Act) or to take proceedings under section one of the 1969 Children and Young Persons Act. However, I was also conscious at the time of working in an office with an unusual awareness of the legal framework which was due to the presence of a particular manager.

14 Kelly's (1990) research in Northern Ireland similarly found that decisions tended to be made in response to pressure and as a result of negotiation.

15 See discussion of Bachrach and Baratz' concept of *nondecision-making* in Chapter 12.

16 Lavery (1986) in quoting this points to a lack of agreement even among advocates of children's rights as to the age at which participation should start. The Family Rights Group has recommended participation at ten years, the former NAYPIC (the National Association of Young People in Care) at thirteen years. In contrast, the Children's Legal Centre appear to argue that age is not an adequate reason to exclude children from the process, and Lavery uses Franklin's (1986a) arguments on voting to suggest that 'there is no case for the exclusion of certain age groups from participation in review' (Lavery 1986, p. 77; see Chapter 4 above).

17 The figures given are not quite consistent, but this does not affect the findings.

18 Thoburn, Shemmings and Lewis (1995) used a modified version of the ladder as originally devised by Arnstein (1969) for evaluating participation by adults. The ladder has also been developed by Hart (1992) for work with children, and is discussed further in Chapter 11.

19 As the authors point out, a particular rating does not imply that preceding stages were achieved. It measures 'highlights' and so 'differs from the more complex cumulative assessment explained by Thoburn, Lewis and Shemmings' (Grimshaw and Sinclair 1997, p. 150).

20 See also Wood (1986) on the limited educational value of teachers' questions.

Chapter 7

1 'Although the research is exploratory in nature, there are a number of testable hypotheses underlying the design. The first is a general hypothesis that some children are more likely to be fully consulted than others, and that this will be related to factors such as their age and the circumstances in which they are being looked after. Second, that children's sense of being included in decisions is associated with certain kinds of agency practice rather than others. Third, that agency practices vary with the attitudes of staff, rather than simply reflecting official policy. Fourth, that the possibility of conflict between children's wishes and their best interests is an area of difficulty and uncertainty for participants in decision-making. Finally, that communication with children is more productive when they are allowed some control over the process and the agenda.' Proposal to Nuffield Foundation, para. 28.

2 Alderson's own writing (1995) on the ethics of research with children was an important starting point for my second study.

3 A rather different typology is developed in James, Jenks and Prout (1998), but in some ways I prefer the original formulation.

4 Additionally when he was consulted about his care he believed that his own desired outcome – a return home to his mother – was off the agenda.

5 Used here in its dialect sense of 'all right' or 'acceptable'.

6 'The data will be analysed for associations between decision-making processes, the background to those processes, the context in which they take place and the eventual outcomes. *Background factors* include the social characteristics of children and their families: their age and sex, their ethnic, class and cultural background. *Context factors* include the reasons for the child's involvement in the care system, and the nature of the decision to be taken (including whether there is conflict or consensus between family and agency). *Process factors* include the form of decision-making used, the extent to which children and others are included, and the nature of any preparation for participation. *Outcome factors* include the decision taken and whether it is implemented successfully to the satisfaction of those involved.' Proposal to Nuffield Foundation, para. 17.

7 Baszanger and Dodier (1997) suggest that ethnographic research is distinguished by openness to elements that cannot be coded *a priori* and by being grounded in a field context rather than in a formal approach (for instance

conversation analysis). On this basis much of the work described here counts as ethnography.

8   For instance Geertz (1975), James (1993), referred to earlier in this chapter.

Chapter 8

1   Some of this material is also presented in Thomas and O'Kane (1999a).

2   Grimshaw and Sinclair found that 'There was no evidence of a link between attendance and a variety of other possible factors, such as the use of the Assessment and Action Record, the child having a disability.' We found that children with a disability or health problem were more likely to attend only part of the meeting rather than all of it, although there was no difference in the proportion not attending at all ($p < 0.05$).

Chapter 9

1   There were 29 boys and 18 girls, and the average age was similar to the larger group although the group was less evenly spread. In all 35 were in care and 11 accommodated; 37 in foster care (including 6 placed with relatives), 6 in residential care, 4 living with their immediate families. As with the larger group, about half had attended their most recent decision-making meeting.

2   A fuller analysis of the interview materials is given in O'Kane (forthcoming).

3   The same point was made by the children surveyed by Shaw (1998). See also Thomas and O'Kane 1998d.

4   I am often reminded of the comment attributed to Beatrice Webb that their marriage was harmonious because Sidney Webb made all the big decisions and Beatrice made all the little ones – including the decision as to which was which.

Chapter 10

1   This ambiguity in the purpose of reviews was noted in Chapter 6 and is discussed again in the conclusion.

2   The publication of ethnographers' field notes is an example of this approach; see Kirk and Miller (1986).

3   See Thomas and O'Kane 1998b, 1999b for further discussion of these issues.

4   Thomas (in preparation).

Chapter 11

1   In fact, analysis of the survey data shows a very strong correlation between the character of decision-making and whether the child is invited ($p < 0.0002$) for the 7–10 age group, and virtually no correlation at all for the 11–13 group.

2   Acknowledgements to Claire O'Kane for initially identifying this type, and for her other contributions to this analysis.

3 Kefalyew (1996) argues more strongly that 'the reliability of research … taking children as a target group is dependent upon the degree of freedom they enjoy to take part actively in a research process'; p. 204.
4 Some of these issues are also discussed in Thomas and O'Kane (1998c).
5 See Chapter 7.

Chapter 12

1 Lukes (1974) points out that the control of the political agenda is wider than Bachrach and Baratz's definition of nondecisions would suggest, and that overall their analysis is limited by its concentration on individuals, on observable and intentional behaviour, and on overt or explicit grievances. However, the concept of nondecisions remains a very powerful one.
2 Shaw (1998) found that children in foster care were more positive about their situation than those in residential care, but less aware of their rights.
3 For instance Norway, Sweden, Denmark and now Scotland (Marshall 1997).
4 House of Lords in *Gillick* v. *West Norfolk and Wisbech Health Authority*.
5 Lee also argues that 'to argue from "rights" is to exclude the social from our consideration' (ibid.); I would argue rather that while 'rights' without analysis of the social are of limited operational value, a sociological account of participation without a concept of rights lacks ethical purpose.
6 See Chapter 3 above. In fact Tesson and Youniss (1995) argue that Piaget's theory is better understood as a sociological one; that his descriptions of stages are not important, but his theory is, and it is a theory of the social development of cognitive structures. They make a direct link with Giddens' theory of structuration, suggesting that both Piaget and Giddens see structure as productive of creativity and innovation, not as simply restrictive of individuality (Engels said something similar).
7 In essence the argument is about economic exchange between generations, and the nature of the changes that happened in societies when economic activity moved out of households and children moved into schools. Qvortrup (1995) argues that to see children as having moved from being net contributors to net beneficiaries, as Caldwell (1982) does, is to misunderstand the nature of these changes through focusing too closely on intra-familial transactions. In particular he insists that society as a whole, and the adult generations in particular, benefit from children's schooling, and that the education process depends on productive activity by children for which they are not paid directly: 'children by means of their school labour are a part of the societal division of labour' (Caldwell 1982, p. 59). The latter point echoes the arguments of Morrow (1994, 1995) and others about children's economic activity in the home.
8 It may also be because 'adults define children's rights' (McGillivray 1992, p. 222). As Flekkoy and Kaufman (1997) point out, children played no part at all in the drafting of the United Nations Convention.
9 Federle (1994) in a challenging paper, criticises the feminist stress on relationships as masking women's power over children. She argues that both interest- and will-based theories of rights depend on assumptions about capacity and incapacity, and – if I have understood her correctly – that

children's rights must be based instead on respect and designed to redress their lack of real power.

10 One child talked of being picked on at school 'because my mother and father aren't real'. He had been in the same foster home for 12 years.

11 It is arguable that as children 'in the public care' they also represent a site for the study of how the public, the state or 'society' think children should be treated; but I am not sure that I would wish this on them.

12 There is also a need for research that asks whether outcomes for children are improved by involving them more effectively in decisions; a question that this research was not able to address directly, but which is surely worthy of attention. Does children's participation in decision-making need to better decisions, or for instance to greater stability? Elsewhere I have suggested that it may do (Jackson and Thomas 1999), but more evidence is needed.

References

Adams, P. et al. (1971) *Children's Rights: Towards the Liberation of the Child*. London: Elek Books.

Aiken, W. and LaFollette, H. (ed.) (1980) *Whose Child? Children's Rights, Parental Authority and State Power*. Littlefield, Adams.

Ainsworth, M. (1977) 'Attachment theory and its utility in cross-cultural research' in Leiderman, P., Tulkin, S. and Rosenfeld, A. (ed.) *Culture and Infancy*. New York: Academic Press.

Ainsworth, M., Bell, S. and Stayton, D. (1974) 'Infant–mother attachment and social development: 'socialisation' as a product of reciprocal responsiveness to signals' in Richards, M. (ed.) *The Integration of a Child Into a Social World*. London: Cambridge University Press.

Ainsworth, M., Blehar, M., Waters, E. and Wall, S. (1978) *Patterns of Attachment: a psychological study of the strange situation*. Hillsdale, NJ: Lawrence Erlbaum.

Alanen, L. (1995) 'Childhood and modernization', paper delivered at ESRC Seminar 'The Future of Childhood Research', Institute of Education, London, 9 December.

Alanen, L. (1998) 'Children and the family order: constraints and competencies' in Hutchby, I. and Moran-Ellis, J. (ed.) *Children and Social Competence: arenas of action*. London: Falmer.

Alderson, P. (1993) *Children's Consent to Surgery*. Buckingham: Open University Press.

Alderson, P. (1994) 'Researching children's rights to integrity' in Mayall, B. (ed.) *Children's Childhoods: observed and experienced*. London: Falmer.

Alderson, P. (1995) *Listening to Children: children, ethics and social research*. Barkingside: Barnardos.

Aldgate, J., Bradley, M. and Hawley, D. (1997) *Supporting Families Through Short-Term Accommodation: draft report for Department of Health*. University of Leicester.

Alston, P. (ed.) (1994) *The Best Interests of the Child: reconciling culture and human rights*. Oxford: Clarendon Press.

Archard, D. (1993) *Children: Rights and Childhood*. London: Routledge.

Ariès, P. (1962) *Centuries of Childhood*. London: Jonathan Cape.

Arnstein, S. (1969) 'Eight rungs on the ladder of citizen participation', *Journal of the American Institute of Planners*.

Bachrach, P. and Baratz, M. (1970) *Power and Poverty: Theory and Practice*. New York: Oxford University Press.

Bandura, A. (1977) *Social Learning Theory*. Englewood Cliffs, NJ: Prentice Hall.

Barrett, M. and McIntosh, M. (1982) *The Anti-social Family*. London: Verso–NLB.

Barthes, R. (1973) *Mythologies*. Paladin.

Barton, C. and Douglas, G. (1995) *Law and Parenthood*. London: Butterworths.

Baszanger, I. and Dodier, N. (1997) 'Ethnography: relating the part to the whole' in Silverman, D. (ed.) *Qualitative Research: theory, method and practice*. London: Sage.

Baumrind, D. (1973) 'The development of instrumental competence through socialization' in Pick, A. (ed.) *Minnesota Symposium on Child Psychology*. Minneapolis: University of Minnesota Press.

Bebbington, A. and Miles, J. (1991) 'The background of children who enter local authority care', *British Journal of Social Work* 19(5), 349–68.

Belotti, E. G. (1975) *Little Girls: social conditioning and its effect on the stereotyped role of women during infancy*. London: Writers and Readers.

Benedict, R. (1934) *Patterns of Culture*. Boston: Houghton Mifflin.

Berger, P. and Luckman, T. (1971) *The Social Construction of Reality: a treatise in the sociology of knowledge*. Harmondsworth: Penguin.

Bernstein, B. (1972) 'Social class, language and socialization' in Giglioli, P. (ed.) *Language and Social Context*. Harmondsworth: Penguin.

Bloch, M. (1965) *Feudal Society Volume I: the growth of ties of dependence*. London: Routledge and Kegan Paul.

Blustein, J. (1979) 'Child rearing and family interests' in O'Neill, O. and Ruddick, W. (eds) *Having Children: Philosophical and Legal Reflections on Parenthood*. New York: Oxford University Press.

Bossard, J. and Boll, E. (1966) *The Sociology of Child Development*. New York: Harper and Row.

Bowlby, J. (1953) *Child Care and the Growth of Love*. Harmondsworth: Pelican.

Bowlby, J. (1975) *Separation: Anxiety and Anger*. Harmondsworth: Pelican.

Bowlby, J. (1988) *A Secure Base: clinical applications of attachment theory*. London: Routledge.

Boyden, J. (1990) 'Childhood and the policy makers: a comparative perspective on the globalization of childhood' in James, A. and Prout, A. (eds) *Constructing and Reconstructing Childhood: contemporary issues in the sociological study of childhood*. Basingstoke: Falmer Press.

Brazelton, T. (1977) 'Implications of infant development among the Mayan Indians of Mexico' in Leiderman, P., Tulkin, S. and Rosenfeld, A. (eds) *Culture and Infancy*. New York: Academic Press.

Bronfenbrenner, U. (1971) *Two Worlds of Childhood: US and USSR*. London: George Allen and Unwin.

Bronfenbrenner, U. (1979) *The Ecology of Human Development: experiments by nature and design*. Cambridge, Mass.: Harvard University Press.

Bruner, J. (1972) 'Nature and uses of immaturity', reprinted in Woodhead, M., Carr, R. and Light, P. (eds) (1991) *Becoming a Person (Child Development in Social Context 1)*. London: Routledge.

Bruner, J. (1983) *Child's Talk: learning to use language*. Oxford: Oxford University Press.

Bruner, J. (1992) Interview in Audiocassette AC1476. Milton Keynes, Open University.

Burkitt, I. (1991) *Social Selves: theories of the social formation of personality*. London: Sage.

Burman, E. (1994) *Deconstructing Developmental Psychology*. London: Routledge.

Butler, I. and Williamson, H. (1994) *Children Speak: Children, Trauma and Social Work*. Harlow: Longman.

Butler-Sloss, E. (1988) *Report of the Inquiry into Child Abuse in Cleveland 1987*. London: HMSO.

Caldwell, J. C. (1982) *Theory of Fertility Decline*. London and New York: Academic Press.

Campbell, R. and Olson, D. (1990) 'Children's explanations' in Grieve, R. and Hughes, M. (eds) *Understanding Children: Essays in Honour of Margaret Donaldson*. Oxford: Blackwell.

Campbell, T. (1992) 'The rights of the minor: as person, as child, as juvenile, as future adult' in Alston, P., Parker, S. and Seymour, J. (eds) *Children, Rights and the Law*. Oxford: Oxford University Press.

Campbell, T. (1994) 'Really equal rights? Some philosophical comments on "Why children shouldn't have equal rights" by Laura M. Purdy', *International Journal of Children's Rights* 2, 259–63.

Cannan, C. (1992) *Changing Families, Changing Welfare: Family Centres and the Welfare State*. Hemel Hempstead: Harvester Wheatsheaf.

Cantwell, B. and Scott, S. (1995) 'Children's wishes, children's burdens', *Journal of Social Welfare and Family Law* 17(3), 337–54.

Carney, T. (1992) ''Reconciling the irreconcilable'?: a rights or interests based approach to uncontrollability? a comment on Seymour' in Alston, P., Parker, S. and Seymour, J. (ed.) *Children, Rights and the Law*. Oxford University Press.

Case, R., Hayward, S., Lewis, M. and Hurst, P. (1988) 'Toward a neo-Piagetian theory of cognitive and emotional development', *Developmental Review* 8, 1–51.

Cazden, C. (1970) 'The neglected situation in child language research and education', reprinted in Skolnick, Arlene (ed.) (1975) *Rethinking Childhood: perspectives on development and society*. Boston: Little, Brown.

Chandler, M. and Chapman, M. (1991) *Criteria for Competence: Controversies in the Conceptualization and Assessment of Children's Abilities*. Hillsdale, NJ: Lawrence Erlbaum.

Children's Legal Centre (1984) *It's My Life Not Theirs*. Children's Legal Centre.

Children's Legal Centre (1988) *Child Abuse Procedures – the Child's Viewpoint*. Children's Legal Centre.

Christensen, P. H. (1998) 'Difference and similarity: how children's competence is constituted in illness and its treatment' in Hutchby, I. and Moran-Ellis, J. (eds) *Children and Social Competence: arenas of action*. London: Falmer.

Clarke, A. M. and Clarke, A. D. B. (1976) *Early Experience: myth and evidence*. London: Open Books.

Cockburn, T. (1998) 'Children and citizenship in Britain', *Childhood* 5(1), 99–117.

Cohen, H. (1980) *Equal Rights for Children*. Totowa, NJ: Littlefield, Adams.

Coleman, J. (1993) 'Understanding adolescence today: a review', *Children and Society* 7(2), 137–41.

Cranston, M. (1967) 'Human rights, real and supposed' in Raphael, D. D. (ed.) *Political Theory and the Rights of Man*. Indiana University Press.

Crompton, M. (1980) *Respecting Children: social work with young people*. London: Edward Arnold.

Cunningham, H. (1995) *Children and Childhood in Western Society since* 1500. Harlow: Longman.

Curtis Committee (1946) Report of the Care of Children Committee. London: HMSO.

Das Gupta, P. (1995) 'Growing up in families' in Barnes, P. (ed.) *Personal, Social and Emotional Development of Children*. Oxford and Milton Keynes: Blackwell and Open University Press.

Davenport-Hill, F. (1889) *Children of the State*. Macmillan & Co.

de Mause, L. (1974) 'The evolution of childhood' in de Mause, L. (ed.) *The History of Childhood*. London: Souvenir Press.

Demos, J. (1970) *A Little Commonwealth: family life in Plymouth Colony*. London: Oxford University Press.

Dent, H. and Flin, R. (ed.) (1992) *Children as Witnesses*. Chichester: Wiley.

Denzin, N. (1975) *Childhood Socialization*. San Francisco: Jossey Bass.

Department of Health (1989a) *The Care of Children: principles and practice in regulations and guidance*. London: HMSO.

Department of Health (1989b) *An Introduction to the Children* Act. London: HMSO.

Department of Health (1991a) *The Children Act 1989 Guidance and Regulations Volume 3: Family Placements*. London: HMSO.

Department of Health (1991b) *Working Together under the Children Act*. London: HMSO.

Department of Health and Social Security (1981) *A Study of the Boarding Out of Children*. London: HMSO.

Department of Health and Social Security (1984) *Review of Children in Care of Local Authorities: a consultative document*. London: HMSO.

Department of Health and Social Security (1985) *Social Work Decisions in Child Care*. London: HMSO.

Dingwall, R. (1994) 'Dilemmas of family policy in liberal states' in Maclean, M. and Lurczewski, J. (eds) *Families, Politics and the Law: perspectives for East and West Europe*. Oxford University Press.

Dingwall, R. and Eekelaar, J. (1984) 'Rethinking child protection' in Freeman, M. (ed.) *The State the Law and the Family: Critical Perspectives*. London: Tavistock.

Dingwall, R. and Eekelaar, J. (1988) 'Families and the state: an historical perspective on the public regulation of private conduct', *Law and Policy* 10, 341–61.

Dolphin Project (1993) *Answering Back: report by young people being looked after on the Children Act 1989*. University of Southampton.

Donaldson, M. (1978) *Children's Minds*. London: Fontana.

Donaldson, M. and Elliot, M. (1990) 'Children's explanations' in Grieve, R. and Hughes, M. (eds) *Understanding Children: essays in honour of Margaret Donaldson*. Oxford: Blackwell.

Donegan, L. (1993) 'See you in court, Dad'. *The Guardian*, date missing.

Donzelot, J. (1980) *The Policing of Families: welfare versus the state*. London: Hutchinson.

Dreitzel, H. (ed.) (1973) *Childhood and Socialization*. London: Collier Macmillan.

Dunn, J. and Kendrick, C. (1982) *Siblings: Love, envy and understanding*. Cambridge, Mass.: Harvard University Press.

Dunn, J. (1988) *The Beginnings of Social Understanding*. Oxford: Blackwell.

Dworkin, R. (1978) 'Liberalism' in Hampshire, S. (ed.) *Public and Private Morality*. Cambridge: Cambridge University Press.

Eekelaar, J. (1994) 'The interests of the child and the child's wishes: the role of dynamic self-determinism' in Alston, P. (ed.) *The Best Interests of the Child: reconciling culture and human rights*. Oxford: Clarendon Press.

Eekelaar, J. and Dingwall, R. (1990) *The Reform of Child Care Law: a Practical Guide to the Children Act 1989*. Routledge.

Elshtain, J. B. (1989) 'The family, democratic politics and the question of authority' in Scarre, G. (ed.) *Children, Parents and Politics*. Cambridge: Cambridge University Press.

Ennew, J. (1986) *The Sexual Exploitation of Children*. Cambridge: Polity.

Ennew, J. (1994) 'Time for children and time for adults' in Qvortrup, J., Bardy, M., Sgritta, G. and Wintersberger, H. (eds) *Childhood Matters: social theory, practice and politics*. Aldershot: Avebury.

Erikson, E. H. (1950) *Childhood and Society*. Harmondsworth: Penguin.

Erikson, E. H. (1968) *Identity: youth and crisis*. London: Faber and Faber.

Fahlberg, V. (1994) *A Child's Journey Through Placement*. London: British Agencies for Adoption and Fostering.

Fairbairn, R. (1952) *Psychoanalytic studies of the personality*. London: Tavistock.

Farb, P. (1971) *Man's Rise to Civilization: as shown by the Indians of North America from primeval times to the coming of the industrial state*. London: Paladin.

Farson, R. (1974) *Birthrights*. New York: Collier Macmillan.

Federle, K. (1994) 'Rights flow downhill', *International Journal of Children's Rights* 2, 343–68.

Feinberg, J. (1980) 'The child's right to an open future' in Aiken, W. and LaFollette, H. (eds) *Whose Child? Children's Rights, Parental Authority and State Power*. Boston: Littlefield, Adams.

Fine, G. and Sandstrom, K. (1988) *Knowing Children: Participant Observation with Minors*. London: Sage.

Fisher, M., Marsh, P., Phillips, D. and Sainsbury, E. (1986) *In and Out of Care: the experience of children, parents and social workers*. London: Batsford.

Flavell, J. (1985) *Cognitive Development*. Englewood Cliffs: Prentice-Hall.

Flekkoy, M. and Kaufman, N. (1997) *The Participation Rights of the Child: Rights and Responsibilities in Family and Society*. London: Jessica Kingsley.

Fletcher, B. (1993) *Not Just a Name: the views of young people in foster and residential care*. London: National Consumer Council.

Fox, L. M. (1982) 'Two value positions in recent child care law and practice', *British Journal of Social Work* 12(2), 265–90.

Fox Harding, L. (1991) *Perspectives in Child Care Policy*. London: Longman.

Fox Harding, L. (1996) *Family, State and Social Policy*. Basingstoke: Macmillan.

Franklin, B. (1986a) 'Children's political rights' in Franklin, B. (ed.) *The Rights of Children*. Oxford: Blackwell.

Franklin, B. (ed.) (1986b) *The Rights of Children*. Oxford. Blackwell.

Freeman, D. (1983a) *Margaret Mead and Samoa: the making and unmaking of an anthropological myth*. Cambridge, Mass.: Harvard University Press.

Freeman, M. (1983b) 'The concept of children's rights' in Geach, H. and Szwed, E. (eds) *Providing Civil Justice for Children*. London: Edward Arnold.

Freeman, M. (1983c) *The Rights and the Wrongs of Children*. London: Frances Pinter.

Freeman, M. (1987) 'Taking children's rights seriously', *Children and Society* 1(4), 299–319.

Freeman, M. (1992) 'Introduction: rights, ideology and children' in Freeman, M. and Veerman, P. (eds) *Ideologies of Children's Rights*. Dordrecht: Martinus Nijhoff.

Freud, S. (1973) *Introductory Lectures on Psychoanalysis* (tr. James Strachey). Harmondsworth: Penguin.

Frost, N. (1990) 'Official intervention and child protection: the relationship between state and family in contemporary Britain' in Violence Against Children Study Group, (eds) *Taking Child Abuse Seriously*. London: Unwin Hyman.

Frost, N. and Stein, M. (1989) *The Politics of Child Welfare*. Hemel Hempstead: Harvester Wheatsheaf.

Frye, D. and Moore, C. (1991) *Children's Theories of Mind: mental states and social understanding*. Hillsdale, NJ: Lawrence Erlbaum.

Fuller, P. (1979) 'Uncovering Childhood' in Hoyles, M. (ed.) *Changing Childhood*. London: Writers and Readers.

Furth, H. (1978) 'Children's understanding of society' in McGurk, H. (ed.) *Issues in Childhood Social Development*. London: Methuen.

Garbarino, J., Stott, F. M. and Faculty of the Erikson Institute (1992) *What Children Can Tell Us*. San Francisco: Jossey-Bass.

Gardner, R. (1985) *Child Care Reviews*. London: National Children's Bureau.

Gardner, R. (1987) *Who Says? Choice and Control in Care*. London: National Children's Bureau.

Gardner, R. (1989) 'Consumer views' in Kahan, B. (ed.) *Child Care Research, Policy and Practice*. London: Hodder and Stoughton.

Gazzaniga, M. (1992) *Nature's Mind: the biological roots of thinking, emotions, sexuality, language, and intelligence*. Harmondsworth: Penguin.

Geertz, C. (1975) *The Interpretation of Cultures*. London: Hutchinson.

Gergen, K., Gloger-Tippett, G. and Berkowitz, P. (1990) 'The cultural construction of the developing child' in Semin, G. and Gergen, K. (eds) *Everyday Understanding: social and scientific implications*. London: Sage.

Gibson, S. (1994) 'Social work, law-jobs and the forms of modern law: the Children Act 1989' in Maclean, M. and Kurczewski, J. (eds) *Families, Politics and the Law: perspectives for East and West Europe*. Oxford: Oxford University Press.

Giddens, A. (1976) *The New Rules of Sociological Method*. London: Hutchinson.

Giddens, A. (1993) *Sociology*. Cambridge: Polity.

Gilligan, C. (1982) *In a Different Voice: psychological theory and women's development*. Cambridge, Mass.: Harvard University Press.

Gilligan, C. (1990) *Mapping the Moral Domain*. Cambridge, Mass.: Harvard University Press.

Glachan, M. and Ney, J. (1992) 'Children's understanding of employment, unemployment and pay', *Children and Society* 6(1), 12–24.

Glaser, B. and Strauss, A. (1967) *The Discovery of Grounded Theory: strategies for qualitative research*. Chicago: Aldine.

Goldstein, J., Freud, A. and Solnit, J. (1973) *Beyond the Best Interests of the Child*. New York: Macmillan.

Goldstein, J., Freud, A. and Solnit, J. (1980) *Before the Best Interests of the Child*. New York: Macmillan.

Goodman, G. and Schwartz-Kenney, B. (1992) 'Why knowing a child's age is not enough: influences of cognitive, social and emotional factors on children's testimony' in Dent, H. and Flin, R. (eds) *Children as Witnesses*. Chichester: Wiley.

Goody, J. (1983) *The Development of the Family and Marriage in Europe*. Cambridge: Cambridge University Press.

Grenfell-Hill, J. (ed.) (1996) *Growing Up in Wales: collected memories of childhood in Wales 1895–1939*. Llandysul: Gomer.

Grimshaw, R. and Sinclair, R. (1997) *Planning to Care: Regulation, procedure and practice under the Children Act 1989*. London: National Children's Bureau.

Gripe (1962) *Hugo and Josephine*.

Gunnar, M. (1980) 'Control, warning signals, and distress in infancy', *Developmental Psychology* 16(4), 281–9.

Hallden, G. (1991) 'The child as project and the child as being: parents' ideas as frames of reference', *Children and Society* 5(4), 334–6.

Hammersley, M. and Atkinson, P. (1995) *Ethnography: principles in practice.* London: Routledge.

Hardman, C. (1973) 'Can there be an anthropology of children?', *Journal of the Anthropological Society of Oxford* 4, 85–99.

Hardyment, C. (1983) *Dream Babies: child care from Locke to Spock.* London: Jonathan Cape.

Harré, R. (1974) 'The conditions for a social psychology of childhood' in Richards, M. (ed.) *The Integration of a Child Into a Social World.* London: Cambridge University Press.

Harris, P. (1989) *Children and Emotion: the development of psychological understanding.* Oxford: Blackwell.

Hart, R. (1992) *Children's Participation: From Tokenism To Citizenship.* Florence: UNICEF.

Harter, S. (1983) 'Developmental perspectives on the self-system' in Mussen, P. H. (ed.) *Handbook of Child Psychology.* New York: Wiley.

Hartley, D. and Elliot, M. (1928) *Life and Work of the People of England: the Fourteenth Century.* London: Batsford.

Hendrick, H. (1994) *Child Welfare: England, 1872–1989.* London: Routledge.

Herlihy, D. (1985) *Medieval Households.* Cambridge, Mass.: Harvard University Press.

Heywood, J. (1965) *Children in Care.* London: Routledge and Kegan Paul.

Hill, M. (1997) 'Participatory research with children', *Child and Family Social Work* 2, 171–83.

Hirschfeld, L. and Gelman, S. (ed.) (1994) *Mapping the Mind: domain specificity in cognition and culture.* Cambridge: Cambridge University Press.

Hitchman, J. (1966) *The King of the Barbareens.* Harmondsworth: Penguin.

Hockey, J. and James, A. (1993) *Growing Up and Growing Old: ageing and dependency in the life course.* London: Sage.

Hodgson, D. (1990) 'Power to the child', *Social Work Today,* 12 July.

Hoggan, P. (1991) 'The role of children in permanency planning', *Adoption and Fostering* 14(4), 31–4.

Holman, B. (1988) *Putting Families First: prevention and child care.* London: Macmillan.

Holmes, J. (1993) *John Bowlby and Attachment Theory.* London: Routledge.

Holstein, J. and Gubrium, J. (1997) 'Active interviewing' in Silverman, D. (ed.) *Qualitative Research: theory, method and practice.* London: Sage.

Holt, J. (1975) *Escape from Childhood.* Harmondsworth: Pelican.

Houlbrooke, R. (1984) *The English Family 1450–1700.* London: Longman.

Houlgate, L. (1980) *The Child and the State: a normative theory of juvenile rights.* Baltimore: Johns Hopkins.

Hughes, J. (1989) 'Thinking about children' in Scarre, G. (ed.) *Children, Parents and Politics.* Cambridge University Press.

Hunt, D. (1972) *Parents and Children in History: the psychology of family life in early modern France.* New York: Harper and Row.

Hutchby, I. and Moran-Ellis, J. (1998) 'Situating children's social competence' in Hutchby, I. and Moran-Ellis, J. (ed.) *Children and Social Competence: arenas of action.* London: Falmer.

Isaacs, S. (1930) *Intellectual Growth in Young Children*. London: George Routledge.

Ives, R. (1986) 'Children's sexual rights' in Franklin, B. (ed.) *The Rights of Children*. Oxford: Blackwell.

James, A. (1993) *Childhood Identities: self and social relationships in the experience of the child*. Edinburgh: Edinburgh University Press.

James, A. (1995) 'Methodologies of competence for a competent methodology', 'Children and Social Competence' Conference, University of Surrey, 5–7 July.

James, A. (1998) 'Researching children's social competence: methods and models' in Woodhead, M., Faulkner, D. and Littleton, K. (eds) *Making Sense of Social Development*. London: Routledge.

James, A., Jenks, C. and Prout, A. (1998) *Theorizing Childhood*. Cambridge: Polity.

James, A. and Prout, A. (1990a) 'Introduction' in James, A. and Prout, A. (eds) *Constructing and Reconstructing Childhood: contemporary issues in the sociological study of childhood*. Basingstoke: Falmer Press.

James, A. and Prout, A. (1990b) 'Re-presenting childhood: time and transition in the study of childhood' in James, A. and Prout, A. (eds) *Constructing and Reconstructing Childhood: contemporary issues in the sociological study of childhood*. Basingstoke: Falmer Press.

Jenkins, S. (1975) 'Child welfare as a class system' in Schorr, A. (ed.) *Children and Decent People*. London: George Allen and Unwin.

Jenks, C. (1982) 'Introduction: constituting the child' in Jenks, C. (ed.) *The Sociology of Childhood: essential readings*. London: Batsford.

Jewett, C. (1984) *Helping Children Cope with Separation and Loss*. London: Batsford.

Johnson, D. (1992) 'Cultural and religious pluralism in the drafting of the UN Convention on the Rights of the Child' in Freeman, M. and Veerman, P. (eds) *Ideologies of Children's Rights*. Dordrecht: Martinus Nijhoff.

Joint Working Party on Pregnant Schoolgirls and Schoolgirl Mothers (1979) *Pregnant at School*. National Council for One-Parent Families/Community Development Trust.

Jordan, B. (1990) *Social Work in an Unjust Society*. London: Harvester Wheatsheaf.

Kagan, J. (1977) 'The uses of cross-cultural research in early development' in Leiderman, P., Tulkin, S. and Rosenfeld, A. (eds) *Culture and Infancy*. New York: Academic Press.

Kamerman, S. B. and Kahn, A. K. (1978) *Family Policy: Government and Families in Fourteen Countries*. New York: Columbia University Press.

Kant, I. (1887) *The Philosophy of Law*. Edinburgh: T & T Clark.

Kefalyew, F. (1996) 'The reality of child participation in research', *Childhood* 3(2), 203–13.

Kellmer-Pringle, M. (1974) *The Needs of Children*. London: Hutchinson.

Kelly, G. (1990) 'Decision-making in child care in Northern Ireland', *Social Work and Social Sciences Review* 2(1).

Kendrick, A. and Mapstone, E. (1991) 'Who decides? Child care reviews in two Scottish social work departments', *Children and Society* 5(2), 165–81.

Kennedy, D. (1998) 'Empathic childrearing and the adult construction of childhood', *Childhood* 5(1), 9–22.

Kessen, W. (1979) 'The American child and other cultural inventions', reprinted in Woodhead, M., Light, P. and Carr, R. (eds) (1991) *Growing Up in a Changing Society (Child Development in Social Context 3)*. London: Routledge.

Kirk, J. and Miller, M. (1986) *Reliability and Validity in Qualitative Research.* London: Sage.

Kitzinger, J. (1990) 'Who are you kidding? Children, power and the struggle against sexual abuse' in James, A. and Prout, A. (eds) *Constructing and reconstructing Childhood: contemporary issues in the sociological study of childhood.* Basingstoke: Falmer.

Klein, M. (1975) *Love, Guilt and Reparation.* New York: Delta.

Konner, M. (1977) 'Infancy among the Kalahari Desert San' in Leiderman, P., Tulkin, S. and Rosenfeld, A. (eds) *Culture and Infancy.* New York: Academic Press.

Kroll, B. (1995) 'Working with children' in Kaganas, F., King, M. and Piper, C. (eds) *Legislating for harmony: partnership under the Children Act 1989.* London: Jessica Kingsley.

La Fontaine, J. (1986) 'An anthropological perspective on children in social worlds' in Richards, M. and Light, P. (eds) *Children of Social Worlds: development in a social context.* Cambridge: Polity.

Labov, W. (1972) 'The logic of non-standard English' in Giglioli, P. (ed.) *Language and Social Context.* Harmondsworth: Penguin.

Land, H. and Parker, R. (1978) 'The United Kingdom' in Kamerman, S. B. and Kahn, A. K. (eds) *Family Policy: Government and Families in Fourteen Countries.* New York: Columbia University Press.

Lansdown, G. (1994) 'Children's rights' in Mayall, B. (ed.) *Children's Childhoods: observed and experienced.* London: Falmer.

Lansdown, G. (1995) *Taking Part: Children's participation in decision-making.* London: IPPR.

Lansdown, G. and Newell, P. (eds) (1994) *UK Agenda for Children.* London: CRDU.

Laslett, P. (1971) *The World we have lost.* London: Methuen.

Laslett, P. (1983) *The World we have lost: further explored.* London: Methuen.

Laslett, P. and Wall, R. (eds) (1972) *Household and Family in Past Time.* London: Cambridge University Press.

Lavery, G. (1986) 'The rights of children in care' in Franklin, B. (ed.) *The Rights of Children.* Oxford: Blackwell.

Layder, D. (1993) *New Strategies in Social Research: an introduction and guide.* Cambridge: Polity.

Le Roy Ladurie, E. (1980) *Montaillou: Cathars and Catholics in a French village 1294–1324.* Harmondsworth: Penguin.

Lee, N. M. (1998) 'Childhood, ambiguity and social exclusion: the case of child protection', Children and Social Exclusion Conference, University of Hull, 5–6 March.

Leiderman, P. and Leiderman, G. (1977) 'Economic change and infant care in an East African agricultural community' in Leiderman, P., Tulkin, S. and Rosenfeld, A. (eds) *Culture and Infancy.* New York: Academic Press.

Leiderman, P., Tulkin, S. and Rosenfeld, A. (eds) (1977) *Culture and Infancy.* New York: Academic Press.

LeVine, R. (1977) 'Child rearing as cultural adaptation' in Leiderman, P., Tulkin, S. and Rosenfeld, A. (eds) *Culture and Infancy.* New York: Academic Press.

Li, A-C. (1937) 'Zuni: some observations and queries', *American Anthropologist* 39, 62–76.

Liedloff, J. (1975) *The Continuum Concept*. London: Duckworth.

Lifechance Project (1994) *Participation Report 1994: report by the Lifechance project working with Oxon Social Services on participation by young people in care*. Oxford: Save the Children.

Light, P. (1986) 'Context, conservation and conversation' in Richards, M. and Light, P. (eds) *Children of Social Worlds: development in a social context*. Cambridge: Polity.

Light, P. and Perret-Clermont, A. N. (1989) 'Social context effects in learning and testing', reprinted in Light, P., Sheldon, S. and Woodhead, M. (eds) (1991) *Learning to Think (Child Development in Social Context 2)*. London: Routledge.

Lindley, R. (1989) 'Teenagers and other children' in Scarre, G. (ed.) *Children, Parents and Politics*. Cambridge: Cambridge University Press.

Lloyd, P. (1990) 'Children's communication' in Grieve, R. and Hughes, M. (eds) *Understanding Children: essays in honour of Margaret Donaldson*. Oxford: Blackwell.

Lofland, J. and Lofland, L. (1995) *Analysing Social Settings: a Guide to Qualitative Observation and Analysis*. Belmont, Calife.: Wadsworth.

Lorenz, W. (1998) 'Children and European social policy traditions', BAAF Conference 'Exchanging Visions', University of Bradford, 22–4 April.

Lukes, S. (1974) *Power: a Radical View*. London: Macmillan.

Lyon, C. and Parton, N. (1995) 'Children's rights and the Children Act 1989' in Franklin, B. (ed.) *The Handbook of Children's Rights: Comparative Policy and Practice*. London: Routledge.

Maccoby, E. (1980) *Social Development: psychological growth and the parent–child relationship*. New York: Harcourt Brace Jovanovitch.

Macfarlane, A. (1979) 'Review of Stone's The Family, Sex and Marriage', *History and Theory* 18, 103–26.

Main, M. (1991) 'Metacognitive knowledge, metacognitive monitoring, and singular (coherent) vs. multiple (incoherent) model of attachment: findings and directions for future research' in Murray Parkes, C., Stevenson-Hinde, J. and Marris, P. (eds) *Attachment Across the Life Cycle*. London: Routledge.

Main, M., Kaplan, K. and Cassidy, J. (1985) 'Security in infancy, childhood and adulthood: a move to the level of representation' in Bretherton, I. and Waters, E. (eds) *Growing Points in Attachment Theory and Research*. Chicago: University of Chicago Press.

Mandell, N. (1991) 'The least-adult role in studying children' in Waksler, F. C. (ed.) *Studying the Social Worlds of Children: sociological readings*. London: Falmer.

Marsh, P. and Allen, G. (1993) 'The law, prevention and reunification – the New Zealand development of family group conferences' in Marsh, P. and Triseliotis, J. (eds) *Prevention and Reunification in Child Care*. London: Batsford.

Marsh, P. and Crow, G. (1997) *Family Group Conferences in Child Welfare*. Oxford: Blackwell.

Marshall, K. (1997) *Children's Rights in the Balance: the participation – protection debate*. London: The Stationery Office.

Maurice-Naville, D. and Montanegro, J. (1992) 'The development of diachronic thinking: 8–12 year-old children's understanding of the evolution of forest disease', *British Journal of Developmental Psychology* 10, 365–83.

Mayall, B. (1995) 'Childhood as a minority group: some issues arising', The Future of Childhood Research Conference, Institute of Education, London.

McDonnell, P. and Aldgate, J. (1984) *Reviews of Children in Care*. Oxford: Department of Social and Administrative Studies.

McFadden, E. J. (1991) 'The inner world of children and youth in care', Seventh International Foster Care Conference Conference, Jonkopping, Sweden.

McFarlane, J. (1964) 'Perspectives on personality, consistency and change from the guidance study', *Vita Humana* 7, 115.

McGillivray, A. (1992) 'Reconstructing child abuse: Western definition and non-Western experience' in Freeman, M. and Veerman, P. (eds) *Ideologies of Children's Rights*. Dordrecht: Martinus Nijhoff.

McGillivray, A. (1994) 'Why children do have equal rights: in reply to Laura Purdy', *International Journal of Children's Rights* 2, 243–58.

McGurk, H. and Glachan, M. (1988) 'Children's conversation with adults', *Children and Society* 2(1), 20–34.

Mead, G. H. (1934) *Mind, Self and Society*. Chicago: University of Chicago Press.

Mead, M. (1943) *Coming of Age in Samoa*. Harmondsworth: Penguin.

Mead, M. (1963) *Growing Up in New Guinea*. Harmondsworth: Penguin.

Mead, M. and Wolfenstein, M. (1955) *Childhood in Contemporary Cultures*. Chicago: University of Chicago Press.

Meadows, S. (1993) *The Child as Thinker: the development and acquisition of cognition in childhood*. London: Routledge.

Merleau-Ponty, M. (1964) 'The child's relations with others', reprinted in Jenks, C (ed.) (1982) *The Sociology of Childhood: essential readings*. London: Batsford.

Mill, J. S. (1910) *Utilitarianism, Liberty and Representative Government*. London: Dent.

Miller, A. (1987a) *The Drama of Being a Child*. London: Virago.

Miller, A. (1987b) *For Your Own Good: the roots of violence in child-rearing*. London: Virago.

Millham, S., Bullock, R., Hosie, K. and Haak, M. (1986) *Lost in Care: the problems of maintaining links between children in care and their families*. Aldershot: Gower.

Minow, M. (1986) 'Rights for the next generation: a feminist approach to children's rights', *Harvard Women's Law Journal* 9(1).

Mnookin, R. (1976) 'Child-custody adjudication: judicial functions in the face of indeterminacy', *Law and Contemporary Problems* 39(3), 226–93.

Mnookin, R. and Szwed, E. (1983) 'The "best interests" syndrome and the allocation of power in child care' in Geach, H. and Szwed, E. (eds) *Providing Civil Justice for Children*. London: Edward Arnold.

Morrow, V. (1994) 'Responsible children? aspects of children's work and employment outside school in contemporary UK' in Mayall, B. (ed.) *Children's Childhoods: observed and experienced*. London: Falmer.

Morrow, V. (1995) 'Invisible children? Towards a reconceptualization of childhood dependency and responsibility' in Ambert, A-M. (ed.) *Sociological Studies of Children: Volume 7*. Greenwich, Conn.: JAI Press.

Moss, H. and Jones, S. (1977) 'Relations between maternal attitudes and maternal behaviour as a function of social class' in Leiderman, P., Tulkin, S. and Rosenfeld, A. (eds) *Culture and Infancy*. New York: Academic Press.

Mount, F. (1982) *The Subversive Family*. London: Jonathan Cape.

Murray, L. and Stein, A. (1991) 'The effects of post-natal depression on mother-infant relations and infant development' in Woodhead, M., Carr, R. and Light, P. (eds) *Becoming a Person (Child Development in Social Context 1)*. London: Routledge.

Musgrove, F. (1964) *Youth and the Social Order.* London: Routledge and Kegan Paul.
Newell, P. (1991) *The UN Convention and Children's Rights in the UK.* London: National Children's Bureau.
Newson, J. and Newson, E. (1974) 'Cultural aspects of child rearing in the English speaking world' in Richards, M. (ed.) *The Integration of a Child Into a Social World.* London: Cambridge University Press.
O'Donovan, K. (1993) *Family Law Matters.* London: Pluto.
O'Kane, C. (forthcoming) 'The development of participatory techniques: facilitating children's views about decisions which affect them' in James, A. and Christensen, P. (eds) *Conducting Research with Children.* London: Falmer.
O'Neill, J. (1998) 'Making civic children', Children and Social Exclusion Conference, University of Hull, 5–6 March.
O'Neill, O. (1992) 'Children's rights and children's lives' in Alston, P., Parker, S. and Seymour, J. (eds) *Children, Rights and the Law.* Oxford: Oxford University Press.
Oakhill, J. (1984) 'Why children have difficulty reasoning with three-term series problems', *British Journal of Developmental Psychology* 2(3), 223–30.
Oakley, A. (1994) 'Women and children first and last: parallels and differences between children's and women's studies' in Mayall, B. (ed.) *Children's Childhoods: observed and experienced.* London: Falmer.
Oldman, D. (1994) 'Adult-child relations as class relations' in Qvortrup, J., Bardy, M., Sgritta, G. and Wintersberger, H. (eds) *Childhood Matters: social theory, practice and politics.* Aldershot: Avebury.
Opie, I. (1993) *The People in the Playground.* Oxford: Oxford University Press.
Owen, M. (1992) *Social Justice and Children in Care.* Aldershot: Avebury.
Packman, J., Randall, J. and Jacques, N. (1986) *Who Needs Care? Social-work decisions about children.* Oxford: Blackwell.
Page, R. and Clarke, E. (1977) *Who Cares?* National Children's Bureau.
Palmeri, A. (1980) 'Childhood's end: toward the liberation of children' in Aiken, W. and LaFollette, H. (eds) *Whose Child? Children's Rights, Parental Authority and State Power.* Littlefield: Adams.
Papadopoulos, T. (1996) ' "Family", state and social policy for children in Greece' in Brannen, J. and O'Brien, M. (eds) *Children in Families: research and policy.* London: Falmer.
Parker, R. (1982) 'Family and social policy: an overview' in Rapoport, R., Fogarty, M. and Rapoport, R. (eds) *Families in Britain.* London: Routledge and Kegan Paul.
Parker, R. (1987) *A Forward Look at Research and the Child in Care.* Bristol: School of Applied Social Studies.
Parker, R. (1990) *Away from Home: a short history of provision for separated children.* Barkingside: Barnardos.
Parker, R., Ward, H., Jackson, S., Aldgate, J. and Wedge, P. (1991) *Looking After Children: assessing outcomes in child care.* London: HMSO.
Parker, S. (1994) 'The best interests of the child – principles and problems' in Alston, P. (ed.) *The Best Interests of the Child: Reconciling Culture and Human Rights.* Oxford: Clarendon Press.
Parton, N. (1991) *Governing the Family: Child Care, Child Protection and the State.* Basingstoke: Macmillan.
Pateman, C. (1970) *Participation and Democratic Theory.* Cambridge: Cambridge University Press.

Paton, H. (1948) *The Moral Law.* London: Hutchinson.

Phillips, M., Shyne, A., Sherman, E. and Haring, B. (1971) 'Factors associated with placement decisions in child welfare', Research Centre, Child Welfare League of America.

Piaget, J. (1926) *The Child's Conception of the World.* London: Routledge and Kegan Paul.

Piaget, J. (1969) 'Advances in child and adolescent psychology', reprinted in Light, P., Sheldon, S. and Woodhead, M. (eds) (1991) *Learning to Think (Child Development in Social Context 2).* London: Routledge.

Piaget, J. (1976) *Judgment and Reasoning in the Child.* New York: Harcourt Brace Jovanovitch.

Pinchbeck, I. and Hewitt, M. (1969) *Children in English Society: Vol. 1.* London: Routledge and Kegan Paul.

Pinchbeck, I. and Hewitt, M. (1973) *Children in English Society: Vol. 2.* London: Routledge and Kegan Paul.

Plumb, J. (1975) 'The new world of children in eighteenth-century England', *Past and Present* 67, 64–93.

Pollock, L. (1983) *Forgotten Children: parent–child relations from 1500 to 1900.* Cambridge: Cambridge University Press.

Pretty, J. N., Guijt, I., Thompson, J. and Scoones, I. (1995) *Participatory Learning and Action: A Trainers Guide.* London: IIED.

Prout, A. and James, A. (1990) 'A new paradigm for the sociology of childhood? provenance, promise and problems' in James, A. and Prout, A. (eds) *Constructing and Reconstructing Childhood: contemporary issues in the sociological study of childhood.* Basingstoke: Falmer Press.

Purdy, L. (1992) *In Their Best Interest? The Case Against Equal Rights for Children.* Ithaca, NY: Cornell.

Purdy, L. (1994a) 'Why children shouldn't have equal rights', *International Journal of Children's Rights* 2, 223–41.

Purdy, L. (1994b) 'Why children still shouldn't have equal rights', *International Journal of Children's Rights* 2, 395–8.

Pye, C. (1986) 'Quiche Mayan speech to children', *Journal of Child Language* 13, 85–100.

Qvortrup, J. (1990) 'A voice for children in statistical and social accounting: a plea for children's right to be heard' in James, A. and Prout, A. (eds) *Constructing and Reconstructing Childhood: Contemporary Issues in the Sociological Study of Childhood.* Basingstoke: Falmer Press.

Qvortrup, J. (1994) 'Childhood matters: an introduction' in Qvortrup, J., Bardy, M., Sgritta, G. and Wintersberger, H. (eds) *Childhood Matters: Social Theory, Practice and Politics.* Aldershot: Avebury.

Qvortrup, J. (1995) 'From useful to useful: the historical continuity of children's constructive participation' in Ambert, A.-M. (ed.) *Sociological Studies of Children: Vol 7.* Greenwich, Ct: JAI Press.

Qvortrup, J. (1998) 'Childhood exclusion by default', Children and Social Exclusion Conference, University of Hull, 5–6 March.

Rapoport, R., Fogarty, M. and Rapoport, R. (eds) (1982) *Families in Britain.* London: Routledge and Kegan Paul.

Rawls, J. (1962) 'Justice as fairness' in Laslett, P. and Runciman, W. G. (eds) *Philosophy, Politics and Society (Second Series).* Oxford: Basil Blackwell.

Rawls, J. (1967) 'Distributive justice' in Laslett, P. and Runciman, W. G. (eds) *Philosophy, Politics and Society (Third Series)*. Oxford: Basil Blackwell.

Rawls, J. (1972) *A Theory of Justice*. Oxford: Oxford University Press.

Raz, J. (1986) *The Morality of Freedom*. Oxford: Clarendon Press.

Rich, J. (1968) *Interviewing Children and Adolescents*. London: Macmillan.

Richards, M. (1986) 'Behind the best interests of the child: an examination of the arguments of GFS concerning custody and access at divorce', *Journal of Social Welfare Law* (March), 77–95.

Richards, M. and Light, P. (ed.) (1986) *Children of Social Worlds*. Cambridge: Polity.

Roche, J. (1995) 'Children's rights: in the name of the child', *Journal of Social Welfare and Family Law* 17(3), 281–300.

Roche, J. (1996) 'Children's rights: a lawyer's view' in John, M. (ed.) *The Child's Right to Resources*. London: Jessica Kingsley.

Rodham, H. (1973) 'Children under the law', reprinted in Skolnick, A. (ed.) (1976) *Rethinking Childhood: Perspectives on Development and Society*. Boston: Little, Brown.

Rogers, C. (1978) 'The child's perception of other people' in McGurk, H. (ed.) *Issues in Childhood Social Development*. London: Methuen.

Rogers, C. M. and Wrightsman, L. S. (1978) 'Attitudes towards children's rights: nurturance or self-determination', *Journal of Social Issues* 34(2), 59–68.

Rogoff, B., Gauvain, M. and Ellis, S. (1984) 'Development viewed in its cultural context', reprinted in Light, P., Sheldon, S. and Woodhead, M. (eds) (1991) *Learning to Think (Child Development in Social Context 2)*. London: Routledge.

Rogoff, B., Sellers, M., Pirrotta, S., Fox, N. and White, S. (1976) 'Age of assignment of roles and responsibilities to children: a cross-cultural survey' in Skolnick, A. (ed.) *Rethinking Childhood: Perspectives on Development and Society*. Boston: Little, Brown.

Rose, S. (1976) *The Conscious Brain*. Harmondsworth: Penguin.

Rotter, J. (1966) 'Generalized expectancies for internal versus external control of reinforcements', *Psychological Monographs* 80(1 (whole no. 609)), 1–28.

Rowe, J., Cain, H., Hundleby, M. and Keane, A. (1984) *Long-Term Foster Care*. London: Batsford.

Rowe, J. and Lambert, L. (1973) *Children Who Wait: a study of children needing substitute families*. Association of British Adoption Agencies.

Ruddick, W. (1979) 'Parents and life prospects' in O'Neill, O. and Ruddick, W. (eds) *Having Children: Philosophical and Legal Reflections on Parenthood*. New York: Oxford University Press.

Rutter, M. (1981) *Maternal Deprivation Reassessed*. Harmondsworth: Penguin.

Ryan, T. and Walker, R. (1993) *Life Story Work*. London: British Agencies for Adoption and Fostering.

Ryburn, M. (1991) 'The myth of assessment', *Adoption and Fostering* 15(1), 20–7.

Rymer, R. (1994) *Genie: a scientific tragedy*. Harmondsworth: Penguin.

Sacks, O. (1995) *An Anthropologist on Mars*. London: Picador.

Saporiti, A. (1994) 'A methodology for making children count' in Qvortrup, J., Bardy, M., Sgritta, G. and Wintersberger, H. (eds) *Childhood Matters: social theory, practice and politics*. Aldershot: Avebury.

Schaffer, R. (1989) 'Early social development', reprinted in Woodhead, M., Carr, R. and Light, P. (eds) (1991) *Becoming a Person (Child Development in Social Context 1)*. London: Routledge.

Schaffer, R. (1991) Talk included in Audiotape AC 1476, Open University, Milton Keynes, UK.

Schattschneider (1960). *The Semi-Sovereign People: a realist's view of democracy in America*. New York: Holt, Rhinehart and Winston.

Schieffelin, B. and Ochs, E. (1983) 'A cultural perspective on the transition from prelinguistic to linguistic communication', reprinted in Woodhead, M., Carr, R. and Light, P. (eds) (1991) *Becoming a Person (Child Development in Social Context 1)*. London: Routledge.

Schildkrout, E. (1978) 'Roles of children in urban Kano' in La Fontaine, J. (ed.) *Sex and Age as Principles of Social Differentiation*. London: Academic Press.

Schofield, G. and Thoburn, J. (1996) *Child Protection: the voice of the child in decision-making*. London: IPPR.

Seligman, M. (1975) *Helplessness: on depression, development and death*. San Francisco: W. H. Freeman.

Seymour, J. (1992) 'An "uncontrollable" child: a case study in children's and parents' rights' in Alston, P., Parker, S. and Seymour, J. (eds) *Children, Rights and the Law*. Oxford: Oxford University Press.

Shahar, S. (1990) *Childhood in the Middle Ages*. London: Routledge and Kegan Paul.

Shaw, C. (1998) *Remember My Messages*. London: Who Cares? Trust.

Shaw, I. (1996) 'Unbroken voices: children, young people and qualitative methods' in Butler, I. and Shaw, I. (eds) *A Case of Neglect? Children's experiences and the sociology of childhood*. Aldershot: Avebury.

Shemmings, D. (1996) *Involving Children in Child Protection Conferences: research findings from two child protection authorities*. Norwich: University of East Anglia.

Short, G. (1991) 'Children's grasp of difficult issues' in Woodhead, M., Light, P, and Carr, R. (eds) *Growing Up in a Changing Society (Child Development in Social Context 3)*. London: Routledge.

Shorter, E. (1977) *The Making of the Modern Family*. London: Fontana.

Shotter, J. (1974) 'The development of personal powers' in Richards, M. (ed.) *The Integration of a Child Into a Social World*. London: Cambridge University Press.

Silverman, D., Baker, C. and Keogh, J. (1998) 'The case of the silent child: advice-giving and advice-reception in parent-teacher interviews' in Hutchby, I. and Moran-Ellis, J. (eds) *Children and Social Competence: arenas of action*. London: Falmer.

Sinclair, R. (1984) *Decision-making in Statutory Reviews on Children in Care*. Aldershot: Gower.

Sinclair, R. and Grimshaw, R. (1997) 'Partnership with parents in planning the care of their children', *Children and Society* 11(4), 231–41.

Skolnick, A. (1973) *The Intimate Environment: Exploring Marriage and the Family*. New York: Little, Brown.

Skolnick, A. (1975) 'The limits of childhood: conceptions of child development and social context', *Law and Contemporary Problems* 39(Summer), 38–77.

Skolnick, A. (ed.) (1976) *Rethinking Childhood: Perspectives on Development and Society*. Boston: Little, Brown.

Sluckin, A. (1987) 'The culture of the primary school playground' in Pollard, A. (ed.) *Children and their Primary Schools*. London: Falmer.

Snow, C. (1991) 'The language of the mother–child relationship' in Woodhead, M., Carr, R. and Light, P. (eds) *Becoming a Person (Child Development in Social Context 1)*. London: Routledge.

Solberg, A. (1990) 'Negotiating childhood: changing constructions of age for Norwegian children' in James, A. and Prout, A. (eds) *Constructing and Reconstructing Childhood: contemporary issues in the sociological study of childhood*. Basingstoke: Falmer Press.

Sommerville, C. J. (1982) *The Rise and Fall of Childhood*. London: Sage.

Speier, M. (1976) 'The adult ideological viewpoint in studies of childhood' in Skolnick, A. (ed.) *Rethinking Childhood: perspectives on development and society*. Boston: Little, Brown.

Stainton Rogers, R. and Stainton Rogers, W. (1992) *Stories of Childhood: shifting agendas of child concern*. London: Harvester Wheatsheaf.

Statham, J. (1986) *Daughters and Sons: experiences of non-sexist child raising*. Oxford: Blackwell.

Stedman Jones, G. (1971) *Outcast London: a study in the relationship between classes in Victorian society*. Oxford: Oxford University Press.

Steedman, C. (1986) *Landscape for a Good Woman*. London: Virago.

Stein, M. and Ellis, S. (1983) *Gizza Say?* National Association of Young People in Care.

Stein, S. (1984) *Girls and Boys: the limits of non-sexist childrearing*. London: Chatto and Windus/The Hogarth Press.

Stevens, O. (1982) *Children Talking Politics: Political Learning in Childhood*. Oxford: Martin Robertson.

Stier, S. (1978) 'Children's rights and society's duties', *Journal of Social Issues* 34(2), 46–58.

Stone, L. (1979) *The Family, Sex and Marriage in England 1500–1800*. Harmondsworth: Penguin.

Stone, J. (1995) *Short-term Family Placement*. London: British Agencies for Adoption and Fostering.

Striker, S. and Kimmel, E. (1979) *The Anti-Colouring Book*. Leamington Spa: Scholastic Press.

Super, C. and Harkness, S. (1982) 'The development of affect in infancy and early childhood', reprinted in Woodhead, M., Carr, R. and Light, P. (eds) (1991) *Becoming a Person (Child Development in Social Context 1)*. London: Routledge.

Tesson, G. and Youniss, J. (1995) 'Micro-sociology and psychological development: a sociological interpretation of Piaget's theory' in Ambert, A.-M. (ed.) *Sociological Studies of Children: Vol 7*. Greenwich, Ct.: JAI Press.

Thane, P. (1981) 'Childhood in History' in King, M. (ed.) *Childhood, Welfare and Justice*. London: Batsford.

The Children Act (1989) London: HMSO.

Thoburn, J. (ed.) (1992) *Participation in Practice – involving families in Child Protection*. Norwich: University of East Anglia.

Thoburn, J., Lewis, A. and Shemmings, D. (1995) *Paternalism or Partnership? Family Involvement in the Child Protection Process*. London: HMSO.

Thomas, K. (1989) 'Children in Early Modern England' in Avery, G. and Briggs, J. (eds) *Children and their Books: a celebration of the work of Iona and Peter Opie*. Oxford: Oxford University Press.

Thomas, N. (1994) 'In the Driving Seat': a study of the Family Group Meetings project in Hereford. Swansea: Department of Social Policy and Applied Social Studies.

Thomas, N. (1995) Participation in Children's Reviews and Planning Meetings. Oxford: Oxfordshire County Council.

Thomas, N. (forthcoming) 'Putting the family in the driving seat: the development of family group conferences in England and Wales', Social Work and Social Sciences Review.

Thomas, N. (in preparation) 'Constructing voices: the interpretation of rich qualitative data in research with children'.

Thomas, N. and Beckett, C. (1994) 'Are children still waiting? New developments and the impact of the Children Act 1989', Adoption and Fostering 18(1), 8–16.

Thomas, N. and O'Kane, C. (1996) 'Children's Participation in Plans and Reviews', paper delivered at National Children's Bureau Conference 'Plans and Reviews: Getting it Right for Young People', London, 31 October.

Thomas, N. and O'Kane, C. (1998a) Children and decision-making: a summary report. University of Wales Swansea: International Centre for Childhood Studies.

Thomas, N. and O'Kane, C. (1998b) 'The ethics of participatory research with children', Children and Society 12(5), 336–48.

Thomas, N. and O'Kane, C. (1998c) 'When children's wishes and feelings clash with their "best interests"', International Journal of Children's Rights 6(2), 137–54.

Thomas, N. and O'Kane, C. (1998d) 'What makes me so different?', Community Care 1253 (17 December–6 January), 23.

Thomas, N. and O'Kane, C. (1999a) 'Children's participation in reviews and planning meetings when they are "looked after" in middle childhood', Child and Family Social Work 4(3).

Thomas, N. and O'Kane, C. (1999b) 'Children's experiences of decision-making in middle childhood', Childhood 6(3).

Thomas, N. and O'Kane, C. (forthcoming) 'Discovering what children think: connections between research and practice', British Journal of Social Work

Thomas, N., O'Kane, C. and McNeill, S. (1998) Voices with Volume. Audiotape from University of Wales Swansea, International Centre for Childhood Studies.

Thomas, N., Phillipson, J., O'Kane, C. and Davies, E. (1999) Children and Decision-making: a Training and Resource Pack. Swansea, International Centre for Childhood Studies.

Thurgood, J. (1990) 'Active listening – a social services' perspective' in Bannister, A., Barrett, K. and Shearer, E. (eds) Listening to Children. Harlow: Longman.

Tulkin, S. (1977) 'Social class differences in maternal and infant behaviour' in Leiderman, P., Tulkin, S. and Rosenfeld, A. (eds) Culture and Infancy. New York: Academic Press.

Tulkin, S. and Konner, M. (1973) 'Alternative conceptions of intellectual functioning', reprinted in Skolnick, Arlene (ed.) (1976) Rethinking Childhood: perspectives on development and society. Boston: Little, Brown.

Turnbull, C. (1984) The Human Cycle. London: Jonathan Cape.

Ukviller, R. (1979) 'Children versus parents: perplexing policy questions for the ACLU' in O'Neill, O. and Ruddick, W. (eds) Having Children: Philosophical and Legal Reflections on Parenthood. New York: Oxford University Press.

United Nations (1989) Convention on the Rights of the Child. 20 Nov., A/RES/44/25, New York.

Van der Veer, R. and Valsiner, J. (1994) *The Vygotsky Reader*. Oxford: Blackwell.

Veerman, P. E. (1992) *The Rights of the Child and the Changing Image of Childhood*. Dordrecht: Martinus Nijhoff.

Verhellen, E. (1992) 'Changes in the image of the child' in Freeman, M. and Veerman, P. (eds) *Ideologies of Children's Rights*. Dordrecht: Martinus Nijhoff.

Vernon, J. and Fruin, D. (1986) *In Care: a Study of Social Work Decision-making*. London: National Children's Bureau.

Vygotsky, L. (1966) 'Genesis of the higher mental functions', reprinted in Light, P., Sheldon, S. and Woodhead, M. (eds) (1991) *Learning to Think (Child Development in Social Context 2)*. London: Routledge.

Vygotsky, L. S. (1962) *Thought and Language*. Cambridge, Mass: MIT Press.

Vygotsky, L. S. (1978) *Mind in Society*. New York: Cambridge University Press.

Waksler, F. C. (1991) 'The hard times of childhood and children's strategies for dealing with them' in Waksler, F. C. (ed.) *Studying the Social Worlds of Children: Sociological Readings*. London: Falmer.

Wald, M. S. (1979) 'Children's rights: a framework for analysis', *University of California Davis Law Review* 12, 255–82.

Ward, C. (1978) *The Child in the City*. London: The Architectural Press.

Ward, C. (1994) 'Opportunities for childhoods in late twentieth century Britain' in Mayall, B. (ed.) *Children's Childhoods: Observed and Experienced*. London: Falmer.

Ward, H. (ed.) (1995) *Looking After Children: research into practice*. London: HMSO.

Welsby, J. (1996a) 'The Children's Planning Initiative', Conference 'Plans and Reviews: getting it right for young people', National Children's Bureau, 31 Oct.

Welsby, J. (1996b) 'A voice in their own lives' in De Boer, G. (ed.) *Children's Rights in Residential Care in International Perspective*. Defence for Children International, Netherlands.

Whiting, B. and Whiting, J. (1975) *Children of Six Cultures*. Cambridge: Harvard University Press.

Wilcox, R. and colleagues (1991) *Family Decision-Making, Family Group Conferences*. Lower Hutt, New Zealand: Practitioners' Publishing.

Wilson, A. (1980) 'The infancy of the history of childhood: an appraisal of Philippe Ariès', *History and Theory* 19, 132–53.

Winefield, A., Tiggemann, M., Winefield, H. and Goldney, R. (1992) *Growing up with Unemployment: a longitudinal study of its psychological impact*. London. Routledge.

Wolf, J. (1992) 'The concept of the "best interest" in terms of the UN Convention on the Rights of the Child' in Freeman, M. and Veerman, P. (eds) *Ideologies of Children's Rights*. Dordrecht: Martinus Nijhoff.

Wolff, R. P. (1968) *The Poverty of Liberalism*. Boston: Beacon Press.

Wolfson, S. (1992) 'Children's rights: the theoretical underpinnings of the "best interests of the child"' in Freeman, M. and Veerman, P. (eds) *Ideologies of Children's Rights*. Dordrecht: Martinus Nijhoff.

Wood, D. (1986) 'Aspects of teaching and learning' in Richards, M. and Light, P. (eds) *Children of Social Worlds: development in a social context*. Cambridge: Polity.

Woodhead, M. (1990) 'Psychology and the cultural construction of children's needs' in James, A. and Prout, A. (eds) *Constructing and Reconstructing Childhood: contemporary issues in the sociological study of childhood*. Basingstoke: Falmer Press.

Worsfold, M. (1980) 'Students' rights: education in the just society' in Aiken, W. and LaFollette, H. (eds) *Whose Child? Children's Rights, Parental Authority and State Power*. Littlefield: Adams.

Worsfold, V. L. (1974) 'A philosophical justification for children's rights', *Harvard Educational Review* 44(1), 142–59.

Wringe, C. (1980) 'Pupils' rights' in Aiken, W. and LaFollette, H. (eds) *Whose Child? Children's Rights, Parental Authority and State Power*. Boston: Littlefield, Adams.

Wringe, C. (1981) *Children's Rights: a philosophical study*. London: Routledge and Kegan Paul.

Wringe, C. (1996) 'Children's welfare rights: a philosopher's view' in John, M. (ed.) *Children in Our Charge: the Child's Right to Resources*. London: Jessica Kingsley.

Yamamoto, K. (1993) *Their World, Our World: reflections on childhood*. Westport, Conn.: Praeger.

Yamamoto, K., Soliman, A., Parsons, J. and Davis, O. L., Jr (1987) 'Voices in unison – stressful events in lives of children in six countries', *Journal of Child Psychology and Psychiatry* 28.

Young, R. (1980) 'In the Interests of Children and Adolescents' in Aiken, W. and LaFollette, H. (eds) *Whose Child? Children's Rights, Parental Authority and State Power*. Littlefield: Adams.

Zigler, E., Kagan, S. and Hall, N. (eds) (1996) *Children, Families and Government: preparing for the twenty-first century*. Cambridge: Cambridge University Press.

Index

activities, *see* communication, methods of

activity days, 135–6

adults
attitudes to children's involvement, 170–1
listening to children, 94–5, 143, 177, 182

advocacy, 87, 129, 153, 162, 169, 189

age, 2, 6, 10–15, 24–5, 29, 31, 32, 36, 38, 44, 45–6, 49, 62, 66–8, 89, 109–10, 115–16, 122–3, 124–5, 126, 127–8, 140, 148, 153, 156, 157, 159, 161,167, 186

agenda for discussion, 89–90, 105, 112, 149, 194

Alanen, Leena, 102, 200

Alderson, Priscilla, 19, 103, 134

Aldgate, Jane, 86, 90–1

anthropology, 2, 16, 102, 114

Archard, David, 41–3, 44–5, 46–7

Ariès, Philippe, 5–8, 9, 11, 17

Arnstein, Sherry, 129, 174

Atkinson, Paul, 99, 114

attachment, 27, 28, 34, 57–8, 82, 93, 94

audiotape, 134, 154, 188

autonomy, *see* children

Bachrach, Peter, 193

Baratz, Morton, 193

Barton, Chris, 51

Baumrind, Diana, 28

Berger, Peter, 16

'best interests', *see* children

Blustein, Jeremy, 52, 58

boundaries, 139, 156

Bowlby, John, 27

boys, 10, 33–4, 118, 126, 136–7, 157

brothers and sisters, 28, 121, 135, 138–9

bureaucracy, 171

Burkitt, Ian, 26

Campbell, Tom, 40

care orders, 123, 139

care system, 70ff, 140, 164

caretaker thesis, 41–2

Carpenter, Mary, 71–2

changes in society, 154

child development, 13–14, 21–35

childhood
and competence, 196–8
in different cultures, 12–15; *see also* culture
theories of, 5–20

children
abuse and neglect, 73, 118, 157
attending meetings, 89, 115–6, 124–5
attitudes to their involvement, 170
autonomy, 18, 29, 31, 40–9, 65–7, 140–1, 154, 176, 194
behaviour, 14, 27, 149
'best interests' of, 57, 62–6, 76, 85, 139, 159–60, 178–87
confidence of, 74–5, 157, 167
with disabilities, 33, 104, 158, 172
disagreement with social workers, 119, 126–7
effect of past experiences, 172
influence of views, 68, 121, 126–7,147, 158–9
invited to meetings, 118, 122–4, 127–31, 161, 167
in need, 60

children – *continued*
looked after, 3, 70–95, 155, 194–5
of middle years, 22, 48–9,
68–9, 74
'of the state', 52, 54
regarded as objects, 58
suspicion of adults' questions, 178
as threats, 59
understanding of difficult issues, 32
as victims, 59
Children Act 1948, 70, 73, 76,
79–80, 81
Children Act 1989, 1, 59–60, 76, 88,
161, 185
children's needs, 31–2
children's participation in decisions,
41, 66–9, 101, 111, 194–6
children's rights, 36–49, 57–69
184–7, 194–6
children's understanding, 15, 22–5,
28, 29, 32–3, 61–2, 64–5, 92–4,
142, 144
children's views, 132ff.
Children's Legal Centre, 61, 87
Childright, 67
choice, 31, 42, 75, 84, 102, 111,
113, 119, 131, 140–1, 144, 148,
174–5, 177, 187
citizenship, 198–200
Cleveland inquiry, 62, 92
'climbing wall' of participation,
175–7
cognitive development, 22–6
Cohen, Howard, 39, 66
Coleman, John, 61
communication between adults and
children, 92–5, 144–5, 171–2,
177–8
communication, methods of:
activities, 94–5, 112, 119–20,
135–6,
drawings, 112, 119–20
games, 112, 119–20
writing, 94–5, 145
competence, 22, 28, 33, 34, 42, 65,
184–7, 196–8
complaints, 119, 151, 165, 187

compromise, 144, 154, 156, 160, 170
consent
to research, 111–2
to sexual activity, 44–5
contact, 57, 60, 84, 121, 136,
146, 179
control, 19, 46, 106, 111, 140, 156,
160, 165, 176
Convention on the Rights of the
Child, 1–2, 36, 49, 59–60, 64,
153, 195
Cranston, Maurice, 40–1
Crompton, Margaret, 93–4
culture, 12–15, 63–4, 103, 158
Cunningham, Hugh, 11–12

decision chart, 107, 135, 136
decision-making meeting, 117,118
decisions, difficult, 32–3, 158
decisions, everyday, 137, 191
decisions, long-term, 137
decisions in child care, 83–92
decisions in children's lives, 136
Declaration of the Rights of the
Child, 36, 37
Dent, Helen, 104
Denzin, Norman, 16, 19
Department of Health, 80, 92,
149, 192
development, concept of, 21
'diamond-ranking', 136, 151,
165–6; *see also* reasons why
children should have a say
Dingwall, Robert, 52, 55, 67
Donaldson, Margaret, 23, 26
Donaldson LJ, 61
Donzelot, Jacques, 53–4, 55
Douglas, Gillian, 51
drawings, *see* communication,
methods of
Dunn, Judy, 28, 29
dynamic self-determinism,
64–6, 185

Eekelaar, John, 52, 64–6, 67, 185–7
emotional development, 28–31
empowerment, 88, 165

ethnography, 17, 99, 102
explanation, 34–5, 144–5, 181

factors relating to adults, 157–8
factors relating to children, 156–7
Fahlberg, Vera, 93, 208
fairness, 41, 144
families, 30, 50–69, 75–6, 80–3,
    83–5, 156, 194–6, 200–1
family group conference, 91–2
family meetings, 142, 156
family policy, 52–5
Farson, Daniel, 38, 40, 46
Feinberg, Joel, 42, 65
Fine, Gary, 104
Fisher, Mike, 84
Flavell, James, 24
Fletcher, Barbara, 87–8
foster care, 77, 151
Fox Harding, Lorraine, 55–7, 88–9
Franklin, Bob, 43–4, 46–7
Freeman, Michael, 37, 40, 42
Freud, Anna, 57–8
Freud, Sigmund, 28
friends, 27, 137–9, 139–44, 150–1
Fruin, David, 83–5

games, *see* communication,
    methods of
Garbarino, James, 25
Gardner, Ruth, 86–7
Gillick Judgement, 61–2
Gilligan, Carol, 33
girls, 10, 33–4, 118, 126,
    136–7, 157
Glaser, Barney, 96–9, 113–5
Goldstein, Joseph, 57–8
Grimshaw, Roger, 88–92, 122,
    174–5, 190–4
group discussions, 89, 109–10,
    132, 134

Hammersley, Martyn, 99, 114
Hardman, Charlotte, 16, 103
Harris, Paul, 29–30
Hart, Roger, 129, 174

Hendrick, Harry, 59, 71, 72
Hewitt, Margaret, 8, 54
Heywood, Jean, 70–2, 75–6
history of childhood, 5–12
history of state care, 70–80
Hodgson, David, 88
Hoggan, Pauline, 92–3
Holt, John, 38, 40, 41–2, 43–5
Hughes, Judith, 44
Hutchby, Ian, 196–7

interview guide, 134–5
interview materials, 106, 111–2, 136
interviewing children, 104–8
Isaacs, Susan, 26
Ives, Richard, 44

James, Allison, 15–19, 102–3,
    104, 196
Jenks, Chris, 16–18, 197
justification for expecting children
    to obey authority, 58

Kamerman, Sheila, 52
Kahn, Alfred, 52
Kendrick, Andrew, 86
Kroll, Brynna, 94–5, 177

La Fontaine, Jean, 13, 15
ladder of participation, 89,
    174–7
laissez faire policy, 53, 56, 57
Lambert, Lydia, 80-1, 83
Land, Hilary, 52–3
language, 24, 28, 32–3, 120, 149
Lansdown, Gerison, 184, 195
Laslett, Peter, 9, 18
Layder, Derek, 98–9, 30, 200
Lee, Nick, 197, 340
liberationist argument, 39,
    41–2, 45
Light, Paul, 18, 23, 197
local authorities, 59, 70–92,
    108–11
Lofland, John, 99, 113
Lofland, Lyn, 99, 113

Looking After Children, 80, 119,
 120, 122–4, 148, 161–3, 188
Luckmann, Thomas, 16

McDonnell, Pauline, 86
McFadden, Emily Jean, 93
McGillivray, Ann, 48–9
Mandell, Nancy, 104
manipulation, 194
Mapstone, Elizabeth, 86
de Mause, Lloyd, 5, 8
Mayall, Berry, 103
Mead, Margaret, 12–13
Meadows, Sara, 24, 29
Merleau-Ponty, Maurice, 29, 197
Minow, Martha, 199
Mnookin, Robert, 63–6, 183, 186
Moran-Ellis, Jo, 196-7
Morrow, Virginia, 19

negotiation, 31, 139, 144, 154,
 156, 159, 200
non-decisions, 84
'nondecision-making', 193
Nuffield Foundation, 110

O'Kane, Claire, 106, 110, 175, 188
O'Neill, John, 198–9
O'Neill, Onora, 37
Oakley, Ann, 103
Oldman, David, 12, 198
Opic, Iona, 104

Packman, Jean, 73, 77, 83–4, 86
paperwork, 164–5, 189
parental authority, 50–2, 57–9
parental autonomy, 54, 55–9
parental responsibility, 50–2,
 59–61, 66–9
parents, 8–15, 50–69, 72–5, 88–92,
 137–9, 161–3
parents' rights, 56, 58
Parker, Roy, 52–3, 74
participation
 political, 196
 as a process, 144–5, 175–7
 typologies of, 129–30, 170–7

partnership, 85, 91, 118, 155, 184
Parton, Nigel, 54, 67
Pateman, Carole, 196
Piaget, Jean, 22–6, 32, 42
Pinchbeck, Ivy, 8, 54
placement, 76–7, 118, 136–7,
 163–5, 178–80
planning meetings, 90–1, 109–10,
 115–6, 163
Pollock, Linda, 9
'pots and beans', 135, 146–7
power, 18, 32, 44, 53–4, 56, 84,
 90–1, 93, 139–44, 155–6, 193,
 194–6, 198–9
preparation for meetings, 125–6,
 127–31, 146–7, 161–2
problem of indeterminacy, 62–6
Prout, Alan, 15–19, 102
psychology, 12, 21–35, 196–8
Purdy, Laura, 38–40
purpose of meetings, 145,
 161, 190–1
purpose of state care, 71–2

qualitative data, 98–9, 166
qualitative research, 96–9, 132
quantitative analysis, 98–9, 132
questionnaire, 116–7
Qvortrup, Jens, 18, 198

rational autonomy, 41–3
Rawls, John, 39, 40–1, 47
reasons for not inviting
 children, 153
reasons why children should have
 a say, 151–2, 165–6
records of meetings, 163
reflexivity, 102, 114, 177
reification, 16
relationships, 301–5
research:
 applied, 96–9
 with children, 101–4
 methodology, 96–114
 methods, 108–14, 115–18, 134–6,
  153–4, 200–1

residential care, 76–7, 118–19, 210,
    239, 261, 340
residential workers, 138
reviews, 79–91, 115–16, 132–4,
    145–50, 161–3, 191–4
review meetings, 85–91, 108–11,
    115–16, 118–31, 145–50, 161–3
'boring', 145–6
Richards, Martin, 18, 57, 197
rights, 36–49, 50–69, 88–91,
    184–7, 194–6
conflicts between different kinds
    of, 45–8
political and sexual, 43–5
of self-determination, 38–40,
    45–8
to welfare, 36–8, 45–8
risk, 158–60, 178–87
Roche, Jeremy, 182
Rodham, Hillary, 36
Rogers, C.M., 45–8
Rowe, Jane, 80–1, 83
Ruddick, William, 50–2
rules, 137–44, 155–6
Ryburn, Murray, 192

safety, 144, 158–60, 180–4
Scarman, Lord, 61, 65–6, 187, 195
Schofield, Gillian, 184–7
school, 10–12, 28–31, 32–3, 48,
    76–7, 93–4, 140–1, 180
Second World War, 55
Seymour, John, 58–9, 62, 185
Shahar, Shulamith, 7, 11
Shemmings, David, 92
Shorter, Edward, 8
Sinclair, Ruth, 88–92, 122, 174–5,
    190–4
Skolnick, Arlene, 63
social development, 26–8
social workers, 84, 92–5, 112,
    116–31, 134–6, 138, 149,
    150–1, 155–6, 158–65, 167–9,
    171, 180–7
sociology, 15–19, 196–8
Solberg, Anne, 18, 197

Solnit, Albert, 57–8
Speier, Matthew, 16, 20
Stainton Rogers, Wendy, 17
state paternalism, 56, 57
state's intervention in parental
    conduct, 55–7
staying with friends, 136, 141
Steedman, Carolyn, 54
Stevens, Olive, 32–3, 44
Stone, Lawrence, 8
Strauss, Anselm, 96–9, 113–5
support, 24, 33, 90, 94, 119–20,
    139–50, 175–7

tape-recording, *see* audiotape
teachers, 137–9
team managers, 138, 163
theories of childhood, 5–20, 103
Thoburn, June, 89, 174, 184–7
Thomas, Keith, 10
Thurgood, Jan, 94–5, 177
time, 136, 139, 141, 144, 149, 150
tutelary complex, 53–4
typologies, 170–4

UN Convention, *see* Convention of
    the Rights of the Child

Vernon, Jenni, 83–5
voice of the child, 67
Vygotsky, Lev, 23, 26, 197

Welsby, John, 158, 171
Wesley, Susannah, 64, 203
wishes and feelings, 1, 62–4, 66–9,
    83–95
Woodhead, Martin, 31
worry, effects of, 35
Worsfold, V.L., 40–1, 90
Wrightsman, Lawrence, 45–8
Wringe, Colin, 48
writing, *see* communication,
    methods of

Yamamoto, Kaoru, 32, 102